TREK BACK FROM BURMA

TREK BACK FROM BURMA

By

WILFRED G *BURCHETT*

GYAN

ISBN : 978-81-212-1557-2(HB)

First Published, 1943

Published, 2018

Published by

Gyan Publishing House
5, Ansari Road
Daryaganj, New Delhi-110002
Phone: 011-47034999, 9811692060
www.gyanbooks.com
E-mail: books@gyanbooks.com

Printed at: G. Print Process, Delhi.

PUBLISHERS' NOTE

Mr. Burchett came out to India to cover the Sino-Japanese War and incidentally drifted into Burma with the Chinese Army. Having been through actual fire he has much to say about the factors which led to the fall of Burma. He relates first hand incidents which finally led to the evacuation of the country.

In this revealing book the author throws a search-light on the faults of the campaign.

CONTENTS

CHAPTER I

Sunday night, December 7th 1941. Chungking's streets as usual at that time of the year almost ankle deep in mud, the air, heavy with fog, raw and damp. Jack Belden—at that time International News Service China correspondent—and myself both feeling profoundly dissatisfied with ourselves and the world at large, trouser-ends turned up over our ankles, left the Press Hostel—Press Asylum would be a more appropriate name—made our way up the long hill that leads to "down-town" Chungking. Belden, morose, taciturn, tempestuous, I found always surprisingly good company, mainly because of his long bursts of silence. Without discussing the matter we each knew why the other was so gloomy and surly. The combination of months of inaction, the sterile atmosphere of the Press Hostel where correspondents sat and glowered at each other in between passing on official communiques and handouts of the Publicity Board; the austere, Methodist, YMCAish atmosphere of China's "New Life" Capital; the absence of female companionship; made us cramped and frustrated.

Up the long hill lined with open-fronted restaurants where naked, browned chickens and ducks, long necks lengthened as they hung in rows from wires; heads cocked speculatively sideways, testified that Chungking still had plenty of food—for those that could pay. The warmth of the sizzling, iron, cooking pans out in front, attracted circles of beggars, gazing hopefully, hungrily and stolidly at the diners within. Restaurants, shops, stalls, Government Offices, with many a gap between where Japanese bombs had blasted other restaurants, shops, stalls and offices out of existence, tumbling them down on to the vegetable patches hundreds of feet below. We paused at one of these kerbside restaurants and Belden roared.

"Wai, Tsa Fang! Jao-tse, yu meiyu? (Have you got any Jao-tse).

And a round, shaven-headed, wispy-bearded little man with greasy white apron, standing over a cooking-pan with iron ladle in hand, roared back.

"Jao-tse yu-a." (Jao-tse, there are).

We sat down while the "tsafang" separated a dozen tiny pallid crescent-shaped meat pies, from several scores more, and dipped them in a pan of simmering brown fat. After a few minutes he ladled them out, set them—golden brown—on a nest of pine needles in a round wooden frame, and brought them over to us, together with the inevitable pot of green tea. With fat trickling down our chins we ate them, ordered another dozen, ate them, wiped faces and hands with steaming hot towels—and continued our way down town.

Past the first class shops, which boasted of glass showcases, displaying thermos-flasks, flimsy cotton socks and singlets, toothpaste and electric torches; food-shops with cheese at three pounds sterling a half-pound tin, condensed milk eight shillings a tin, coffee two pounds a tin, butter three pounds for twelve ozs. Past the second-hand shop selling anything from a fur coat to a bottle of whisky for twenty pounds and in into the Moscow restaurant. We ordered two cups of good hot coffee, and Belden made the gentle, mournful-looking "tsafang" jump, when he slapped the table with open hands and yelled.

"And bring us a couple of women as well."

A party of pale, plump well-fed Chinese with enamel-cheeked ladies at the next table looked at Belden with pained surprise. The "tsafang" hovered over the table brushing away non-existent crumbs, murmuring that girls very difficult to get; very, very expensive when got. Six, five, four (very cheap) pounds would be minimum, the "tsafang" humbly murmured.

"We want girls to come and talk and laugh with us."

The "tsafang" rushed to the door to chase away a shivering bundle of rags who'd squeezed in with bowl and chopsticks, begging a little rice. He joined a row of others, children and old women, whose flattened noses and cheeks, were pressed against the cold glass front of the restaurant, their eyes magnified to saucer-size as they impassively watched the generous remains of dish after dish being borne away.

"Kuniang, yao buyao?" (Do you want a flowery virgin or don't you?) "Three hundred fifty dollars," he murmured as he filled up our coffee cups.

We didn't. We wandered into the street again, walked about for hours, hardly exchanging a word. At length, when we were already half way back to the Press Hostel, Belden asked the question, we'd both been waiting to ask all night.

"D'you think the Japs really mean it this time?"

"What do you think?"

"I don't see how they'd be so crazy to start anything. But they've gone so far, it's hard to see how they can back down now! In fact I don't see how they can, and I don't see how they can't."

And that's about as far as we got in dozens of talks we'd had extending over six weeks since I arrived in China, trying to work out just how much Japan was bluffing and how far she was in earnest. It seemed impossible that she would take a smack at the United

States and Britain, but then six months earlier it had seemed just as impossible that Germany would attack Russia.

There was tension in the air that Saturday night. The vibrations from those aircraft-carriers speeding towards Pearl Harbor, and the transports moving into the Gulf of Siam were felt more strongly in Chungking than at Pearl Harbor or Singapore or Manila. Maybe because Chungking had always hoped Britain and America would be involved in the war with Japan; because her spokesmen had warned America time and time again that the Japs would one day strike cunningly and treacherously; there was a feeling in the air that night that "der Tag" was about to dawn. It was that feeling that kept "Lousy" Peng, director of Chungking's short-wave radio station, awake that night and made him tune in to San Fransisco in the early hours of Monday morning.

5-30. Check on that cold, drizzling, Monday morning, I was awakened by confused shouts from "Lousy." Jumbled thoughts and amazing words. Pearl Harbor, Bombs. Japanese. War. I grabbed "Lousy" as he was passing my door, his face solemn and green and shining with misty rain, his eyes unnaturally large behind his thick, horn-rimmed glasses.

"Lousy, what's all this about?"

"Boy, oh, Boy! The Japs have bombed Pearl Harbor."

More and more pyjama-clad figures. Wider and wider eyes.

"But how" "Where from" "It's a hoax." "How far's Pearl Harbor from Japan." "They can't be so crazy." "Lousy, you've been drinking." "The Yellow sons of bitches."

Only Belden wasn't excited. I turned him over

several times, trying to drum the news into his heads. It's dangerous to talk to Belden before 11 a.m., at the best of times. At 6 a.m., it's suicidal. It was midday before he finally realised he was at war. Most of us trooped down to the radio station with Lao C—"Lousy" —Peng. Lousy, incidentally had tried unsuccessfully to have his Christian name changed to Mike (for Microphone) but Lao C was joyfully corrupted by all and sundry to "Lousy" and will remain so.

"Lousy" invited me to broadcast Sunday night, and tell the world how Chungking reacted to the outbreak of war in the Pacific. I wandered around the streets, after a few hours, listening to what was coming in over the radio......from Tokio, San Fransisco and London. Crude posters were displayed all over the streets announcing the news. "Extras" on blue sheets were rushed out and newsboys (and girls) mobbed as they rushed from the newspaper offices. "Lousy," unprecedentedly pasted bulletins outside the broadcasting station. He was the most important figure in China for those first brief hours, until regular reports started to come through. He telephoned Hollington Tong, got him out of bed and persuaded Holly he wasn't drunk, and Japan had really attacked Pearl Harbor. "Holly" who as Vice Minister Publicity ("Publicity" became "Information" after the Pacific war broke out) has to keep the Generalissimo informed of any special information that comes his way.

He telephoned the Generalissimo. The Secretary, who answered the phone; said unless it was very important he didn't like disturbing the Gissimo at that hour of the morning. The Gissimo had to be disturbed, however. He listened to "Holly's" account of the radio report. Without asking for repetition, or speaking more than half a dozen words he put down the receiver. He straight away gave orders for a meeting of the Military Affairs Council (China's War Cabinet). That was a typical reaction from the Generalissimo. No time wasted in idle discussion. His capacity for quick mental decisions, and their immediate translation into action, is one of the factors that fits him to be China's war-time leader.

Chungking was an inferno of exploding fire-crackers. It suddenly sprang into life. "ABCD Front." The idea caught on like wild-fire. We're no longer alone. America, England, Australia, Dutch East Indies—and as a matter of course Russia will soon be in it. Japan will be smashed in a few months. Hooray. More fire-crackers.

The press went in a body to "Holly" for official reaction. "All for one and one for all—that's our slogan from now on," said "Holly"; and that was all we could get from him. Every-body was jubilant—that is the Chinese were. Officials and people alike were caught up on the crest of a tremendous wave of enthusiasm. The Japanese bombs on Pearl Harbor had achieved in five minutes what Hollington Tong's Publicity Department had been trying to achieve for five years. America and Britain were on China's side at last. The war was as good as over. If the Chinese armies, miserably armed, fed, clad and doctored, could hold up the Japs for five years, the ABCD alliance could clean them up in five months. I'd never seen Chungking so animated before. There were broad smiles on all Chinese faces. Chinese, and foreigners too, became sentimental. Slapping each others backs, fervently shaking hands......"We're allies now."

"Holly" and his staff of propaganda experts held a hurried meeting which I imagine was one huge sign of relief......"At last" the long job was over—but not quite. Britain and America were ("ipso facto") at war with Japan. But what about the Russians? That was the remaining task for "Holly's" department. Try and get the Russians in as well, then China and "Holly" could sit back and take a complete rest. So the word went out to newspapers, periodicals, and patriotic societies for a Russian declaration against Japan.

My broadcast was to go over in the evening. I started off......"The news of the treacherous Japanese attack on Pearl Harbor was received in Chungking with mixed feelings. Coupled with warm sympathy for the victims of the attack is a tremendous upsurge of relief that China no longer stands alone......"

I learned afterwards that at the end of the first sentence. Wang Shih Chieh, Minister of Publicity, telephoned "Lousy" Peng and said:

"What's this fellow talking about saying the news was received here with 'mixed feelings?' He knows darned well there's only one feeling here about this."

And Wang Shih Chieh was right. There was only one feeling—of unadulterated relief. Mouths *did* droop at the corners a little when news of the sinking of the "Repulse" and "Prince of Wales" filtered through.

At first none believed it. At the British Embassy, cipher clerk Crofton accused people of fifth columnism, for even suggesting that the ships might have been sunk.

Word was passed round the Press Hostel, that there would be a special Press Conference on December 9th. Among the foreign correspondents were Leland Stowe, Chicago "Daily News," Gunther Stelin, "Manchester Guardian," expansive, dimpled Harrison Forman, "Columbia Broadcasting System;" the three Tass men, Nomerotsky, Monin and Yakshamin, Spencer Mossa, "Associated Press," "Mac." Fisher making one of his last appearances as United Press Correspondent, before Office of American War Information acquired him, Roderick MacDonald, "Sydney Morning Herald" Jack Belden "INS" and myself for London "Daily Express" and Sydney "Daily Telegraph."

Lights had failed, as often before, and candles were dotted around the conference table. There was a host of Chinese correspondents and photographers, foreign embassy officials and publicity board representatives. An excited babble of sound died away as small, neatly-dressed, Foreign Minister Dr. Quo Tai-chi entered the conference room. He adjusted horn-rimmed glasses, looked around the room, smiled at a few correspondents he recognised and started reading.

"Whereas......Whereas......Whereas......"

At one stage the candles flickered and he pushed his near-sighted eyes almost on to the paper he was reading. Two correspondents grabbed candles and set themselves on either side of Dr. Quo peering over his shoulder and throwing a dancing light on the papers. "Whereas......Mumble.......Mumble.......Mumble........ therefore the Chinese Government has decided to declare war on Japan, Germany and Italy.

Unprecedented scenes. The Chinese cheered, Britain, American—Yes, Russian correspondents—cheered too, and wildly applauded Dr. Quo, as he wiped his glasses and set down his papers. After nearly five years of unofficial warfare, China declared war on Japan, and for good measure on Germany and Italy too. That's how certain China felt about the outcome of the war in her first flush of enthusiasm. Rumour had it that cautious members of the Military Affairs Council and the Waichiaopu (Foreign Office) advised against rash plunging into war against Germany and Italy—just in case. But, it was done. Measures were announced shortly afterwards for the dismissal of all German Military and other advisers, to the Government, and for the internment of Axis nationals.

A few days earlier when I felt affairs in the Pacific were approaching a crisis I had seen Quo Tai-chi about China's part in Allied strategy, in case Britain and America were involved in war with Japan. Dr. Quo was very emphatic, and assured me that China would be prepared even to send Chinese troops outside her own territory—wherever they could be best used by the Allies. This was the first indication that China was able and willing to raise an expeditionary force—the first to serve outside China since 1883, when Chinese troops fought the French in Indo-China—then a Chinese protectorate. Quo's statement made headlines in the London Press, and incidentally won me a job with the "Daily Express," where I'd sent the story "on spec." Later I was to have something to do with that Chinese Expeditionary Force when it entered into action. At the time it was moving down the Burma Road towards the Yunnan-Burma frontier.

CHAPTER II

Most nights at the Press Hostel, Spencer Moosa, and his Russian wife Nina, kept open house for the correspondents. Spencer was one of the most envied men there. Not only did he have a wife, but also two rooms—one with a charcoal stove. After dinner we usually drifted down from the Press dining room and played "hearts" till about 2 a. m., when the last edition of "Central News," and the Chinese war communique were issued. With gin, vodka, a warm fire and a few packs of cards, Spencer and Nina greatly helped to prevent complete demoralisation of the correspondents, until the Pacific War provided some sort of outlet for their repressed and rusty minds. Explorer and writer Harrison Forman was a regular sitter-in for a "hearts" game. With great good humour he accepted the "slings and arrows" directed at him. His chief claim to fame was his book on Tibet, in which country, he was reputed to have travelled widely. Accepted in America as an authority on the forbidden country, he acted as technical director of "Lost Horizon." The press pretended to believe Harrison had never really been further than the Chinese Province of Silang, and any coupling of his name with Tibet was always sure to produce a good laugh. Baby-faced Leland Stove with his innocent, bluest of blue eyes, pink skin and halo of snowy white hair was another regular "hearter." Also Roderick MacDonald, "Sydney Morning Herald," who affected a broad, horsetail type, fair moustache and a prolonged pose of Byronic gloom. Roderick was always brimming over with "inside dope," but was always so pleased with himself that he couldn't contain his news. After a few drinks he was always ready—with upraised portentious forefinger and after a ponderous preface......" "As a matter of fact, I am in a position to reveal......" to spill his story. Underneath his affectations and poses Mac. is a first class reporter with a keen nose for news. It was he who suggested we should camp on the airfield till the first CNAC planes arrived from Hong Kong, with firsthand news of the situation there.

Our "hearts" game that first night of the Pacific war was subject to many interruptions. Attention was mainly focussed on the radio, as Tokio, San Fransisco, Manila, BBC and Bendsong poured out their versions of the day's happenings. Early next morning we were waiting on the airfield for the first arrivals from Hongkong. Amongst the first bunch was the beautiful, petité, American born Chinese wife of Jack Young,—assistant to Theodore Roosevelt on his panda-searching expeditions to China. It was freezing cold on the airfield, so we went along to Chialing House—Chungking's only foreign style hotel—to talk in reasonable comfort.

"It all happened so bewilderingly quickly, it's hard to know where to start," she said, as we sat huddled in our overcoats in the draughty Chialing House lounge. "So much has happened since yesterday morning."

"Just try and tell me how things started. When you first knew the show was on: How people acted; what the Japs did; how you got away?"

"I suppose it was about 8 a.m. when we heard planes first. I said to a friend who was staying with me 'looks like the British have got some planes here at last.' We went out and had a look, and they looked grand, their wings flashing in the sun against the blue sky.

They didn't seem in a hurry, just silvery and fat and leisurely, they circled round. We counted nine—then eighteen, twenty-seven. Lots of people were standing about watching them. Then they went into dives and were coming up again before we heard the explosions, and saw great clouds of smoke spouting up. At the same time the air raid sirens sounded."

"Did they drop bombs on Hong Kong island or across in Kowloon?"

"They seemed to be dropping near the airfield at Kowloon. But even then nobody thought we were at war. Thought it must be an accident. Then after an hour or so news passed around about Pearl Harbor and Singapore, and we realised it was war. I telephoned friends and people that they should know what was happening. Some said the Royal Scots had been fighting on the edge of New Territories since dawn. Some people over Kowloon side had heard explosions since near midnight. There was no official news of what was happening. People poured down town buying up foodstuffs. The ferries across from Kowloon were jammed with people trying to squeeze into Hong Kong. For a while they stopped running but Chinese ferried people across in sampsas at terrific prices. Everybody wanted to be in Hong Kong because they reckoned the New Territories might fall, but Hongkong can hang out until help comes. In the afternoon the CNAC Manager rang and told me to bring one bag with not more than 20 lbs. of baggage, and be at the aerodrome prepared to leave about midnight for Chungking.

"That was a job—to decide what should be put in that one bag. I have a feeling that those things I left behind, I'll never see again.

"It was pretty awful, waiting down at the aerodrome.

There were whole bunch of us there, all with our little bags—some of them had big suitcases, and kicked up an awful row when they were told they couldn't bring them. We could hear the rumbling of the guns and the chatter of machine-guns away over on the edge of the New Territories. The field was blacked-out, of course, in case of Jap raids. We waited and nothing came, and we thought maybe they'd decided it was too dangerous. We waited about four hours altogether and then we heard the drone of a plane. Gee! Were our hearts in our mouths? .Searchlights went on, and their pale fingers swept around sort of restlessly, till one of them picked up the plane. It looked like a little white moth. Then another beam spotted it and two streaks of light held the plane in a cross. We didn't know what to think. If it was a Jap, it'd bomb the airfield, and spoil our chances of getting away. If it was our plane, we feared our own anti-aircraft guns might open up and shoot it down. We felt pretty good when the searchlights went off, leaving the field ten times as black as before. Then the ground-lights came on and the plane swooped in. Lights went off again, while we piled in. I didn't feel so good when we were all set to go and the 'drome lighted up again. I held my breath and hoped hard the Japs wouldn't come over till we got off. Well, they didn't and here we are, and if you don't mind, I'm going to have a wash and pile into bed. If you want to ask any more questions, you'd better come back after I've had a good sleep, and maybe I'll think of something else."

Mrs. Jack Young was one of two hundred and seventy-five people snatched away from Hong Kong under the very noses of the Japs, by those tough, carefree pilots of China National Airways. For four days and nights—till the Japs were almost on the edge of Kai Tak aerodrome itself, these pilots maintained a shuttle service between Hongkong and Chungking and Hongkong and Namyung—the tungsten export aerodrome in Kwantung province, and nearest aerodrome, in Free China to Hong Kong.

The Australian pilot Sydney de Kantzow made many trips during those days. He told me of one Chinese woman, who camped out at the field and slipped into every plane before it took off. Several times, she nearly got away, sitting quiet as a mouse in the darkest corner of the plane, and mournfully unprotesting as she was inevitably turned out.

"She had stiff luck when I flew Madame Kung and Madame Sun Yat Sen out," de Kantzow said, "I only saw her at the last moment. She only had to say she was one of the Madame Kung's party and I would've let her stay. Even if she'd stayed out she could've gone with us. As it was, as soon as I spoke to her she just got up quietly, put her cloth bundle under her arm and climbed out without saying a word. Maybe she was luckier with some other plane afterwards."

One who did not get away was Australian journalist Dorothy Jenner, who'd left Chungking on November 28th for Hong Kong and Manila. "Andrea" as she was known to readers of her column in the Sydney "Sun" tried to leave with Colin MacDonald of London "Times" on a destroyer a few hours after the first air raid. A destroyer, trying to run a blockade of Jap warships, which'd moved to the Harbor entrance, was no place for a woman, even such a delightful, courageous, unconventional soul as Dorothy Jenner.

"Andrea" was told she had a much better chance flying across to Manila by Clipper—scheduled to leave the following morning—then risking a hazardous journey by destroyer. Next morning as she made her way across to the waiting Clipper, Jap planes swooped down, machine-gunned and sank the plane while its Captain dived about in the water dodging bullets Her hopes of leaving Hong Kong were sunk with the Clipper. The Sydney "Sun" did everything possible to get her out. Wired to Madame Chiang to send in a special plane. Madame was willing to do it, but by the time she received the wire it was too late. Today Dorothy Jenner is making unhappy the lives of Japanese guards at Stanley Prison, Hong Kong. Other prisoners of war who escaped, have told me of her forthright vigor in sticking up for such rights as prisoners of war in a Japanese camp may expect.

China National Airways' first concern, was to get out their own personnel, with their families and such notables who were particularly in danger from the Japanese. Madame Kung, sister of Madame Chiang Kai Shek was offered passage on the first plane out, but was frightened it might not get through. With the third sister Madame Sun Yat Sen, she left on the following night.

In Chungking we kept in touch with every plane arriving from Hong Kong. They provided the only means of keeping us informed about happenings in the beleaguered city. After CNAC personnel were evacuated, Kuomintang officials with their wives and concubines monopolised the planes. Much criticism was levelled at some of these for bringing out immense quantities of trunks and baggage (including dogs), when important personalities, many especially hated by the Japs, were left behind. Hong Kong had been the chief centre for Chinese who didn't see "eye to eye" with the Kuomintang, and I think many Central Government officials were secretly relieved that at one blow, they were rid of so many dissident elements. There was great pleasure, in liberal and foreign circles in Chungking, when it was known that Madame Sun Yat Sen had escaped—her sister Madame Kung repeatedly refused to leave unless Madame Sun was taken in the same plane. I tried to see Madame Sun (Soong Ching Ling) as soon as she arrived, but she was sick at heart for all her friends, and her husband's friends, who'd been left behind. She saw no one but most intimate acquaintances for weeks.

CHAPTER III

A few days after Pearl Harbor, I received notice that General Chou En Lai, the Chungking representative of the Chinese Communist Party, and one of the party's "Big Three" was holding a Press Conference. I had seen General Chou several times before, and always found anything he had to say, well worth the trouble of a trip to his Headquarters. With Mao Tse Tung and Chu Teh he is the third member of the triumvirate of the officially non-existent, but actually tremendously powerful Communist Party in China. An aristocrat, son of a Kiangsi Mandarin family, he has a fine logical, analytical mind and is intellectually one of the most honest officials I've met in China.

I think most members of the Press Hostel attended that conference. Kung Peng, and Chia Kang, two of the Communist Party secretaries were also there. The purpose of the conference, General Chou explained, was to clarify the Communist Party's attitude to the Pacific war, and to outline its ideas as to how the war should be won.

If the programme laid down by Chou En Lai that afternoon had been adopted by the War Councils in Chungking, London and Washington, I believe hundreds of thousands of lives would have been saved, and the Pacific war shortened by many months. I cabled a brief summary to Australia, and received a terse reply from my paper.

"Public here uninterested in Chinese Communist Party Pronouncements."

We were so sure of ourselves. We'd lick the pants off these little yellow monkeys in a few months, and send them scurrying back to their cherry blossom islands. What need had we for advice from a Communist Party in any country—Chinese communists at that? It didn't count, that with practically their bare hands, the Chinese communists had been holding up a far greater force of the Japanese army, than that which later drove the Americans out of the Phillippines and the British and Dutch out of Hong Kong, Malaya, Dutch East Indies and Burma. When General Chou gave us his talk that afternoon, he gave us the essence of nearly fourteen years' experience of successfully fighting superior forces with inferior arms. But we weren't interested. We had real armies, real navies and air forces, what need had we for "Bow and Arrow" guerilla methods?

General Chou is of medium build and height. He has the reposeful appearance of a man who knows just where he's going and why. This day, as on most occasions I've seen him, he wore the long blue robe, worn by most Chinese functionaries. He speaks a halting English with a bad accent, difficult to understand until one is used to him. He deliberately searches for the most expressive word. And this selectivity of language enables him to put across his meaning with the greatest economy of phrases. Of course, the Communist Party of China pledged fullest support for the United Nations against Japan. He emphasised that the war in the East was likely to develop more as a political than a military effort, as far as the Japs were concerned. In the most closely populated area in the world, it was ridiculous, he said, to entrust defence to a handful of white troops. If we couldn't sufficiently enthuse the local peoples to defend their countries, we would lose them. The only way to enthuse them in defence, was to give them something to defend. The United Nations were in the happy position of being able to give something. Japan couldn't. But Japan could make promises—and would make promises. She would promise Malaya to the Malayans, Burma to the Burmans. More; she would probably promise a little of Burma to Thailand, a little of Thailand to Malaya, part of India to Burma. Having nothing, she could promise all, Malayans, Burmans, Javanese, Indians—also having nothing, would prefer to believe Japan's promises than to continue having nothing. The United Nations, having something to give, and everything to lose, should part with some power and save themselves, and the countries under their control. People would be prepared to fight for the little that was given them, for something substantial, rather than collaborate with the Japs, for something that was promised in the future. That was the first point Chou made. That we should give these people something to fight for. Not necessarily independence, but dominion status or at least a definite offer, bound by reasonable time limit. Something at least better than the people in South East Asia at present had. Not ask them to "wait and see" after the war, but give now. Cut the ground away from the main basis of Japanese propaganda.

The second point was the organisation of the people into guerilla bands. Here General Chou was speaking as an expert on a subject whereon he has no peer. The Chinese communists already had well knit organisations in several countries in South-East Asia. They were willing to utilise these as the nucleus for guerilla forces in Indo-China, Malaya, Thailand and Dutch East Indies for a start. If the United Nations would supply arms, they could soon set things moving. Organisers could be sent in from China in some cases. In most places they were already on the job. Chou revealed that in one of the most important Japanese bases—Hainan Island—there were 15,000 communist guerillas who could make things very hot for the Japs, if only they had some arms. Communist partisans—the Pao-an guerillas in Kwantung Province along the Canton Kowloon railway—had already been ordered to attack and were in action. (The items about Hunan Island and communist partisans operating along the Canton-Kowloon railway were struck out of our messages by the Ces nor, because "there were no communists in China." The troops operating in Kwantung were always represented as Central Government troops.)

That was the gist of General Chou's statement to the Press. That the Japanese having nothing to give were prepared to promise everything. That the United Nations having everything to give should give something and inspire the people of South-East Asia to defend their own homelands. That the communists would place their experience in guerilla warfare at the disposal of the Uni-nations and help the people to defend themselves.

With two exceptions none of these things were done. The Americans *did* announce independence for the Phillipines and as a result got a fuller measure of cooperation from the Fillipinos than was achieved elsewhere in the Pacific Zone between white troops and the native population. Guerilla warfare was still being carried on there twelve months after the Japanese occupation but limited because few arms were available. In Malaya the British authorities eventually released Malayan communists from prison, legalised the Communist Party and agreed to allow Chinese and Malayan communists to organise guerilla bands. With scanty arms they set to work and very good reports came to hand of the work in the latter days of the campaign. Tokio Radio has since made reference to the activities of bandits in Malaya and escapees who reached China in May 1943, reported that Australian troops operating with Chinese and Malayan guerillas were still causing the Japanese trouble in several parts of Malayan mainland.

Mac. Fisher of United Press, and I had a long talk after Chou's conference. Mac. (short for MacCracken) is, I think, the best informed newspaperman in China today. He brings the sturdy good sense of a Midwest American farm background, to bear on a tremendously varied knowledge of the Far East in general and China in particular. He knew as I did that the British were unpopular in India, Malaya and Burma, as the French were unpopular in Indo-China, the Americans in the Phillipines and the Dutch in the East Indies. We agreed to do what we could, he in the American Press, I in the Australian and English Press to awaken public opinion to the potency of the political weapon Japan was using throughout South East Asia. Buying the active and passive cooperation of hundreds of millions of dissatisfied colonial peoples by promises of "imminent liberations." I started off with a long article to the "Sunday Express" about Burma, trying to point out the type of problem we were up against there.

I used a second-hand illustration given to me by an Australian Buddhist friend of mine, who'd spent many years in Burma. In the Southern Shan states near Loikaw, dwell the giraffe-necked women. Their necks are stretched by means of rings, gradually added between their shoulders and chins, till the neck bone is more than twice normal length. One of these women developed an ulcer on her neck, and the doctor cut away the rings to treat the ulcer. She soon got better, but one morning sitting up in bed she leaned forward and coughed—and broke her neck.

"You see," said an earnest English administrator telling this story to some Burman friends, "that's what would happen if we withdrew British support and capital from Burma. It would be like removing those rings from the woman's neck. The country would just break its neck."

"Ah, yes", smiled a Burman lawyer, between puffs at his cheroot, "but who put these rings round Burma's neck in the first place ? In any case, we don't want them all removed at once. Remove one at a time—and tell us when you are going to remove them, and we won't break our necks."

That's all the Burmans wanted. They wanted to know that the rings round their necks were going to be removed. They'd have been quite happy, if one ring had been removed before the Japanese invasion, and a definite time-table laid down for the removal of the others.

My article was well received—at least by the "Sunday Express". They even cabled me that it made a "grand leader-pagor," but, of course, for all the results it had, it might as well never have been written. No rings were removed; and as a result we ran into some trouble during the Burma Campaign. We were terribly shocked that some of the Burmans preferred to believe in the slender hope of Japanese promises, than the certainty of nothing that we offered. Some of them even took up arms against us, and so the Burmese people were branded by many as a nation of traitors, who according to many army people "should be wiped off the face of the earth."

I don't know why we didn't offer these people in Malaya and Burma some good reason to fight for themselves. If it was just shortsightedness, and because we thought we could beat the Japanese ourselves, without enlisting the support of the local populations, that was bad enough. But it was no worse an error of judgement than we have made elsewhere. I have an idea, however, that the "powers that be" reasoned something like this:

"If we give Malaya and Burma their independence or Dominion status, or even the promise of those things, it may mean the people will fight like hell, and even the Japs. But it also means that we'll have sacrificed a lot of Power in those countries. Now that's going to be devilish awkward afterwards. It's best, in the Empire interest, not to give up anything. We'll fight the Japs as well as we can ourselves. Of course, they'll probably drive us out, but sooner or later we'll be strong again, and together with our allies we'll beat them. We'll get Malaya and Burma back again without having to concede an iota of power. Of course, the fact that tens of thousands of good English and Dominion lives would be lost, and the war prolonged for another year or so would be regrettable, but on the whole prefer able to the other course".

I think this is what must have been in their minds when they refused the offer of the Chinese in Hong Kong on December 8th to provide twenty to fifty thousand Chinese to fight the Japs. It could have been the only reason why Gen. Wavell at first refused the offer of unlimited Chinese aid in Burma. I suppose we thought if we save Hong Kong and Burma with Chinese support, the next thing is we'll have to get Hong Kong and Burma back from the Chinese. At least many of our officers and officials from those colonies explained things that way to me. Looking at things from an Imperial standpoint perhaps they were right. But lots of members of the United Nations no longer consider such questions from an Imperial standpoint. In fact, according to the Atlantic Charter they are pledged to fight for the rights of self-determination for all nations.

On the 22nd December Chungking got all "hot up" when it was known General Sir Archibald Wavell and Major-General George E. Brett, Chief of United States Air Corps had arrived for talks with the Generalissimo. It was a fairly safe bet that the talks had something to do with Chinese participation in the Burma Campaign, but nothing definite was announced. The usual blurb about "routine talk" and "exchange of views" was put out for the Press. Jack Belden, Harrison Forman and myself went down to the landing strip on the Yangtse on Christmas Eve in the hope of having a few words with Wavell when he left. The head of the British Military Mission to China, Major-General Lancelot Dennys (later killed in an air crash at Kunming) introduced us to the General. I had an impression of a tough, hard-bitten soldier with tons of physical and moral courage. He wasn't divulging much in the way of information, and seemed more inclined to ask questions than answer them. That sent him up in our estimation. At that time he was Commander-in-Chief of India—officially. Actually I'm sure he already knew of his appointment as Supreme Commander of Allied Forces in South West Pacific Area, announced a few days later.

There were only a few people on the bitingly cold airfield, and we had nearly an hour with Wavell, because Japanese fighters were up around Kunming, delaying his departure. He asked a good deal about the Chinese Army and Foreman and Belden—Belden particularly—were qualified to speak about that. He was gracious enough to ask what we thought should be done out here and I'm afraid I expounded rather fully an idea which had been developing in my mind for some time.

I felt that in the Pacific War the Japanese had a great weapon in the colour of their skin. They are Asiatics. Their skins are yellow, and they are fighting in an area where ninety-nine percent of the population are Asiatics, with yellow, brown and black skins, and most of them ruled by a tiny minority of people whose skins were white. The slogan of the Japs was Asiatics against the Whites." The Japanese were not fighting for themselves alone, but to liberate all "Asiatics from the subjection of the white races. "The Japanese in the vanguard of the fight to emancipate their yellow and brown-skinned brothers."

The Japanese were pouring this stuff out in scores of Eastern dialects twenty-four hours a day from their broadcasting stations. They had been dropping leaflets on the Chinese and Indians in Hong Kong, the Malayans, Indians and Chinese, in Malaya, telling them just that sort of stuff—and it was going down. Apart from lots of other reasons they had for disliking us, these peoples, Annamites, Malaya, Javanese etc., hated our assumption of over-all superiority based on the colour of our skins. They must have had a pleasant thrill of anticipation, when the Japs promised them that, soon they were going to kick our white behinds so hard that we would tumble over each other to get away from the heavy-shod yellow Japanese feet.

I reasoned the best way to counter-balance these weighted scales would be to make another Asiatic, Chiang Kai Shek, Commander-in-Chief of the whole Asiatic area. With one blow we'd have castrated the most vigorous of the Japanese propaganda agents.

There were good reasons why Chiang should have

been given that job. Firstly, he is a top-notch soldier and strategist. He's been educated in a Japanese Military Academy and knows their methods so well, that together with some tricks he has developed himself, his poorly equipped armies lost less territory to the Japs in five years, than the United Nations did in five months. Secondly, there are over eight million Chinese scattered throughout South East Asia and they would have rallied to Chiang's leadership and provided useful armies. In Malaya, for instance, there are as many Chinese as Malays. Thirdly, and most important, as pointed out above, Chiang's appointment and China's assistance, would have effectively countered Japanese claims to leadership in the "Asia for the Asiatics" campaign.

In more condensed form I tried to put this idea across to General Wavell as we stamped up and down the landing strip on the edge of the Yangtse, trying to keep our feet warm. His only comment was "Hmm Hmm." A few days later it was announced that he'd been appointed Supreme Commander in the South West Pacific, and "was my face red?"

Much later I learned what happened at the Wavell-Chiang Kai Shek talks. The Gissimo had the 5th and 6th armies already in Yunnan. I'd seen them marching down the Burma Road two months earlier when I was coming up into China. He offered to send them both into Burma for a start, and as many more armies as Wavell wanted. China naturally regarded Burma as more important to her at that time than to anybody else. It was her only contact with the outside world. Lease-Lend goods had just started to arrive in quantity —to the tune of about seventeen thousand tons a month. Work on the Yunnan-Burma railway was going on well. If China was to carry on, and if the United Nations were to make use of Chinese bases, to attack Japan proper, the Burma Road had to be kept open. Therefore, Chiang was anxious to send everything possible to help hold Burma. He even agreed to send down two squadrons of the precious first-fruits of United States Aid to China—the American Volunteer Fighter Group Squadrons. There have been various stories about why Wavell was chary in accepting the Gissimo's offer. One is that he was very hopeful about the whole situation in Burma. He would be pleased to have the 5th Army, but that was all. There were two more divisions coming out to reinforce Burma—the 18th from the Middle East, the 77th from South Africa—so there was really nothing to worry about, "thanking you very much all the same."

Actually neither of these divisions reached Burma. The 18th was on its way to Burma when things started to go wrong in Malaya, so it was switched to Singapore instead. The 77th unhappily was delayed until after Rangoon had fallen, and was transferred elsewhere. The Chinese armies (for Wavell eventually had to ask for the 6th and as many more troops as could be spared) never entered Burma until the country was virtually lost. Rangoon had fallen, long before the Chinese got to grips with the Japs, and no further reinforcements or supplies could be brought in. Apologists for our non-acceptance of the first Chinese offers have said to me since.

Another at least as likely explanation was that the 5th and 6th armies were the only Central Government troops in Yunnan at that time and as the local provincial troops have always been considered unreliable, Wavell feared to have both Central Government armies shifted out of Yunnan while there was a chance of the Japs driving through from Indo-China to outflank the whole Allied armies in Burma.

A third explanation offered by old "die-hards" in Burma and elsewhere seems the least likely of all.

"Naturally," they said, "we don't want Burma overrun with Chinese. Never......etc."

"But General Wavell couldn't be expected to know that things would go so badly in Malaya, at the time he was in Chungking."

Maybe not. But Malaya was part of his theatre. The campaign there was already in full swing, and swinging backward as far as we were concerned. It was an error of military judgement. Certainly, everyone makes errors, but there in Chungking at the end of December 1941, General Wavell was offered something which would help to compensate for any error of judgement. The chance to make "doubly sure" was politely declined. Other apologists reason "but naturally we didn't want Burma over-run with Chinese. Never get the beggars out again. Old Wavell, you know damned shrewd. What's the good having Japs out if you've got Chinese in. When we've won the war, sure to get the Japs out, but don't want to have to start fighting all over again to get the Chinese out."

I've skipped far ahead of my conversation with General Wavell and had better return to describe things in their chronological sequence.

Wavell was travelling in an ordinary CNAC plane with the veteran CNAC pilot "Scotty" at the controls. (Scotty was afterwards killed in the same crash that killed Major-General Dennys). They took off fairly late in the afternoon, but soon returned because Jap fighters were still hovering about. Later that evening they flew to Kunming, leaving early next morning for Rangoon, flying off their course to steer clear of the Japs. Somehow they got over Thailand and didn't discover their mistake till approaching Japanese occupied Bangkok. They turned back to Rangoon, and landed at Mingaladoon aerodrome in the middle of a Jap air raid. Bombs were dropping all over the drome, and Wavell and party had to dive for a slit trench till the raid was over. That was the second Jap raid on Rangoon; the first had knocked out the control tower and so "Scotty" got no warning that a raid was in progress. Fortunately none was injured.

CHAPTER IV

Chungking declined into its usual New Life dullness and normality after the brief flutter of excitement during Wavell's visit. I was still doing some work at the broadcasting station, and on Xmas Eve "Lousy" Peng had asked me to go down and help him with a special Xmas programme.

XGOY, the International Broadcasting Station presents a brave exterior situated on a hill near the Generalissimo's headquarters. But like most other buildings in Chungking it has suffered from bombings. At Xmas 1941 most of the windows had been blasted out; workmen were still trying to patch up holes in its roof, and liberal scaffolding inside kept it from collapsing altogether.

"Lousy" had brought from Chengtu (capital of Szechuan, and free China's Chief University and Missionary Centre), a mixed octet of singers to broadcast carols and songs of Xmas cheer. In the little studio a cabinet organ was set up and by about 7-30 p.m. everything was ready for the Xmas broadcast. While our audience was being "warmed up" with gramophone selections, the electric power cut out. Lights went and "God Rest You Merry Gentlemen" moaned despairing to an end as the gramophone turntable ran down. In most places this would have upset the whole evening's programme. Not so in Chungking. Candles were lit, the diminutive Chinese girl announcer, long straight hair falling untidily round her shoulders, had a portable gramophone on the table, "God Rest You Merry Gentlemen" transferred, and the switch thrown, all in a few seconds, so that the Broadcast was hardly interrupted. Later in the evening when the Chengtu Conservatorium of Music graduates, candles in hand, were grouped round the organ fervently singing their carols and chorales I persuaded "Lousy" to broadcast a brief description of what seemed to me a good picture on Chinese improvisation. Impossible really to broadcast such picture. "Lousy," tall and bent, with a thick brown scarf wrapped round his throat to keep out the cold, anxiously flitting from controls to microphone, the eight overcoated singers, huddling together for warmth and economy of light. Hammer blows percolating through the chinks in the soundproofness of the studio, as carpenters still worked to hold the building together. Candles instead of electric light, hand cranked gramophone instead of electric turntable. Above all, eight Chinese struggling through the "Hallelujah" Chorus. That's improvisation if you like, and an example of how the Chinese "get by." The students sang beautifully. Their voices were perfectly blended, and even if they lacked volume for the "Hallelujah," a turn of the rheostat dial at the controls adjusted that.

After it was over "Lousy" took me out to dinner at one of the sidewalk restaurants, lining the road between the Broadcasting House and the Press Hostel. "Lousy" gets sentimental at times and like many westernised Chinese, Christian feasts meant more to him than to lots of nominally Christian "foreigners." As a special concession to the "foreign friend" (in New Life China all Westerners are referred to as "foreign friends" instead of the heartier former "foreign devils") "Lousy" was allowed to open a bottle of "pai ka" at the table. "Pai ka" (white and dry) is a potent Chinese wine. It looks like water, but each drop ploughs a fiery furrow as it rolls down your throat and seems to bore a hole in your stomach linings. One can hardly claim to have lived in China until one can toss down "pai ka" by the cupful. I'd seen this bottle poking out of "Lousy's" pocket while he was superintending the carol singing and feared I'd have to share it with him. Fortunately, Chungking's New Life austerity feeding regulations only permit two people to have two dishes and a soup, so there wasn't much opportunity for drinking. Normally one drinks a cupful as each fresh dish is brought in, and at a big dinner running to fifteen or twenty dishes this becomes demoralising. "Lousy" went back to celebrate Xmas with his wife and brood of delightful impish children, and I went back to the Press Hostel to mope with the rest of our community of mopers. Hong Kong had fallen, and most Chinese I knew in Chungking had good and valuable friends in Hong Kong. It was little wonder that Chungking was even more depressed than usual during those Xmas days.

One joyous surprise we had towards New Year was when "Lao Ma," Colin McDonald of London "Times" reappeared at the Press Hostel. "Lao Ma" (Old Horse) was his Chinese nickname to distinguish him from "Hsiao Ma" (Young Horse) as "Sydney Morning Herald" Roderick MacDonald was called. Representing the "Grannies" of their respective countries, Colin Mac. was born in Australia and removed to Scotland in his childhood, while Roderick Mac. was born in Scotland and removed to Australia while still a babe. Colin MacDonald was the Doyen of China's foreign journalists. In his late forties, he'd been in China since the outbreak of the Sino-Japanese "incident." Punctilious about his brand of shaving cream and tooth-paste and changing to woollies at the correct moment in the change of season, his appearance is mild, and gently melancholy. Whilst protesting that he always tried to avoid excitement, he contrived to be in the centre of any particular hell that was being raised. He was on the water tower at Shanghai the day Pembroke Stephens of the "Daily Telegraph" was machine-gunned by the Japs. He was on the U. S. "Panay" when she was sunk by Japanese bombs, and American officers who were there tell of his bravery, covering with his body a wounded marine when the planes came down to machine-gun the decks.

The last time I'd seen MacDonald was at the Yangtse landing strip on November 28th, when he and Dorothy Jenner were waiting to take off by air to Hong-Kong. We were none of us very well. In fact I counted it one of the heroic deeds of my life that I'd dragged myself out of bed by 9 o'clock that particular morning and accompanied them down to the aerodrome. The previous evening the British Press Attache had given a farewell dinner to MacDonald and Jenner. It was the first dinner that the Press had had for a long time and the most successful I can remember. Not that I remember much about that one. History records that after all was over the Press Attache W. G. Harmon broke his wrist, descending the steps to the Yangtse Ferry; Ferdinand MacCracken Fisher passed the night on the sodden ground of an air raid shelter. Towards the end of the dinner, Chungking history pitilessly records that the London "Times" and the "Daily Express" became involved in most sentimental valedictory exchanges in fluent—or fluid—French, climaxed by noisy kissing of stubbly cheeks. Dorothy Jenner was rescued by Leland Stowe from an amorous, Chinese journalist, who was pleading with Dorothy that he pined for a "western emotional experience."

I had a confused feeling of being plunged into the icy air, and arm in arm with Betty Graham, tall, beautiful, blond-haired American journalist (free-lance at that time) and struggling up and down interminable stairways, striking dozens of matches that refused to light, looking at room numbers in a vain search for Rewi Alley, Founder of China's Industrial Cooperatives. I don't know why we were looking for him, but Betty insisted it was for some immensely important discussion. I think we never found him, because we were in the wrong street. But Betty, who was caught in the vortex of one of her long, passionate rows with Jack Belden, was certain that Jack was responsible for the elusiveness of Rewi Alley. We wandered back to the Press Hostel, and she entered into a long and bitter argument with Belden. It was loud too, because Belden was inside Spencer Moosa's room, and we were outside in the garden. It was bitterly cold, and ungallant as it was, I left her in the garden and didn't remember anything till I woke next morning, clad in shoes, socks and hat, with nothing in between. Dorothy Jenner who lived in the next room but one swore that I'd entered into a long, one-sided political argument with her during my last minutes of consciousness.

Next morning the inmates of the Press Hostel awoke, grey and haggard and mostly decided to go to sleep again. Mac. Fisher found his way home from the air raid shelter, Lao Ma and Dorothy Jenner shudderingly prepared to leave for Hong Kong. When the time came for them to depart, a few terribly ill people straggled out of the hostel in pyjamas and dressing gowns, and a mournful knot gathered by Spencer Moosa's door to make the final adieus. Betty Graham maliciously loaned over the balcony with her Leica and made a series of pictures which have been her secret joy ever since.

I've written somewhat at length about this party, because such events, regrettably, are Chungking's time marks, as far as the foreign population is concerned. Now that air raids have stopped there are only two factors by which the passage of time is marked in Chungking, the arrival of important visitors, or the incidence of a good dinner party.

"Don't you remember," people will say, in recalling some event, "it was about the time Wendell Willkie was here," or "it must have been just before the Soviet Embassy gave that big dinner. You remember? when Jarrison Forman fell over trying to get a flashlight picture of the Ambassador toasting General Tai Li."

And here was MacDonald back again. He'd spent four days in bed in Hong Kong on arrival. He just recovered in time to welcome the first Japanese bombs on the city. He escaped on board a British destroyer together with phlegmatic Guy Wint from the British Ministry of Economic Warfare, and they practised handing up shells to the guns in case the blockading Jap warships spotted them. I don't know what happened on that voyage. Something that can't be told till the end of the war. I know "Lao Ma" went to the Dutch East Indies, across to Singapore in time for a good bombing there, then to Rangoon where he just got comfortably settled in the Strand Hotel in time for the first Japanese raid on Rangoon. The wharves in front of the Strand were turned into a slaughter house of Indian coolies. And so "Times" MacDonald came back to Chungking, the most bombed city in the world and now the safest capital in the Far East.

To show the Chinese they weren't forgotten, even if Japan was fighting the British, American and Dutch elsewhere, Japanese forces in the Yangtse Valley had started another push down the railway line which runs—or did till the Chinese pulled up chunks of it—between Hankow and Canton. The objective was Changsha, capital of Hunan Province, which had already defied two previous Jap attempts at its capture. It seemed for prestige purposes that this time the Japs must capture Changsha. Military circles in Chungking admitted that the Japs were battering almost at the gates of the city, but were confident they'd be beaten back. Some of us who hadn't been to the Chinese front were keen to get down to Changsha, and approached "Holly" tong about it. He promised to do what he could. Earlier I'd asked the "Express" to let me go to the Burma Front, but as they already had veteran O. C. Gallagher down there, they wanted me to stay in China.

CHAPTER V

After New Year I cabled the "Express" again, suggesting that I go down with the Chinese armies into Burma. Leland Stowe had already left Rangoon and Rod. MacDonald was expecting to leave shortly. I didn't want to have the Sydney "Morning Herald" in Burma and the "Telegraph" unrepresented. Then came news that "Holly" had arranged for a party to go down to Changsha. The night before we left I got a cable from "Express", enthusiastically agreeing to my proposal to go to Burma with the Chinese armies. I cabled back that I was on my way to Changsha, but would go to Burma immediately I returned. Jimmy Wei, Holly's energetic secretary was leading our party to Changsha. There were several Chinese journalists and photographers, whose names I don't know, Francis Yao, from the Official Chinese News Agency—Central News—Harrison Forman with bags of cameras Nomerotsky from Tass News Agency, Robert Payne from the British Embassy and covering for London "Times," George Wong for United Press, Maurice Lie photographer, acting for Associated Press, and myself. Lt. Col. David Barret, Military attaché at the United States Embassy and Captain McMullan from the British Military Mission were also with us. We reckoned the news from Changsha must be good, otherwise the government wouldn't be keen for us to go down there.

We were to fly in a specially chartered CNAC DC2 plane to Kweilin. There's probably no country in the world like that surrounding the Kwangsi capital.

It's basically flat but covered with thousands of fantastic, inverted ice-cream cone type outcrops of rocky pinnacles. Some are small and seemingly needle sharp, others are mountain size, but all taper off to sharp peaks. It looks as if a plateau had been gradually worn away leaving only the hardest sharp cores of rock to point to the original level. In the base of these freak hills and mountains, the Chinese have tunnelled out workshops, aeroplane hangars, and fuel storage depots, well out of reach of Japanese bombers. Kweilin's newspapers are also published in these rock tunnels. It's usually misty round Kweilin and I've never flown there without fearing, any minute that the belly of the plane will be ripped out, on one of those needle peaks. This Changsha trip was the first I'd made to Kweilin and I got an uneasy feeling in my spine, peering down at those pinnacles, when the plane suddenly started plunging down. One of the propellers had stopped revolving. We skimmed along on one motor for about ten minutes, seemingly just clearing the mountain tops. Then for a few minutes, we actually dodged in between peaks. After one or two false starts, the propeller whirred again and we soared up towards the clouds.

Months later, in the bar of the Great Eastern Hotel, Calcutta I heard some pilots discussing the 'ceiling' of Douglas planes on one and two motors respectively, and heard one of them say:

"I scared the "daylights" out of a bunch of journalists way back in January, flying them down to Kweilin. I always wanted to see how much those buses would drop if one motor cut out with a full load on so I switched one engine off. We only dropped a couple thousand feet, and she picked up immediately I switched her on again."

I went across to tell that pilot what I thought about

him and discovered that it was the Australian, Syd. de Kentzow, so there wasn't much I could do about it except to agree that he *had* scared the "daylights" out, of at least one journalist.

At Kweilin aerodrome a fleet of cars was waiting to rush us to the Lo Chun Hsie, Kweilin's ace hotel. We were the guests of the Kweilin garrison commander for lunch and I tasted for the first time Kweilin's famous Putao Jao, grape wine. I believe it's actually made from berries, but tastes something like a diluted port. At any rate it was a welcome change from the eternal rice wine. Afterwards we went to see the grand old man of Kwangsi Province, General Li Chi Sen. He is regarded as one of China's "Elder Statesmen" and with Generals Pai Chung Hai (Deputy Chief of Staff) and Li Tsung Jen (Commander 5th War Area) completes the famous trio of Kwangsi generals. While he was explaining the progress of the fighting at Changsha, the air alarm went and we were hurried into a magnificent air raid shelter, hewn out of Kweilin's rock. Only one reconnaissance plane came over and we were soon back poring over maps and trying to grasp the complexities of the strategical situation in the Hunan fighting. Later that evening we were taken to the train in which we were to travel to Hengyang (Hunan Province). This train was one of the major surprises I had in China. A special "blue" coach had been reserved for us, and one had to keep looking out of the window and see the rice-fields to realise that one was still in China. It had a regular wagon-lit sleeping car, and I think most of us agreed next morning that we'd had the most comfortable night's sleep since we arrived in China. About 7 a.m., just as we were pulling into Hengyang, there was another air alarm and our train shunted back into some cuttings a few miles away. We piled out, and hearing planes coming, stretched out in a rice field hoping we were invisible among the green stalks. I think there were three planes, but they never bothered us. We went on to Hengyang, where we changed trains for Chuchow, the furthest point towards Changsha to which trains were running at that time. From Chuchow we travelled by motor launch, going northwards down the Hsiang river to Changsha itself.

It was bitterly cold, but the air was clear. Frost on the rice-stubble, but hard blue sky above. The Hsiang river flows into the Yangtse at Yochow—which is the Jap base for their drives on Changsha. The river is famous for its boat-builders, and we passed fleets of beautiful gondola-shaped sailing boats, slim and curved, the grain of the camphor wood showing through heavy layers of tung oil. They carry a great deal of sail for their size and make a brave showing, with a good wind behind them, ploughing their way upstream through the steely, blue waters of the Hsiang. Like most rivers in China, the Hsiang seemed to be teeming with fish. Most ingenious of the many methods used to catch them, seemed to be that employed by the cormorant fishers. We saw scores of boats, black with the huge variety of cormorant one finds in China. I counted twenty-two on one boat. They perch on the sides and oars, ruffling out their feathers; every now and again diving overboard, deep into the water, almost always returning with a fish which was quickly retrieved by the fisherman. Other boats had a large scoop-shaped net set in a frame—like a huge landing gaff—with the frame attached to a ladder-like arrangement. This lay flat in the bottom of the boat when the net was out of the water. When the net was lowered, the ladder automatically rose till it stood almost vertical. After about ten minutes, the fishermen started walking up the ladder which gradually subsided to its position at the bottom of the boat—and the net with the water streaming through it, and a residue of fish in the bottom, came up out of the water. A very simple and efficient arrangement, and another example of Chinese ingenuity.

For most of that down-river trip we sat huddled together in the cabin of the launch, the Chinese drinking their fiery "Pai Ka" wine, and playing a Chinese variation of chess, the rest of us telling stories—most of them unprintable. Now and again we squeezed out and crossed over to the barge which carried our baggage, and which was lashed alongside the motor-launch. Stamping our feet and clapping our gloved hands to keep the blood circulating, we sang all the river songs we could think of. Big, upstanding Nomerotsky was the only one who seemed to enjoy the cold, and when we'd run out of river songs, he went through his repertoire of Russian songs. He taught us the air of some Red Army choruses, and we roared them out as lustily as we could, to the amazement of the fishermen, many of whom had never seen "foreign devils" before.

It was midday on the third day after leaving Chungking, that we arrived at a long stretch of silver sand beach a few miles northward of Changsha. We disembarked north of Changsha. The name Changsha means "Long Sands" and the gleaming sand strips on either side of the river are sufficient justification for the name. While the rest of the party were dumping their baggage ashore, I retired to the shade of a ferry house to change my camera lens. When I returned to the beach, I was surprised to see it deserted. Then I heard an aeroplane, and someone shouted to me to hurry and get into a ditch. My feet hardly touched the ground as I leaped over the sand and jumped into a slit trench a hundred yards from the river's edge with the plane following. It hovered around for a while, but did not drop anything.

We had a long walk to the headquarters of General Hsuen Yueh (the "Little Tiger" as he was fondly called) thrice defender of Changsha. We were quartered in a foreign-style building, which in peaceful times had seen the headquarters of a forestry school. A terrific lunch had been prepared for us, and I was introduced for the first time to the pleasant Hunan custom of eating from the bubbling "huo kuo" (fire pan or chafing dish). In China, soup is always served at the end of the meal. It's often served several times during the meal also, but invariably a proper Chinese dinner ends with a soup. In Hunan, towards the end of the meal, a large powter bowl is brought in and set in the middle of the table. On a twelve inch high stand it looks like the old type of kerosene lamp with the small cylindrical chimney glass. Instead of a glass chimney, the bowl has a pipe down the centre where glowing coals are placed which keep the soup-filled bowl at simmering point. The guests help themselves from the communal dish, and as its contents are reduced, the remainder of various delicate dishes which still adorn the table, are shovelled in. Sweet-sour pork, pigs skin, fish heads, chickens' blood, frogs' legs, pieces of Pekin duck, doves' eggs, mushrooms, chillies—all go in together while the table boy, from time to time, keeps the bowl filled to its proper level by adding more soup. On a cold winter's day, the "huo-kuo" is a fine institution.

After lunch we went across to the "Little Tiger's" lair. General Hsueh Yueh is not at all the popular idea of a great commander. Small, slight, boyish-looking, in different surroundings one might have picked him for a hard-bitten jockey. His bullet head was close-shaven, and he was wearing the greenish-khaki uniform of Chinese officers, with a pair of soft, black knee boots. He had an impressive-looking collection of staff officers with him. One particularly struck me—and other correspondents afterwards mentioned the same thing—by his extraordinary facial resemblance to Napoleon Bonaparte. With the heavy, thoughtful "man of destiny" expression, he also wore his dark forelock swinging in a crescent across his temple. I discovered later that "Napoleon" was Assistant Chief of Staff. The Adjutant-General, was also a fine-looking man with the lofty forehead and triangular face of an intellectual. After preliminary courtesies (during which with traditional Chinese politeness Hsuen Yuen apologised for the poor way in which we'd been received, the miserable lodging into which we'd been thrown and the despicable food which would be offered us during our stay in Changsha) maps were unrolled, and we were treated to an exposition of the Hunan campaign, as it had progressed up till that day.

The previous Changsha-campaign had taken place in September, 1940 when the Japs actually got inside the city and were forced to withdraw mainly because of difficulties with their rear communications. Hsueh Yueh, told us that immediately after the September campaign he began to prepare for another Jap attempt. He maintains that he worked out his strategy, had it approved by the Generalissimo, and orders were given to his various armies in the field with such exactitude, and in such detail that once the campaign actually started no fresh orders had to be issued.

Roughly the plan of campaign was as follows. The Japanese had to push about 60 miles southwards from Yochow to Changsha, crossing four rivers running approximately at right angles to their line of advance. The main Japanese drive was along the torn up road-bed of the Yochow-Changsha section of the Canton-Hankow railway. Chinese troops, on the south bank of each of the four rivers, had orders to oppose the Japs, but not at too great cost to themselves. The idea was to progressively reduce the forces which would eventually reach Changsha. All roads and tracks were destroyed so that at the Sintsiang, the first river crossing, the Japs had to leave all their artillery behind—except mountain guns and mortars which could be carried on horse-back. Chinese troops on the South bank of the rivers were posted like gates along the path of the Jap advance—gates which at first resisted, but swung open when pressure was strong enough.

Two of Hsuen Yueh's best divisions remained in Changsha, with their backs to the river and their fronts to the enemy. They were dug in the city itself and also in a cemetery just outside the city boundaries. Their orders were in accordance with Chiang Kai Shek's revolutionary strategy "make the enemy's rear your front." They either had to advance, stay where they were, or die. With the half mile wide Hsiang River at their backs there was no other alternative. To the South of Changsha the "Little Tiger" kept his "counter-attacking" armies in reserves. By the time they neared Changsha, the Japanese armies were well strung out. Those "gates" which had swung open to let them through, became fences, running North and South between the rivers parallel to Jap supply—and communication lines, which latter were constantly attacked. From probably sixty thousand men that set out from Yochow (the Chinese claimed a hundred thousand), only about thirty thousand actually took part in the assault on the city.

The Japs' biggest shock must have come when the Chinese blazed away at them with six inch field guns, posted in the hills on the opposite side of the river from Changsha, and well out of range of the Japs' mountain guns and mortars. The battle for Changsha itself was short and fierce. The Japs occupied the famous American endowed Yale-in-China Hospital in the outskirts and battled their way through to the South gate of the city. Their planes came over and heavily bombed the Chinese defenders, but they were so well dug in that little harm was done. At the height of the battle the fighting was so mixed that the Japs couldn't drop bombs without hitting their own troops. Fiercest fighting was for possession of the cemetery, portions of which changed hands seven times during the battle. When the opposing armies had almost fought themselves to a standstill, the "Little Tiger's" two armies of "counter-attack" were swung into the fray. The Chinese forces strung out along the Jap supply lines had done their work so well that the Jap troops at Changsha began to run out of food and ammunition. Planes came over and dropped supplies every day, but much of that dropped was pounced on by Chinese peasants. Soon the remnants of the Jap army were in full retreat. Chinese troops between the four rivers swung round into position again. This time they were not to be "gates," but "barriers" along the North banks of the rivers barring the Jap path of retreat. This time there was to be no giving way to pressure, but annihilation of the enemy.

After Hsueh Yueh's exposition of the situation (this was just two days after the Japs had been pushed back from Changsha and fighting was still in progress at the Liuyang River 12 miles North of the city) we went along to have a look at his artillery battery. We were all surprised to see good six inch Krupp guns stamped "Made in Germany 1936." I am sure the Japanese would have been edified to know that their defeat was at least partly due to the excellence of their Axis partners' guns. They were well camouflaged, and Jap planes never spotted them although they wasted bombs on dummy batteries of petrol drums and bamboo poles, the Chinese had rigged up about half a mile away. One of the artillery officers told me that when they fired their first salvos, there seemed to be a mass meeting of Jap soldiers and officers in a walled-off compound, when the smoke and dust cleared from the shell bursts, the ground was covered with dead Japs and the walls of the compound had disappeared.

Next day we set off early to have a look at Changsha and the battlefield in the immediate vicinity. It's a fine, big city with about 250,000 population. Much of it was destroyed in an unfortunate fire during the first "Battle for Changsha" in October 1939. Orders had been given to Governor Chang Chi Chung to burn the city, rather than let it fall into Japanese hands if the situation got desperate. While the Japs were still a long way from the city, it was set on fire and much of it destroyed. The Japs never got within 40 miles of Changsha that time. Some say the Hunan governor panicked. Others that he fired the city to trap General Chou in Lai and other communists from Hankow, who were in the city and narrowly escaped death. Whatever the real reason was, the Generalissimo had Chang Chi Chung shot.

The wide streets of the city were completely deserted as we tramped through that morning, except for troops. There seemed a fair number of the latter, clad in rags, but tough as nails. We passed lines of them carrying plain pine coffins, containing remains of comrades killed in battle. The whole of the civilian population of Changsha had been evacuated in seven days, long before the Japs approached. Special evacuation trains and boats were provided and less than five hundred civilians remained. The city had been turned into a fortress, with machine-gun nests and pill-boxes at every street corner. Bricks and stone barricades, and bamboo pallisades had been thrown across the streets; shop doorways and windows bricked up, so that troops infiltrating would have no cover for street fighting. Whole shopping streets were practically turned into solid walls. Our military observers were impressed with these internal city defences and said it was obvious that even had the Japs got into the city they would have had to fight every inch of the way through the streets. Bombing had done little to destroy the defences, only knocking out shops and houses here and there. Gaps caused by bombs in the street wall were soon patched up with bricks and stones cemented together. At the city's South gate there was evidence of fierce fighting. The conducting officer told us, a Chinese detachment defending here, had been reduced to nineteen men, but they didn't budge, holding the Japs off till reinforcements arrived. I'd never before realised what tough stuff bamboo is, till I saw how it had held up the Japs round this South gate. Plenty of rifle bullets had flattened themselves against it without penetrating. The Japs had got so close that they had hacked away with their bayonets, but made little impression on it. I think they'd have needed anti-tank or mortar shells fired point-blank to have torn through that pallisade. The Chinese had made a sort of trellis with it, driving long stout sharpened bamboo poles well into the ground, and laying split bamboo through horizontally.

Through the South gate, in the outskirts there'd been heavy street fighting. Wooden shutters and doors were splintered and scarred where bullets had whipped along, telegraph poles spattered like target cards in a shooting gallery. Furnitures, and doors hastily ripped off their hinges, had been thrown together for barricades, and every here and there, were patches of blood and scraps of blood-stained padding torn from coat linings lying, where some wounded soldier had sought temporary shelter. There were a power house and an arsenal nearby, about a mile from the South gate, and these were the nearest points to the city, occupied by the Japs. A little further along, we came on a burying part, but this time it was Japs they were burying. They'd laid out about twenty of them, all—starknaked—and were burying them a few inches under the ground. Of the hundreds of Japanese corpses I saw that and the following day, all but about a dozen were naked. Those that still had on uniforms were ones that hadn't been discovered by burying parties, I discovered for myself. The uniforms are always stripped off and taken back to headquarters, so that a tally can be kept of Jap casualties.

I was surprised at the little emotion I felt, looking for the first time at bodies of men who'd died violently. Maybe if they'd been men of my own race I'd have felt differently. I hope I would. They looked so much part of the yellow earth on which they were lying that it was difficult to believe they'd been breathing and eating and drinking a few days earlier. Our military observers carefully examined the corpses' feet. Because Japanese wear slippers with a thong separating the big toe and the rest of the foot, the division formed between the toes is an easy way to distinguish between Japanese and Chinese. Despite obvious superficial resemblance between Japanese and Chinese there *are* points of dissimilarity not difficult to define. Japs have more hair on their bodies for one thing, and many of them wear luxuriant whiskers. The Chinese usually have straight, lank hair. The Japs' hair is often quite crisp. The Chinese have a franker, more cheerful expression in their faces, and those who've lived long in the East can usually distinguish between the two.

The cemetery hill was a veritable graveyard of Jap troops, scores of whom were still sprawling about, just as they'd fallen. Every square yard looked as if it had been fiercely contested. In trenches and dugouts and shell holes there were bodies many of them wounded in half a dozen places. Lt. Col. Barrett, who has been in China since long before the Sino-Japanese "incident" incidentalised, and been on most of the important battle-fields since "allowed" he'd never seen evidence of bloodier fighting. The bodies we saw represented only a tiny fraction of the Jap casualties, because they were only the unburied remnants of those left after the last Jap retreat from the cemetery. Those killed during the earlier fighting had been taken away and cremated by the Japs themselves. A gruesome touch was added to the general bloodiness, by the fact that most of the corpses had a limb, usually an arm, hacked off. The Japs have to have some ashes to send home in a little white casket to the hero's family, and if they can't drag away a complete corpse, they like to hack off a limb so as to have at least something to burn.

General Li Yu Tang, a big, intelligent-looking Hunanese, who was in charge of the divisions inside Changsha, proudly took us over to a machine-gun nest, topping a small rise on the edge of the cemetery, and told us that although the cemetery changed hands several times, this one Chinese machine-gun nest was never lost. In the final Japanese assault the whole of the cemetery was lost except this one point, and only one machine-gunner remained alive, but he succeeded in holding the position until help arrived.

How the Japs must have cursed the Chinese peasants who turned out in force and destroyed the roads leading to Changsha, forcing them to leave their artillery behind. With the position they held near the cemetery, and decent field places, they could have blasted away at Changsha defences as long as they pleased.

We walked across to a small village to see some of the Japanese cremation grounds. The two we saw were about one hundred feet long and fifteen wide, the whole area covered with blackened bones and skulls and scraps of charred flesh. Near one of these charnel strips I saw a group of excited peasants—the first civilians I'd seen around Changsha—talking and pointing at something, lying alongside a small pond. I went over and saw the bodies of two blue clad peasants stretched out on the ground. Their hands were tied behind their backs, and there were ropes round their necks. I think the latter were put there by the villagers to drag them from the pond. Their foreheads had been battered in—probably by rifle butts. I called an interpreter over and the villagers told us that these were a father and son, and were two of eighteen peasants from the village the Japs had caught and killed. All the bodies were thrown in the pond. The peasants from the village wanted to take me across to a house where lay the body of the wife of the young man. The Japs had caught her too and raped her to death. I didn't go to see the body.

Later that morning, we visited the burnt out headquarters of one of the Jap regiments that had got closest to the city. Some Chinese soldiers had crept up at night, silently killed the sentries and set fire to the thatch-roofed building. Incidentally, Japs in China as in Burma were found notably careless about posting sentries. The regimented commander—Colonel Kato—tried to rush out, but was shot. The rest of his staff perished in the flames. Their shrivelled torsos were there still.

Often, especially in the village streets, we found naked Jap bodies that had been split open from crutch to throat, opened up like a pig or sheep hanging in a butcher's window. At first I thought that must be a very efficient hari-kiri, but it was gently explained to me that it was more likely to be wounded Japs who'd been discovered by Chinese peasants. After seeing those bodies dragged from the village pond, I could understand the peasants' feelings.

On the way back to General Li Yu Tang's headquarters for lunch, we walked along one of the main roads of the Jap advance. It had been under fire from the "Little Tiger's" six inch guns. It must have been wet at the time, because the print-marks of Japanese boots were clearly visible. Dried out puddle holes and foot-marks were all caked with dried blood. I've seen a fair number of battle-fields since, but none where the earth was so blood-soaked as that round the cemetery and road at Changsha. On evidence we saw that morning, our two military observers (both of them shrewd and conservative in estimating casualties) reckoned the Japs suffered at least ten thousand casualties around Changsha itself.

After an enormous lunch we set out to see what the Japs had left of the Yale-in-China Hospital and Middle School. We ran into Dr. Pettus on our way. He was in charge of the hospital and had just returned from Hsiangtan to look over the damage. He and his wife had evacuated a couple of hundred school children 20 miles up the river to Hsiangtan, and jubilantly told us he'd been able to take away the best part of the hospital equipment. I suppose it was the first chance the Japs had in China, adequately to express their feelings towards America. In previous campaigns they'd always been afraid to go too far in damaging foreigners' property, because their government had to pay out compensation. They'd done their best to make up for lost opportunities at Changsha. Most of the buildings at Yale-in-China were totally destroyed. They'd tried hard to burn the hospital, but even after liberally pouring cans of petrol about the place, it was hard to destroy a brick building as solidly built as the Yale-in-China Hospital. After a rough checking over, Pettus estimated the damage at about one million American dollars.

With the exceptions of a break for lunch and another hour's spell to examine booty captured from the Japs, we'd been tramping about since sun-up that morning. By the time we finished with Dr. Pettus, it was just getting dark, and we were relieved to find a string of horses waiting to take us back to the boat. We were fairly exhausted by the time we'd crossed the river and tramped three miles back to Headquarters. Next morning we were due to leave on an excursion to the Liuyang River.

The Liuyang trip was postponed because there were still a few Japs about, and it would be a terrible "loss of face" for Changsha generals if any correspondents got wounded. The "Little Tiger" had given orders for the Japs to be mopped up so we could go the following day.

As compensation for the delay he sent over a Japanese prisoner for us to question. We were interested to know how he'd let himself be taken prisoner.

Normally a Jap fights to the last and commits hari-kiri rather than fall into enemy hands. He explained that he and five of his comrades were cut off in the Changsha Power House after the main force of Japs had retreated. He'd had nothing to eat, he said, for five days, and feeling very weak and dizzy didn't realise that the soldiers advancing towards him were Chinese. I asked him what his first thoughts were when he found himself prisoner. He said he tried to pull the pin out of his hand grenade so's he could kill himself. He didn't have anything very interesting to say, except that the army provided Japanese prostitutes for them—even at the front. I've lost my Changsha notes now, but I remember that the price of a prostitute was a big proportion of the soldiers' monthly pay. He complained that as he was used to getting three meals a day in the Japanese army it was difficult to get used to the Chinese custom of only two meals a day. He asked us for and received some sugar and cigarettes. He'd been an insurance clerk in Tokio before he was grabbed for the army, and his father was a pawn-broker. He didn't know much about the Pacific war and said the only thing he and his comrades were interested in was getting back to Japan to be with their families.

After he was taken away, I discussed with some Chinese journalists this peculiar idea of the Japs always wanting to commit suicide as soon as they were captured. The Chinese maintained that, apart from the fact that a Japanese soldier was never allowed to return to Japan once he'd been made a war prisoner, it was quite a natural reaction to want to kill oneself when captured. I argued that with Westerners, the first reaction would be to reason.

"Well, here I am. I'm still alive. I'd better keep

myself as fit as possible, so that I can take the first opportunity to escape."

They couldn't understand that attitude and were certain if they were captured they'd try and kill themselves at the first opportunity. The old axiom "while there's life there's hope" doesn't seem to find favour in oriental philosophy.

We filled in the rest of the day, making up notes, writing despatches and preparing ourselves for the ordeal of a three mile walk at night, to attend a dinner, given in our honour by the gentlemen of the Changsha Press. That was a fine dinner. I think it's an appropriate stage in this book to reveal some of the pitfalls into which the unwary visitor to China may fall, when he attends an "honest to goodness" Chinese dinner.

There are certain formalities which both guest and host are expected to observe. For instance, the host will certainly apologise before dinner commences, for the unpalatableness of the dishes he's about to set before his guest. The tables are usually round and the guest is seated facing the door, the host with his back to the door. The guest by his position facing the door assures himself that no assassin can sneak in unseen and strike him down. The host by turning his back to the door, shows he fears no such thing. If there are friends of the host present, there will be a polite scuffle amongst them when the time comes to be seated. None will consider himself of sufficient importance to be placed next to the guest of honour. They will want to occupy the humbler positions each side of the host. When the placing of the guests is politely settled, warm wine will be brought in little pewter kettles and before the dinner starts, the host will lift his wine cup, bow to his guest and say "Kam pae" (dry cup) which means that everyone must empty his cup. If the guest of honour doesn't succeed at the first throw, the host will remain standing politely inclining his head, with his cup in the air, until honour is satisfied and the guest—probably wildly spluttering—has swallowed his wine. The host will murmur "Ah hsi hsi ni" (Ah, thank you) put down his cup and refill all the guests' cups and his own. The first dishes have been brought in by this time and placed in the centre of the table. The host picks up his chopsticks, everyone else follows suit, he chants "Shih tsai" (to the food) and everyone plunges in with their chopsticks and the dinner has started. Every now and again, someone picks out a particular delicacy—a succulent piece of pig's entrail for instance—and lays it in the bowl of the guest of honour. As the dinner wears on, each of the host's friends solemnly requests the guest to "kam pae" with him. At first he politely refuses, but they look so hurt, emptying their own cups and standing with cups poised in mid-air, that the guest eventually relents and tosses off cup after cup. As each fresh dish is brought in everybody drinks, but the guest is always several cups ahead, because he has to drink separately with every other diner present. When everybody is feeling pleasantly merry, they start playing the finger game. The host starts with the guest. Simultaneously, they fling one hand forward, with a certain number of fingers stuck out, at the same time shouting what they believe to be the total number of fingers showing in both hands. They probably have to throw their hands out several times before one of them guesses the right number. The loser has to toss off a cup of wine. At a big dinner party with a dozen or so tables, and half a dozen pairs at each table playing the finger game, each couple shouting their guesses at the tops of their voices, the noise is terrific.

The Press dinner at Changsha followed the usual form. The wine was frightfully strong "pai ka." Towards the end of the dinner I was asked to make a speech—to propose the toast of the ABCD Front. ABCD Front was very popular in China at that time. I had already responded to everybody's toast at my table, as well as toasts from several other tables. I was very willing to make a speech. I only had hazy recollections about it afterwards. I remembered speaking very deliberately, and stopping after every sentence while Francis Yao from Central News translated for me. He wasn't in a very good condition either. The speech seemed terribly well received, and I remember some argument when I finished it. I wanted to drink a toast to the ABCD Front, but it seemed I was persuaded to drink a separate cup for ABC and D. I don't recall another thing after that. The next thing I knew was waking up next morning at our headquarters, feeling very ill, and with plenty of evidence around me that I was ill. Maurice Lieu and Francis Yao came in while I was sitting up wild-eyed in bed and assured me that I'd made a smashing speech the night before, not only at the dinner, but all the way home and as I was carried upstairs. It was cabled back to Chungking by Central News and all the Chinese papers carried it next day. I suspect what Francis Yao gave out as a translation of my speech was really a speech of his own concoction. When I returned to Chungking, Chinese friends of mine, and Publicity Board officials, all congratulated me on the magnificent oration I had delivered at Changsha. I always intended to get a translation made and find out with what statements I had been credited, but I never did. Whatever Francis Yao's speech contained, it established my reputation among Chinese newspapermen.

Those of us who felt able to move after celebrating the "Third Victory of Changsha" left early in the morning for the three-mile walk to the river, where a launch was waiting to take us across to the Changsha side, where we were to pick up horses and ride out twelve miles to the Liuyang River crossing. We wanted to see something of the Jap line of retreat, and the Liuyang was the scene of a violent battle as the Japs tried to force their way back across the river. It was terribly cold, the countryside was blanketed in frost and the road slippery with ice. We were a silent and downcast company. Even veteran Dave Barrett's normally rubicund shining countenance was pallid and drawn, and MacMullan's endless repertoire of risqué stories was received in frigid silence. The river crossing was fairly rough and several hardier spirits who'd tackled breakfast before they left, were soon hanging over the rail.

The jolting up and down on the backs of the small, rough-riding Chinese horses, soon cleared our stomachs of any remnants of the night's debauch, and after an hour's riding most of us began to pick up again.

The path of any retreating army is a mournful enough sight, but this one leading back to the Liuyang river was particularly bad, because of the remains of dead Jap horses scattered all over the place. Whether they'd slaughtered them for food, or because they reckoned on retreating faster without them, was hard to say, but there were bits and pieces of dead horses everywhere. It was difficult and dangerous riding, because of the way the road was destroyed. Chinese roads are built well about the level of the rice-fields, as the latter are under water for most of the year. When the cry goes out to destroy roads, the peasants cut them down to the level of the rice field, all except a track left in the middle ranging from six to fifteen inches wide. Sometimes, to make progress harder for horses, the central track is left in an S formation, so that horses even in daylight can't go faster than walking pace, and at night-time can't move at all without slipping off and bogging in the rice-fields. The path leading out to the Liuyang was very narrow and studded with "cavalry traps." Every few hundred yards it was intersected by wide ditches. In some places these had been bridged by long, nine inch wide, flagstones, over which the horses nervously picked their way, at other places there was just a yawning gap and you had to look for a detour. Chinese horses are very small, but extremely sure-footed, and can negotiate these paths fairly well, but the big, raw-boned Australian-bred nags of the Japs find it terribly hard going. We saw the remains of several that had slipped off the path, and been shot when they couldn't struggle out of the natural bog of the paddy-field. I'll have more to say about Chinese road destruction in a later book on China. I think it's one of the chief factors in their successful resistance to the Japs.

The Liuyang cattle-field was a minor edition of the one we'd seen at the cemetery. Sanitation squads, with masks strapped round their faces, were busily dragging corpses together, and shoving them under the earth. As at Changsha, most of the bodies had a limb hacked off, and some of them seemed to have been caught by the villagers before they died. One body lying face upwards—the escorting officer told us he was a Japanese major—caught my attention. The jaws weren't quite closed and peeping out behind his teeth were five revolver bullets. He'd apparently been leading a charge, revolver in hand with extra bullets in his mouth, when he was struck down.

I think we'd all had our fill of seeing mutilated bodies by this time, and were content to recognise that the Chinese had scored a first class victory over the Japs —incidentally the first victory the United Nations had to their credit since the Pacific War started. We were glad enough to turn our horses' heads back towards Changsha. It seemed a long ride back. Muscles long out of use began to stiffen, the saddles had developed spikes and razor-edges we'd not noticed before, straps of haversacks and cameras cut deep furrows into shoulders and necks, and all in all, we were mightily relieved when we straggled back to our launch again. It was pitch dark by the time we crossed the river, and Harrison Forman and I were nearly frightened to death walking back along the road. About half a mile away from headquarters, we were walking ahead with a tiny torch spotting the ground ahead of us, when a wild figure, letting out an unearthly yell, leaped from the side of the road, shoving his bayonet into my waistcoat button. With his lips drawn back, baring his teeth in a snarl, he looked more like a ferocious animal than a man. He kept on yelling at me and prodding my stomach with each yell, until an officer rushed up and gave the password. That was my first experience of a Chinese sentry. I've been challenged by them plenty of times since on various fronts, but I'm always terrified by their animal ferocity. Even if I know the password, they usually scare me so much that I stand and stutter. I should think if I get killed in this war, it'll be at the hands of a Chinese sentry.

General Hsueh Yueh gave us a farewell breakfast, if one can so term an enormous banquet with about 20 dishes, gallons of wine and which lasted for two and a half hours. After breakfast we were each presented with a Japanese tin helmet and a gas mask neatly tucked in canvas bags on which our names were stencilled, with a signed photograph of the "Little Tiger" and a piece of embroidery for which Changsha is famous. Our names were embroidered on the edge, together with an inscription commemorating the third victory of Changsha. Our homeward trek commenced.

Down on the white sand banks of the Hsiang River was an amazing spectacle. Word had quickly passed round that the Japs had been driven from Changsha. Thousands of people were streaming back to the city. All night they'd been piling up at the river's edge waiting for daylight to be ferried across. Old ladies, in trim black toques, were being carried down in sedan chairs, suitcases and packages piled up on the shafts. Family men trotting along, with their household goods packed in baskets, suspended each end of a carrying stick swung across their shoulders. Often a child was sitting in one basket—an equivalent weight of goods in the other. Wheelbarrows, mountainously piled with baggage, were being urged through the sand, one man yoked in front pulling, another behind pushing—a rope passed under the shafts, and over his back, to take the weight. Young children hardly out of the toddler stage, but looking very independent and grown-up in their padded coats and cloaks, staggered along with loads appropriate to their strength slung over their shoulders, like the grown-ups. Rickshas, their wheels buckled out under the strain of their heavy loads were shoved along through the sand. Changsha was returning to take up residence within a few days, shopkeepers would have dug up their buried stocks, streets and doorways cleared, shops and houses cleaned up, and life revolving as normal. I've entered plenty of Chinese towns and villages after Japanese occupation. I've never seen Chinese people waste time on tears and lamentations. If their home's destroyed, they immediately go about to salvage what can be used again, and they start rebuilding. Thousands of years of sorrows and sufferings have imbued them with Spartan stoicism.

Hunan with its yellow rice-fields and yellow mud villages which seemed to have grown up out of the soil rather than been built on it was soon left behind. The perfect organisation of the Chinese Publicity Department whisked us back to Chungking again. Trains connected with boats with magic precision, and a plane was waiting to take us to Chungking an hour or so after a train landed us at Kweilin. We were back in Chungking within eight days of our departure.

I was anxious to get away to Burma as soon as possible. Roderick MacDonald had already gone, and I didn't want to hang around Chungking a day longer than necessary. We arrived back from Changsha on January 15th, and the first plane on which I could get booking to Lashio was leaving on the 23rd. Stories were already drifting back about Chinese troops in Burma, and both the "Express" and myself were fuming at the delay in getting down.

CHAPTER VI

I left Chungking on January 22nd feeling pessimistic regarding the immediate future in China. There was so much disillusionment following British and American failures against Japanese in the Far East that anything seemed likely to happen. There were plenty of people in high places in Chungking, trying to persuade the Generalissimo that he'd picked the wrong horse in backing the democracies. Many of his immediate entourage were German or Japanese trained and still had close sympathies with the Axis.

Of course, these malcontents had a strong case. What was China getting out of the war? She'd hoped for so much. After five years of hanging on alone, she'd hoped for miracles to happen after she got allies. Now she found her allies were liabilities rather than assets. Hong Kong from where she'd been receiving a trickle of aid—now blocked. The Philippines, Malaya and Dutch East Indies from where she'd received enormous financial contributions from the eight million odd Chinese living there, were either occupied or being occupied. The Burma Road which was to carry all that wonderful stuff promised under Lease-Lend and British credits threatened. The only substantial help she'd received—the AVG (American Volunteer Group) was now being largely transferred to Burma. Some of China's best equipped troops were going to Burma. The democratic idols had feet of clay. The Gissimo had made serious the wrong blunder. Thus they argued.

"In any case," they whispered, "don't let's get too closely involved with the democracies. We should play a waiting game. Sit tight against the Japanese. Keep clear of other involvements and while Britain and America have their hands full elsewhere, we can quietly settle accounts with the communists. Russia's on the point of collapsing and couldn't interfere even if she wanted to."

Reactionaries in Chungking have often told me that it was only British and particularly American sentimental affection for the Chinese Red Army which prevented Central Government troops from crushing them. Incidentally they blame Edgar Snow chiefly for American "sentimentalism" towards the Chinese communists.

There was always a strong pro-Axis feeling in Chungking, especially in Army circles, and after United Nations 'Pacific defeats,' it began to be more vocal than before. Rumour had it that the real reason for Quo Tai Chi's dismissal as Foreign Minister late in December was due to pressure from pro-Axis Kuomintang officials who thought he'd been too precipitate in pushing for declaration of war against Germany, Italy and Japan. I believed even then—and argued this with many of my friends—that the Gissimo and Gissima were both hard-headed and realistic enough to know that the 'Uni-nations' were going to win. That they were strong enough to persuade the malcontents of this and force them to see that China should throw in her lot with the winning side. The question was how many more United Nation defeats would China stand? Malaya wasn't looking too good and Burma was starting badly. Would the Gissimo hold things together if the Burma Road was closed?

These were questions running through my mind as I set out for Burma.

As long as you're not expecting any forced landings, the flight from Chungking to Lashio is a wonderful experience. At first you sweep along the Yangtse Valley until the plane's got sufficient height to clear the mountains round Chungking, then it swings away to the South towards Kunming. You can best appreciate the work of China's humble peasant cultivators from the air. Tough-looking mountains are ringed almost to the very tip with rice terraces, reamed out of the mountain side. They look like inverted spinning tops. Most of the year they're flooded with water, for rice is grown under water till a few weeks before harvest time. And before the green shoots poke through one has the amazing spectacle of mountains turned into stepped lakes. Where rice is cultivated the whole countryside is swathed in rhythmic sweeps of clear mirrors of green stalks or gold stubble according to the season. At any time it presents a mosaic of incomparable pattern and beauty. Much of the land between Chungking and Kunming, however, is too wild and rugged for even the ingenuity of the Chinese cultivator. South of Kunming the country's even grimmer, and one is reminded of telescopic photos of the surface of the moon. The whole landscape is pockmarked with fantastic mountains and craters, and there's little sign of human habitation. Parts of Szechwan and Yunnan Provinces are the most undeveloped areas in China.

Fellow-travellers in the plane included the last members of the United States Navy in China. They were naval personnel from the Yangtse gunboat "Tutuila" which had just been beached, and its guns handed over to the Chinese. Also travelling was Colonel "Fill" Meyer, Military Attaché at the American Embassy. It had been icy cold when we left Chungking, but when we arrived at Lashio, it was boiling hot. An American

Navy truck met the plane, and was greeted with rousing cheers, when the travellers saw it was loaded with free beer for the marines. They probably hadn't seen beer for years—it's unprocurable in Chungking—and soon every man was draining a bottle.

I had to contact Colonel Hobson—"Hobbie Old Boy" to the Americans—who was liaison officer for the Chinese Army. He was supposed to have been warned of my arrival by the British Embassy, Chungking, and was to arrange for me to see the Chinese troops. He came to see me at the CNAC. Hostel (the only hotel worthy of the name at Lashio) but had received no word from Chungking.

"In any case, old boy, I couldn't possibly do anything for you, till you've seen them at headquarters Rangoon, and I receive instructions from there. Sorry old boy!"

And that was that.

I met some friends of mine at the hostel—members of the Magruder Mission to China—Lt. Col. Haas, head of the anti-malarial section of the Yunnan-Burma Railroad, Major Ausland Chief Adviser for the Railroad Construction and Captain Wilson, Adviser to the Yunnan-Burma Highway Administration. The Hostel was full, but Captain Wilson offered me a bed in his room for the night. He looked slightly greyer at the temples than when I'd seen him three months earlier, when he arrived with General Magruder. Tall, slim and fortyish, he had the incredibly difficult job of overhauling the South West Transportation Company—the "Boss" Transport Company on the Burma Road and reputedly the biggest "squeezer" of them all. Wilson's job was to turn it into an efficient graft-free organisation, capable of coping with the increasingly heavy shipments of Lease-Lend goods to China.

Enough has been written about the scandal of the Burma Road, so I'll only give the briefest outline of some of the things Wilson was up against. Trucks, run by Chinese Government subsidised organisations, were only hauling a fraction of the urgently needed military supplies, filling up with prohibited luxury and commodity goods instead and selling them at enormous thousand percent profits at Kunming. The road was not running at half capacity. Valuable ten-wheel trucks with a drive in each of its three sets of wheels were being pitched over the edge of the road, day after day, through sheer carelessness. Trucks were running without oil, tyres without air, everything without overhaul. Craft, gangsterism, inefficiency, "squeeze" all along the line. These were the things Wilson had to fight, and was successfully fighting. Things were beginning to run with something like efficiency by the time Rangoon was lost and the road closed. Captain (later Major) Wilson's job was virtually finished when he was blown to pieces in April by a Japanese bomb at Mandalay. But I'm anticipating the story and must get back to order again.

I had to go 1400 miles then and back to Rangoon to get permission to see the Chinese troops. Early next morning I grabbed a taxi, thus cutting 24 hours off the Lashio-Rangoon train journey, and motored one hundred and fifty miles to Mandalay, catching the Rangoon train at six p.m. the same day.

Next day at Pegu station a young weary-looking Burma Rifles Second Lieutenant got into my compartment. He had just come from Mergui and Tavoy area, where his company had been routed by the Japs. He was returning to headquarters to arrange for replacement of kit. I was eager to get some information about the Japs.

"How were they armed? Were they carrying gas

masks? Were they using mountain guns or mortars? Were there many of them? Was it true that they had Burmans with them? Was it true they were using elephants?"

He had no idea. He hadn't seen any Japs. None of the troops with whom he'd talked had seen any Japs. They had no idea there were any Japs near them, but at night firing burst out all round them, and they found they were surrounded. They beat it, abandoning their kit.

"Were petrol stores and supplies destroyed at Mergui aerodrome?"

No. Everything had been prepared for destruction. Gelignite laid etc. A demolition Squad was ready waiting for the word to blow everything. Word never came. Before they knew what was happening the Japs were on top of them—and they had to beat it, leaving a fine aerodrome, thousand gallons of petrol and stores of bombs for the Japs to use against us. He didn't know if Burmans were helping the Japs. Some of the men said that they'd seen yellow-robed phoongyis creeping about in the jungle a few days previous to the night attack.

I found out later that most of the detonations his men heard were caused by fire-crackers which the Japs used extensively in their "psychological night attacks."

The train was held up several times near Rangoon by air raids. I found the Strand Hotel closed, but got a room at the Allandale Hotel. There were no taxis available, but my Australian Buddhist friend, David Maurice of Imperial Chemical Industries came to my rescue and put his car at my disposal while I was in Rangoon. At Army Headquarters, a Public Relations Officer, Flight-Lieut. Wallace Crabbe—one time staff member of "Melbourne Herald"—presented me with a sheaf of forms which I filled out. He looked up my dossier, found nothing too obviously to my discredit, and within ten minutes I was accredited as a War Correspondent to his Majesty's Forces in Burma, and had a rail warrant and movement order, entitling me to proceed to Lashio and report to "Hobbie Old Boy," who was to pass me on to the Chinese Army.

I found David Maurice very worried about the political situation. He had many Burmese friends and knew what was going on inside Burmese minds. Several of his friends had warned him that trouble was brewing and urged him to seek shelter in a Phoongyi Kyaung (Buddhist Temple). When I was in Burma three months previously, Maurice told me that pro-Japanese elements were getting control of the Thakin party—the chief nationalist political party in Burma. He complained at that time that the Burma Government had locked up all the wrong people. Genuine anti-fascist Thakins were gaoled because of leftist activities—including issuing anti-war pamphlets and alleged fomenting of strikes. The Thakin party which for years past had been anti-fascist, slightly pro-communist, towards the end of 1941 was shorn of its leftist leaders, and the way paved for pro-Japanese elements to capture the leadership of the party.

The situation was aggravated because anti-Japanese propaganda in Burma was sternly frowned upon, right up till the outbreak of the Pacific War. Pro-Chinese propaganda was prohibited, even Chinese propaganda films banned. (This absurd deference to Japanese sensitiveness was not only confined to Burma. In the middle of 1941, I submitted an article on the Chinese cooperatives to a well-known Australian newspaper, to which I contributed a weekly column. The editor told me he couldn't publish any articles expressing sympathy for China. He's been circularised by the British and Australian governments requesting him not to publish any articles likely to give offence to Japan). Many members of the Thakin party, interested only in obtaining independence for Burma, were beginning to listen to those who advanced the Japanese sponsored arguments that the Japs weren't interested in conquering Burma. They only wanted to chase the British out, and then they'd hand Burma over to the Burmans. Why shouldn't the Thakins help the Japs throw the British out, and then they'd be the ruling party in Burma. There were plenty that argued otherwise, but their leaders—people like Thakins Kyaw Sein and Mya Thwin and others, with international outlook, and who knew something of Japanese activities in Korea, Manchuria and Formosa, were in gaol, because they'd written anti-war pamphlets. Leftists in many countries who were against war, changed their ideas after Russia was pulled into the conflict, and they considered the line was at last clearly drawn between the fascist and anti-fascist powers. Some of those Thakin leaders—Thein Pe, for instance,—had also written anti-Japanese pamphlets. The main body of the leaders, however, was now engaged in Pro-Japanese activities. David Maurice who in his spare time acted as volunteer Water-Police Officer, passed on relevant information to responsible authorities.

"What? Thakins turning anti-Japanese? Don't worry old boy. We've got 'em all taped. Pick 'em up tomorrow if we want to. What's that? Whispers of a Burma Independence Army being formed in Thailand? Ha! Ha! They've been pulling your leg this time alright."

Maurice wanted to take a more active part in things,

although he was already doing an important job, in charge of explosives for Imperial Chemicals. He'd done a good job down at the wharves during the first bombing of Rangoon, when he led a gang of terrified coolies to unload a cargo of gelignite. The stuff was on a jetty, surrounded by a sea of blazing tung oil. They had to run a gauntlet of flames, and step over twisted, mangled bodies of scores of coolies still spurting blood, lying where they'd been decimated and hurled by Jap bombs. Because Maurice stayed with them and helped to carry the cases the coolies kept on with the job till the last case of gelignite was carried to safety. A goodly portion of Rangoon's docks were saved from destruction, solely because of Maurice's extraordinary influence with the coolies. I felt and he felt too, that his contacts and influence with the Indian coolies and especially with the Burmans should be better exploited. As an active Buddhist and one of the few British in Rangoon who spoke Burmese really well, Maurice genuinely liked and was liked by the Burmans. Many of them came to him for advice. They also came to him and passed on useful information. I suggested to military and civilian authorities that he would be a useful man to acquire. I suggested to the British ministry of Information and Intelligence Officers that it would be useful if he just walked about the bazaars, and kept his finger on the pulse of Burmese public opinion—as in most places in the Far East, the pulse of public opinion beats strongest at the bazaars and markets. Like so many other valuable men who offered their services in Burma, Maurice was always turned down.

The night I arrived in Rangoon we talked till dawn the following morning, and I got a gloomy picture of the way things were developing. With no anti-Japanese propaganda allowed before war broke out, the government expected a miraculous change in public opinion overnight on December 8th. From ignorance and apathy in Pacific affairs they expected an informed hatred against abominable Japanese aggression. Information services were either non-existent or functioning badly. During air raids, locals saw planes tumbling down out of the sky in flames. Japanese whisper-mongers spread the word around that they were British planes. Actually, they were almost invariably Jap planes shot down by the AVG and RAF. News about raids was held up—sometimes for several days—and by the time the correct story was issued, people had forgotten about that particular raid, in the excitement of seeing more and more planes crashing to earth. Ninety percent of the non-European population, according to Maurice, genuinely believed that the British and American air forces were always worsted in the clashes with the Japs.

"A month ago," he said, "75% of my Burmese friends believed we were going to lick the Japs. Now 90% of them believe we're the ones that are going to be licked. And the information services do nothing to correct that impression."

There were air raids twice daily for the two days I was in Rangoon. The first day, I went to a hill near the Shwé Dagon Pagoda, hoping with my telefoto lens to get some pictures of a dog-fight. Twenty minutes after the sirens sounded the heavy dum-ba-dum-ba-dum of Japanese bombers could be heard, and nine of them passed overhead their wings flashing silver in the sunlight. They were up about 15,000 feet. I heard machine-gun fire before I saw three fighters pounce on them. Almost immediately three of the bombers went down in steep dives, and the rest passed out of sight. At intervals I heard the rattle of machine-guns, and reckoned the AVG probably cleaned them all up.

The next day I went to a Buddhist temple with Maurice, when the planes came over. Some of the phoongyis approached Maurice and talked earnestly with him and he told me afterwards they were asking him to come and live with them in case of trouble. Within a few minutes of our arrival we heard machine-gun and cannon fire and the phoongyis came running over to us, telling us that two more of our planes had been shot down. I saw the planes that did the shooting and knew they were American Tomahawks—and those shot down were Japs. Maurice told the phoongyis that they were Jap planes being shot down. They nodded politely, but looked as if they didn't believe him.

I travelled back to Mandalay with a British major who'd been knocked out in the first Jap raid on Rangoon. He hadn't believed they were Jap planes until bombs started falling. Then he jumped into a slit trench. Shortly afterwards he saw some Japs parachuting down, and jumped out of the trench with his revolver out, to try and pick them off. He thought they represented the beginning of a parachute attack on the city. As he jumped out an anti-personnel bomb burst 50 yards away, and he was hit in the thigh and face.

CHAPTER VII

Back in Lashio, the Hostel was full again and I had to share a room with Major Ausland. Shortly after I arrived, three Chinese officers arrived, one a three star general, the others colonels. One of the colonels was trying to arrange accommodation for the two officers, but the worried American manager of the Hostel was sorry, there were no rooms available. I found out that the officers who wanted rooms were General Tu, Commander of the Chinese 5th Army and Col. Gordon Chu, his ADC. They were supposed to meet "Hobbie Old Boy" the British liaison officer, who was to have arranged accommodation for them and transportation to Rangoon. A captain deputising for Colonel Hobson came down and had a few drinks with them, but after a lot of "haw-hawing" and "Old Boying"—which left the Chinese bewildered—he went away without arranging anything for them. General Tu is a fairly important person and this was his first visit to Burma. I had a talk with Ausland and Dr. Tseng Yang Fu—the Director-General of Yunnan Burma Railway—and we agreed that if I got accommodation elsewhere, with a bit of shuffling about, room could be found for the General and his aide.

I rang Hobbies' deputy and told him I thought we were under some sort of an obligation to find accommodation for the Chinese general, as we'd invited him down. After explaining that by squeezing guests together we could fit them in, I asked if he'd arrange for me to sleep at the RAF mess.

"Quite right old boy. Dashed nuisance there's no place for them, but what can I do? Hobbie's away and there it is. Dashed decent of you. Yes, Yes. I'll ring you back in five minutes. Cheerio."

I waited half an hour and then had to go into Lashio to the bank, leaving a message with the hostel manager to empty my things out of the room as soon as the Captain rang back, and make things ready for the Chinese. I came back late in the evening. The Captain hadn't telephoned, the Chinese officers had been back twice looking for rooms, and eventually gone off in disgust, to get a room in some third class dump. Next morning a plane was supposed to take Tu and Chu to Rangoon, but the RAF said they had no room for them. They were packed off in a car to Mandalay, and then the RAF decided they could take them after all, so another car was sent speeding after the first one to bring them back and put them aboard the plane. I wondered what a British general and his aide would have thought if they'd been treated like that on arrival in China. Even relatively unimportant visitors to China are embarrassed with the wholeheartedness of Chinese courtesy.

This was about the 29th of January. After inspecting my accreditation card, Col. Hobson's deputy decided I was a fit person to be entrusted with military secrets. All the talk of Chinese troops in Burma was "Hooey." Newspaper reports of Burma's great welcome to Chinese troops moving down the Burma Road were incorrect. Except for a small body which had come in by a caravan trail to the Kengtung area, near the border of Yunnan, Indo-China and Thailand, the Chinese Army was still sitting in China in camps stretching from Wanting on the Yunnan-Burma border right back along the Burma Road to Kunming.

The Japs were steadily pushing their way forward from Mergui and Tavoy through our thinly spreadout troops forwards towards the Salween River, while thousands of good Chinese troops were sitting on the frontier, 120 miles north of Lashio.

A truck loaded with rice and onions carried me to Kiukok, the town on the Burmese side of the frontier, opposite Wanting. A very disgruntled British Liaison Officer met me at Kiukok and introduced me to the Chinese Colonel I'd seen the day before at Lashio, trying to arrange General Tu's accommodation. His name was Liang, and when he learned I came from Australia, we were soon on good terms. Till he left to help China drive out the Japs, Col. Liang had spent most of his life in Australia where his father had an importing business in Sydney. He and the British captain were on the best of terms—and the latter whom I'll call Mac. for convenience's sake, was one of the few liaison officers I met in Burma who really understood the Chinese, and didn't treat them like market gardeners or laundrymen. Mac. was righteously indignant when I arrived, because he'd just received a signal from headquarters and had no idea what it meant. Headquarters sent all signals in code, but he hadn't sent Mac. a codebook. He had to send them 120 miles to Lashio by truck; and if he was lucky got them back decoded within 48 hours.

I stopped with Mac. in the Public Works Department House at Kiukok for 3 days. The evening I arrived a team of Asiatic Petroleum Company agents from Kunming also put up at the P. W. D. Bungalow, coming from Rangoon and Bhamo—old Irrawaddy Port and oil distribution depot for China. Kuikok was a convenient place for them to meet, and discuss policy in view of the deteriorating situation in Burma.

Rations at Kiukok were rather low, but the APC. decided to celebrate their coming together by sending out for a huge Chinese meal, which together with drinks brought by Dick Frost—the Rangoon Manager—they invited Mac. and myself to share. Before the party developed into a musical and later a maudlin stage, conversation mainly centred on the advisability or otherwise of destroying oil installations in Burma. I found it illuminating to hear how reluctant capital is to have its creations destroyed. Most of the oil men were against demolitions. Their argument was that even if the Japs conquered Burma, we certainly expected to drive them out again. In any case it was little use destroying oil installations—the Japs would have them working again within six months. I'd heard the same arguments used in Malaya, where most of the rubber planters with whom I spoke were against destroying the rubber plantations. It seemed a naive attitude for hard-headed businessmen to adopt even if *they* left installations intact hoping the Japs would be driven out, to believe that the Japs themselves wouldn't destroy them before they withdrew.

With Colonel Liang and Mac., I drove across the frontier twenty miles to visit one of the Chinese camps. They were good-looking troops and their, camp buildings were cleaner and tidier than any buildings I'd seen in China. Most of them they'd built on the spot, from bamboo. There was plenty of bamboo growing there, and what a Chinese soldier can do with a knife and bamboo is something to be seen rather than described. Some of them were busy when we arrived, splitting and stripping bamboos, making food-carrying baskets, straw slippers and their famous wide hats. These latter are lined with broad leaves, coated with tung oil to make them waterproof and camouflaged with green and brown paint. Long bamboo barracks, with split cane walls and thatch-roofs had bamboo beds, neat rifle racks, even pleated bamboo fences surrounding them. Sentry stands had huge bamboo umbrellas protecting them from rain and sun. They were better fed than most Chinese troops, getting 2½ lbs. of rice per day. They even had a neat ration, normally unheard of for soldiers in China. While we were watching some of the troops being put through volley-ball and hurdling exercises, we could hear a lot of yelling, then two rifle shots. Colonel Liang went off to investigate and came back rather red in the face. He apologised to Mac.

"I'm afraid another of those bullocks has been giving trouble. It just broke loose and they had to shoot it."

Mac. tried to assume an indignant expression and told the Colonel that they'd have to make the bullock last until their next meat ration was due.

"There's been too many of these blasted accidents," he added.

The Chinese soldiers found it too great a strain on their gastric juices, to have a good meaty-looking bullock tethered near them too long.

We went on to a market near the camp, run by Shans—the greater part of the population in the Yunnan-Burma border region is either Shan or Kachin. The Shan women are most attractive and clean-looking people, fairly tall and straight with round faces and creamy complexions. The Yunnan Shans have a distinctive dress of white blouses, dark skirts and usually tall black hats. Although they have no common language with the Chinese, they seemed to be getting along alright with the soldiers, selling them eggs and vegetables—and I suspected other commodities always in demand near soldiers' camps. Chinese officers asked Col. Liang and Mac. when they were going to be shifted into Burma. They all seemed anxious to get cracking, but no one seemed to know when—if ever—they'd be going across the frontier.

We stopped at Wanting on the Chinese side of the frontier on our way back, and had lunch in a Chinese restaurant. As we left the restaurant Col. Liang was stopped by an acquaintance and asked if he could make the Chinese frontier police release his mechanic. The mechanic turned out to be a young Austrian refugee. He was one of thousands of German and Austrian Jews who fled to Shanghai in 1939. He'd drifted to the interior of China, and worked as a motor mechanic. Then the police discovered he had no papers, and he was flung into gaol. He was allowed out on condition he left China, so he travelled down the Burma Road to Rangoon, hoping to get a job with the British or American forces, but had no luck. It was hard enough for British or Americans in the Far East to get jobs with their respective forces, so an alien obviously had little chance. A Chinese garage proprietor from Kunming, who happened to be in Rangoon, offered to guarantee for him in China and give him a job in Kunming, but that was no good to the police—at Wanting. They'd arrested him again for having no passport, and would certainly shove him in gaols. Chinese are bad enough for Chinese—but for Europeans they must be unendurable. There was nothing Col. Liang could do, so I expect the Austrian was put into gaol and is still there. Once you're in gaol in China you're a forgotten man—until the day when you're struck off the lists of the living.

There were big arches decorated with pine branches and Chinese characters on the Burma side of the frontier. Col. Liang translated the latter: "We welcome our gallant Chinese brothers." Mac. told me a story about those arches. The Chinese on the Burma side of the border asked one of the Assistant Superintendents of the area for permission to erect arches to welcome the Chinese troops when they entered Burma.

The official refused—Lord only knows why, and the Chinese were naturally indignant.

Here were their compatriots coming to Burma to save Burma for the British—so they reasoned. Not only were their officers treated badly by the British, but they weren't allowed to express their gratitude to their own people—their own flesh and blood. (Their reasoning was not quite correct. The Chinese were coming to Burma chiefly to try and save the Burma Road. But still the indignation of the Burma Chinese was justified.) They began to hold meetings. Not long afterwards the Assistant Superintendent came to Kiukok and Mac. tackled him about the matter.

"I've said 'No' once, and I don't see why I should change my mind," was the reply.

Later the question was raised with a superior official, who said in effect:

"By all means let the Chinese put up welcoming arches. If it pleases them, why should we object."

The Chinese were told of this and joyfully began erecting their arches. The local police hadn't been informed of the changed decision and set about with their batons, beating up Chinese and tearing down the arches. The Chinese started having protest meetings again. Eventually things were sorted out and the arches finally established, but the Chinese on the frontier weren't quite so enthusiastic about the ABCD front after that. The welcoming green branches incidentally, were shrivelled and browned by the time the Chinese troops did cross the border.

It was a wonderful sight watching from Mac.'s

verandah the trucks piling up at the frontier. Wonderful too, to contemplate the money old Governor Lung Yun—Governor and virtual warlord of Yunnan—raked in each day in taxes. Some trucks were held up for weeks at a time by the various custom's authorities. There was the British Custom's on one side, and the Central Government and Yunnan Provincial Government Custom's on the other side. If you were prepared to "play the game" and pass across plenty of "squeeze", you'd get your trucks through reasonably quickly, and Lung Yun would be cheated of some of his revenue. Honest traders—and there were some—who refused to pay "squeeze," had to have every parcel of goods opened, and their trucks delayed for days. The big racketeers and grafters could easily afford to pay big sums for the privilege of a quick run through with their smuggled goods. Sometimes they were caught by a Central Government agent and then—if they happened to meet an incorruptible one—there were shootings.

The AVG boys were the only ones that had crossing the frontier reduced to a fine art. With "AVG" in huge letters plastered across their windscreens, they drove straight through, every man bristling with Tommy guns and .45's. Some of them were in the racket too, but their prestige and Tommy guns allowed their smuggled goods to pass through without hindrance. I guess most of the stuff they carried was for their own well-earned appetites and thirsts, anyway.

Mac. suggested we should drive over to Loiwing, where the China Aircraft Manufacturing Corporation (CAMCO) was building, assembling and repairing planes for the AVG. He thought I might like to call in and see Dr. Seegrave on the way to Loiwing and hear about his idea for helping the Chinese armies in

Burma. Dr. Seegrave, an American Baptist Missionary, operated a hospital and training school for nurses at Namkham in the Northern Shan States, and supervised other smaller hospitals scattered widely over the Shan States.

The road to Namkham and Loiwing was terrible but the country the most beautiful I'd seen in Burma up to that time. Rolling green hills, willo-line streams, clean and neat Shan villages. Looking at the Shans, I find it easy to believe that people acquire the characteristics of their environment. The Shans rank with the Tahitians as the handsomest people I've seen. The women particularly carry themselves with the same grace and dignity that is so remarkable with the Tahitians. Their skins are light and smooth, their figures straight and well developed, very regular, well moulded features and a wonderfully clear skin. The Shans are an easy-going people, independent, proud and conscious of their long continuous history as a racial entity. Their bamboo huts have a high platform at the rear of the house, shaded by a half-dome shaped, overhanging cave. I liked to stroll along through Shan villages in the evenings to watch mother and father, probably grandma and grandpa as well, and all the little Shans gathered together on the platform, eating their platters of rice and fish, with smoke from their cooking fire lazily merging with the blue haze in the background.

Towards Namkham, the road follows the jade-green Shweli River —which thereabouts forms the boundary between Yunnan and Burma. It got from bad to worse and 7 miles from Namkham there was the sickening bump which denotes a broken spring. After that we had to creep along arriving at Dr. Seegrave's at mid-day. He received us with open arms, and as lunch was just being served, insisted that we join him at table.

A shortish, stocky man, he impresses one immediately with his restless energy. He told me he "figgered" he ought to be doing something about this war. He "allowed" he'd be pretty useful as a surgeon down at the front with the Chinese armies, as he understood they had no properly organised medical service. He'd gathered about him several young American Baptists—who'd been teaching at the American Baptist Mission endowed Judson College at Rangoon University—and given them a grounding in "first aid." He'd equipped a mobile surgical unit, had trucks packed, everything ready for the word "go." He'd picked fifty of his girls trained as nurses in his own Nursing School to go with him. They included Shans, Burmans, Kerens, who, he reckoned, between them could handle most of the Chinese dialects, they were likely to run across. While he was telling all this he was plying us with beer, meat, cheese and salad.

"Boy, it just burns me up, all this delaying business," he complained between mouthfuls.

"We've been all set to go for weeks. Burma's being lost and there's armies sitting up there on the frontier doing nothing, and while they're doing nothing, we're doing nothing."

After lunch he packed me in another car, set some people working on our broken spring, and sent me on my way to Loiwing. Mac. stayed with the Doc.

Loiwing is only just in Chinese territory. It was close enough to Lashio and Bhamo to allow aeroplane parts and raw materials to be delivered at the factory within a few hours of their arrival at railhead and riverhead respectively. At present it was working flat-out, repairing AVG planes damaged by the Japs. The organisation was just in process of being absorbed by the Chinese. Originally CAMCO was founded by the

American Pauley Brothers to assemble and manufacture under licence Curtiss Wright fighter and trainer planes. It was first established in Hangchow near Shanghai and was chased from pillar to post in China till finally in 1940 it set up at Loiwing. In September 1940 the Japs came over from Indo-China, pasted Loiwing with bombs, killing a lot of civilians, but not doing very much damage to the plant. Fear of continued Jap raids hindered development until the Pacific war started and AVG pilots kept raiders away and incidentally creating more repair jobs. The idea was to have mainly American technicians on the job, at first under American supervision, but assimilating as many Chinese as possible, so that later the Chinese could take over the whole plant themselves and establish the nucleus of an aircraft industry in China. There were very few Americans left when I visited the plant, and within six months the Chinese were expected to take over the whole show, retaining some American technicians as advisers. There was an excellent hostel for the Americans, huge dining and club room, billiard tables and all complete.

CAMCO had a difficult time in China and it must have been heartbreaking for those who'd been with the plant from the pioneer day, to have to blow up the whole thing in May 1942, a few days before the Japs took over.

It was dark by the time I got back to Namkham, and Mac. and I—thinking of our bullybeef meals—found it hard to resist Dr. Seegrave's invitation to stay to dinner. He hadn't been able to find a spring to fit the car, but his Shans had fixed it up with some slivers of bamboo. After dinner, Doc. suggested that we stay for a while and join his girls in their Sunday evening sing-sing. I think it was a long time since either Mac. —who used to run a hotel in Tientsin—or myself had sung hymns. Fifteen or twenty of the Doc.'s nurses filed in and sat around on the floor. They took turns in requesting their favourite numbers, and sang with obvious enjoyment. They were very sweet, and shy in front of strangers, and mostly sang with their eyes demurely fixed on the floor. Later I was to see these girls in action down at the front. With bombs falling about them, and fires ringing their hospital, they worked in blood and filth, dressing wounds of Chinese soldiers straight from the front line. They were just as demure and sweet and shy at the front as they were that night at Namkham, but they did a job that would have tried the courage and nerve of hardened veterans, without turning a hair.

I'm not a great friend of missionaries. I've written unpleasant things about them in the past, and probably shall do so again in the future, but old Dr. Seegrave was one whose conduct almost persuaded me to become a missionary advocate. If Doc. Seegrave's idea of being a missionary—an ideal of good practical earthly service that dealt first with problems of filling bellies and healing wounds—was the universal one, I'd be a convert.

We drove back to Kiukok very slowly, partly because of the broken spring, partly because our lights had failed. Fortunately it was moonlight. We stopped for a few minutes to have a look at a Shan dance, but the dancers stopped when we approached so we left them to celebrate their moonlight revels undisturbed.

Mac. and Colonel Liang were going to Lashio next day and offered me a lift. Col. Liang, who stayed on the Chinese side of the frontier, was bringing a car at 9 a.m. to take us. At 10 a.m. no car had arrived. At 10-30 a British Custom's officer strolled over to see Mac. about something and mentioned accidentally that a Chinese officer had tried to drive a car with Chinese number platés across the frontier. The Custom's man was very proud that he'd noticed it in time and had sent the fellow back. It was, of course, Col. Liang. Mac. raised hell, and asked how the "blue blazes" we expected any cooperation from the Chinese when we subjected their officers to such pin-pricking annoyances all the time. We walked over the frontier and found Liang resigned to official obstructionism and trying to tie Burma number plates from an old car over the top of the others. We jumped in the car and tried the AVG method of driving straight through, roaring abuse at anyone who tried to stop us. It worked.

As I'd contracted to submit any stories written in Burma about Burma to Rangoon censorship, I wrote a story about Chinese troops on the Chinese side of the frontier and sent it back to Chungking, hoping that it would have a better chance of reaching London that way than via Rangoon. As it was not—technically at least—a Burma story, I considered I was justified in evading Rangoon censorship especially as I felt London should know what was happening on the frontier. On our way into Lashio we found that cars containing Chinese refugees from Rangoon were being held up by Kachin police at the Bhamo Road turn-off, and only allowed to proceed after an unauthorised levy—pure blackmail—had been paid. There was nothing we could do, except to make a mental note for the future.

Back at Lashio the Yunnan-Burma railway people were in despair about rice supplies which Burma government had promised for their hundred-odd thousand coolies working on the railway. The rice wasn't arriving and the coolies were faced with starvation. The story of the Yunnan-Burma railroad is a subject for a book on its own, but as it has little to do with the war, and had to be abandoned when the Japs reached the Northern Shan States, I don't propose to deal with it in this book. I only want to mention certain of its personnel who were engaged in other projects more directly concerned with the war.

Tseng Yang Fu—the Director-General of the Yunnan-Burma Railroad—is a podgy Cantonese, graduate of Pittsburgh University. He leapt into brief notice abroad in 1938, when he was mayor of Canton. Following the terrible Japanese bombing of Canton, he issued a famous appeal to the mayors of the world, calling for international protests against Jap barbarity. He's a great admirer of the Generalissimo, was his personal secretary at one time—and has occupied almost every imaginable position in China from Minister of Communications to newspaper editor and soldier—he has the rank of Lieutenant-General in the Chinese Army. More than anything else is he proud to display his membership card in the U. S. United Mine Workers Union, which produced the CIO and John Lewis. After taking his D. Sc. degree in Pittsburgh University he worked as a common labourer in the mines, before returning to China. When I saw him first with drooping stomach, shiny blue suit, and felt hat turned up all round, his walking stick held in front of him as he walked with the handle crook turned outwards, and heard his fat cackling voice, I greatly under-estimated Tseng Yang Fu. Later I learned to appreciate his shrewd mind and his inexhaustible fountain of ingenious ideas. In his own way he's got ideals too—which is rare in an official, who's climbed as high up the ladder as has Tseng. In addition to building the railroad, Tseng Yang Fu was acting as personal representative for the Generallissimo in Burma.

At the time he arrived back from Wanting, he had

just been requested by the Gissimo to investigate complaints that Chinese from Rangoon were being pulled off trains at the Goktiek Gorge, because they didn't have permits. Thousands of Chinese were said to be held up for this reason between Maymyo and Lashio. For prevention of sabotage, trains stopped at the Goktiek Gorge, and non-British subjects, of countries other than those bordering Burma, had to produce permits to cross the viaduct. As China bordered Burma, permits were not required for Chinese citizens, and pulling them off trains was just one more case of wilful pin-pricking by Burmese authorities.

Tseng Yang Fu was travelling down to Maymyo and Mandalay the following morning and as I wanted to go to Rangoon again, he offered to give me a lift as far as Mandalay. Major Ausland—Tseng's American adviser—drove the car, and he and Tseng passed the time singing and reciting American song and verse of doubtful origin. Ausland had a fine tenor voice and had a grand repertoire of Wild West saloon ballads. Tseng Yang Fu's chief contribution was of a more serious nature: "Lincoln's Gettyburg Speech." That put both Ausland and me to shame.

I was going to Rangoon this time to see Governor Dorman-Smith and give him a picture of the situation on the frontier and Sino-American gossip drifting back from Lashio to Chungking about our treatment of the Chinese. Tseng thought it would be a good idea if I also took a letter from him to the Governor, about Chinese being pulled off the trains, and also the lack of rice supplies for the Yunnan-Burma Railroad coolies. I had my typewriter, and as we turned and twisted round the hairpin bends between Maymyo and Mandalay, Tseng, in the front seat, twisted his fat body round and dictated a letter to the Governor. It was 4.55

when we left Maymyo station and the train left Mandalay at 6.00 p.m. The Maymyo station-master refused to telephone through, to book a seat because—he said—it was impossible for us to cover 42 miles of the twistiest stretch of road between Lashio and Rangoon in an hour and five minutes. We arrived just at 6.00 as the train was slowly moving off. I jumped in, Ausland throwing my bags in after me, and Tseng waddling along like a well-nourished duck, with his legs lagging behind his body, signing letters as he ran, and shouting in my ear last-minute instructions for Dorman-Smith.

Governor Sir Reginald Dorman-Smith, when he heard that I'd come down from the Yunnan-Burma border, decided to receive me almost immediately. On behalf of that much-maligned Governor of Burma, I must say that I always found him readily accessible, and quick to act when he was convinced of the necessity of action. Clad in blue double-breasted coat and cream trousers, he looked something like a popular cricket hero. He is tall, well-built and handsome, with a dark moustache, and has a man-about-town twinkle in his eyes. When he strides across the room to shake hands, he has a way with him that makes you feel you're the one person in the world whose visit is important to him. With tons of charm and personality, he has the knack of setting one at ease immediately, and shows a careful and sympathetic interest in the minutest details of one's story. I poured out my tale of woe about lack of cooperation with the Chinese. I told him of our officials' superior attitude to Chinese officers, ranging from faintly amused patronage to frank contempt. I told him of the incidents at the CNAC Hostel, the trouble over the welcoming arches at the Yunnan frontier, the Kachin police extorting money from Chinese refugees. I asked him why Chinese troops weren't in Burma, and passed on some of the stories that floated about among Chinese and American officers, who accused us of unjust suspicions that we didn't want Chinese in Burma because we mightn't be able to get them out again. At this the Governor chuckled, rubbed his hands together and said:

"Well...... ?"

I took it to mean that the Government of Burma did feel that way about the Chinese. When I asked Dorman-Smith about this later, however, he assured me that Burma Government had nothing to do with the delay in getting Chinese troops down to the front and were indeed anxious to have them in. He made notes as I spoke and within a few hours a long cable was sent to Lashio ordering that everything possible be done to make Chinese officers and officials feel welcome in Burma. He gave me a chit to a Brigadier at GHQ and I poured out my story again, this time with greater emphasis on discourtesy to Chinese officers, and the grumblings of Chinese officers and officials that Burma was being lost while their armies were doing nothing except sitting on their backsides in the worst malaria belt in the world.

The Brigadier was impressed and sent for another Brigadier, who was Chief Liaison Officer between British and Chinese armies. He seemed to be something of an "old woman" and after listening while I retold the story he querulously demanded if the Chinese couldn't appreciate our difficulties in arranging rice supplies for their troops. He cursed "incompetency" of junior officers for discourtesy to the Chinese and said he was leaving immediately for Lashio and the frontier to "straighten things out."

A great deal has since been made of the difficulty of arranging food supply for the Chinese army, in excusing the delay in bringing the troops in. I have heard the same reason given in explaining the original refusal to have more than one Chinese army in Burma. The Chinese army is the easiest army in the world to feed. The troops need only rice—anything else is by way of an extra. Burma exports normally 3,500,000 tons of rice yearly, enough to feed ten million soldiers for a year, yet the distribution of sufficient rice to feed forty or fifty thousand troops for a few months was too great a problem for the Army to handle! Small wonder if Chinese eyebrows were raised when we used this alibi!

I probably made a nuisance of myself around Headquarters that day. The thing that annoyed me most was the absurd, defeatist ideas the army seemed to have about the quality of Chinese troops. Time and again, when I posed my question:

"Why aren't the Chinese armies in Burma?" I got the reply:

"Will the beggars fight when we *do* bring them in?" or "What's the use of bringing them in when they won't fight."

This, at a time when we were getting pushed from pillar to post around the Pacific, prized out of every corner we held, and surrendering our "impregnable" fortresses to the very people the Chinese had been fighting more or less successfully for 5 years, and when our troops in Burma were throwing away arms and equipment and fleeing ahead of the Japs.

Those hotels that were still functioning in Rangoon were filled, so I stayed in David Maurice's humble little house in the Burmese quarter. It was near full moon and the Japs were coming over two or three times nightly. The first night I was there, bombers came over fairly low, and as they passed overhead we saw their interior suddenly light up as the bomb traps opened. We snuggled down in the trench as the bombs "whooshed" down and exploded about a quarter of a mile away in a market. Many of Maurice's neighbors had evacuated, and I think about half the population had left Rangoon by this time—early February.

CHAPTER VIII

Although this was not my area—O. D. Gallagher, veteran "Daily Express" correspondent was "covering" British military activity in Burma while I was supposed to concentrate on the Chinese—I wanted to have a look at the front while I was in South Burma. We'd evacuated Moulmein on January 31st, and were holding a line stretching from Martaban to Pa-An along the North bank of the Salween River. I had to go by railway from Rangoon North-East to Pegu, then South to Thaton to Brigade Headquarters. Maurice drove me to the station, where we had a couple of hours to wait because of an air raid. Just as the train was moving off he rushed over with a young Lieutenant-Colonel and shoved him into my compartment. The Colonel didn't seem anxious to talk at first, but after some preliminary discussion about what ought and ought not be done in Burma, I found out he was off on a dangerous and exciting mission. He'd been in Burma for several years and knew and liked the Kerens. (There are about a million Kerens in Burma living mainly in the hills along the Burma-Thailand frontier. They are pro-British because they're Christian, and they're Christian mainly because of the activities of the American Baptist Mission. They don't like the Buddhist Burmans.) After months of unsuccessful agitating in the army, he'd finally got permission to organise Keren irregulars, to hamper the Japanese rear and operate as independent guerillas in Japanese occupied areas. It had been a hard fight to persuade the army that such unorthodox methods might have a chance of success, and I gathered they'd let this Colonel go because he'd made such a nuisance of himself that they were glad to get rid of him. He had bags of silver rupees, caches of arms planted in various parts of the country and unlimited enthusiasm and faith in his Kerens. He spoke Kereri like a native. He begged me to publicise the importance of guerilla warfare right throughout the Pacific area. He soon found out he didn't have to waste time trying to convert me to that point. I was with him from the start. He'd known David Maurice for a long time and appreciated his influence with the Burmans. He was dismayed to know that better use was not being made of Maurice's talents, and had given him a note that morning to the Oriental Mission—the Cloak and Dagger outfit, as they were nicknamed—who encouraged and supplied funds and arms for various projects too unorthodox for the Army to handle.

The Colonel left me at Pegu. The last I saw of him and his bearded face was hung over a steering wheel, as he was bumping happily along a road in a Jeep with some of his beloved Kerens. Later he and his levies did splendid work wrecking Jap communications in the Southern Shan States and in demolishing lead and silver mines near Loikaw. As far as I know he—or at least his men—are still operating in the Shan States, and the last I heard of them, they were very much a "thorn in the Japs' side". Lean, bearded and tough, with tons of initiative and resource, on excellent terms with his men, he seemed a splendid man for his job. His Kerens were the only organised body still operating in areas 12 months after Jap occupation. I was sorry to lose contact with him.

I got to Brigade H/Q, and the G. 2. (Intelligence Officer) said if I came back in the evening, he'd have something of interest for me. After dark a market place burst into flames near Brigade H/Q, and they told me that wherever Headquarters moved, fires broke out in the vicinity in the evening, marking the target for Japanese bombers.

A Burmese constable and his assistant were brought into the Intelligence Officer's room for questioning. The constable had an ancient double-barrelled shot-gun. In the dim light thrown by a kerosene lantern, they were a tough-looking pair. It appeared they'd crossed the Salween earlier in the day to see what was happening in Pa-An village on the South bank. As they made their way into the village, two men, clad in Burmese coats and *loongyis* (long skirt wrapped round waist and worn by Burmese men) approached them and made signs of wanting food. They didn't speak Burmese, so the constable questioned them in Keren. Suspicious, when they didn't understand Keren, the constable handed his shotgun to his assistant and grabbed a note-book out of the pocket of one of the men. While he was examining the note-book, its owner reached for a revolver, but it got caught in the loongyi. The assistant fired at point blank range, and shot him to pieces. The other turned and ran, stopping twice and firing at his pursuers, but missed and hit a villager. The assistant gave him the other barrel and winged him, but he kept running. Villagers with their *dhas* (long knife swords used mainly for peaceful purposes, cutting shrubs, grass, splitting wood etc. but kept razor sharp and a terrific weapon in a close-in fight.) took up the chase and by the time the constables caught up, there wasn't much of the second man left.

We crowded round as the constable pulled out of his pocket articles and documents they'd taken from the dead men. They were soaked in blood—not surprising, considering their owners' fate. Most important were excellent maps of the district showing disposition of Jap troops, and their fairly correct estimate of our positions and strength. Documents in Japanese were sent off to Rangoon for translation. The policemen were complimented on their courage and resource, given a cash reward and a promise of immediate promotion. From the description they gave of the bodies, it was evident that the "Burmans" were two Japanese Intelligence Officers. That was a nice little story to reward me for my visit to the front. I wrote it and sent it back by Army courier that same night. It was an interesting point that the villagers joined in polishing off the Japs, but whether from patriotic motives or because they obeyed mob instinct to join in the chase, wasn't clear.

An Intelligence Officer took me by car the following day to the positions we were holding on the Salween opposite Pa-An village. The car had a punctured tyre when he went to collect it, and an hour was wasted while he hunted round for tyre levers and repair outfits and had it repaired. We'd originally planned to go to Martaban as well, but had to wipe that out because of the punctured tyre. We passed a convoy of ancient, wooden limbered eighteen pounders, rattling along on their way to Martaban. I don't think the Japanese got a very rich prize when they captured them. The Salween is about eight hundred yards wide at Pa-An, and the Japs held positions at the South bank. We parked our car out of range of their mortars—or at least out of sight. As we walked along a road parallel to, and a score of yards from the river, I was trying to remember how accurate rifle fire is at eight hundred yards, when suddenly a bullet whanged past me. We snuggled down pretty close to the ground after that, keeping on the far side of the road and our bodies below the road level. Jap snipers have a reputation for "getting their man."

The 7th Gurkhas were holding the position, and as always, seemed very cheerful, licking their lips and whetting their knives, waiting for the day the Japs tried to cross the river. The C. O. seemed cheerful enough too. But I think he felt as I felt, when he showed me on the map how thinly strung out his men were, that they didn't have a chance of holding the Japs once the real push started. They'd already turned back a couple of small parties, attempting night crossings, but the Colonel was convinced that some were already across and probing about in the area. I asked him whether he had any contact with the local people. Were they friendly or hostile? He said that they seemed friendly enough. Several times parties of his men had been cut off. The Burmans had helped them, showed them paths, given food and water without payment. I said:

"Surely we can exploit this friendly feeling. They should be invaluable in bringing us information about the Nips," and I told him the story of the Burmese constable and the Pa-An villagers.

"That's true," the Colonel agreed, "but unfortunately we've no real contact with them. We've got no one here that speaks their lingo. I often wish we did have. I think they'd cooperate with us alright."

The Japanese had plenty of people that spoke Burmese and the tribal dialects. Apart from members of the Burma "Independence" Army, who accompanied them from the first days, they'd enlisted interpreters from among Burmans and Shans living along the frontier regions in Thailand. I knew personally several forestry officers who know the country and the dialects, as well as the locals; police officers and people like David

Maurice, all speaking the language fluently, who time and again offered their services to the Army, but were turned down. The Army afterwards complained that they had to fight a hostile native population as well as the Japanese. But they made no attempt to establish any contact with the Burmans, Kachins, Shans etc., let alone win them over.

Driving back to Thaton, the staff car blew another tyre, and as there was no spare and no pump or repair outfit, we had to sit at the side of the road until we were lucky enough to be picked up by a truck. I couldn't help wondering what would have happened if the Intelligence Officer had an urgent despatch to make to Headquarters.

I caught a train back to Rangoon about midnight that night, and wrote a doleful despatch about insufficiency of men, the tendency still to trust to "natural" defence lines, such as rivers and mountain ranges. I went to Public Relations Office (the organisation that handles everything pertaining to correspondents' wants and otherwise, from issuing rail warrants to censoring and despatching our messages) just to make certain my message from Thaton, had been received, censored and telegraphed. It had been received and censored, but "due to an oversight" not despatched. (When I arrived from Lashio, I went across to Public Relations Office just to check that all messages sent from Lashio had gone through. The Public Relations Officer looked at me blankly, and swore he'd received no messages. I went across to the Telegraph Office, and with the Superintendent, spent half a day checking through incoming telegrams. He showed me the numbers of my messages received from Lashio and the signature of acceptance from Public Relations. With this information I went back to the Office, and the messages were found in the Officers' drawer. Out of sight out of mind. I wasn't there to push them through, so he just shoved them in a drawer.) The Public Relations Officer apologised profusely and sent the message off. Shortly afterwards he was relieved of his job and made a recruiting officer. Lt. Col. Foucar, a Rangoon lawyer and author was placed in charge, and although he had no experience of handling correspondents, he was a success, and Public Relations worked more smoothly in Burma under great difficulties than in most theatres.

The Japs crossed the Salween on February 8, a few days after I left. They pushed across near Pa-An swinging in a semi-circle towards the coast trying to bottle up our troops. It was during this fighting that a curious incident occurred, which well illustrates the confusion of the Burma fighting.

We'd evacuated Thaton. The enemy was reported to have occupied the town in force. The Moulmein Express was on its way down from Pegu, and orders were given for it to be stopped many miles North of Thaton and sent back. Some mistake occurred and instead of the train being stopped, it was seen chugging its way on down to Thaton. Word was sent to the General-in-Command, that it had gone down—and would probably return full of Japanese troops.

With commendable speed, steps were taken to ambush the train. Explosives were laid under the track, and troops posted in strategic positions. Everything was set to blow the Japs sky high. Before it reached the ambush, someone noticed their were women and children leaning out of the windows. Orders were given to hold fire and the train was stopped. It was packed with rejoicing evacuees. The train had gone on down to Thaton station as usual. Everything was in order. No Japs there, but a crowd of people waiting on the station who immediately mobbed the train. The engine-driver was very proud of his quite unconscious heroism, when the position was explained.

It was that sort of confusion that later resulted in the destruction of the bridge over the Sittaung River while most of our troops were on the wrong side of the water. How many of our men were lost in that action, no one knows. Many of them were wiped out by Japs before they even had a chance to try and get across. Many more were either drowned or machine-gunned in the water. No doubt the Japs made mistakes too—but they were always advancing past them covering them as they went; and we never knew.

CHAPTER IX

There was nothing to keep me in Rangoon, so I went back to see what was happening to the Chinese armies. Back at Lashio, Tseng Yang Fu was in trouble. He'd had a radio-telephone in Lashio for swift communication with the Gissimo in Chungking. Burma Government had seized it—it contravened their censorship regulation, I think—and the Gissimo had to rely on ordinary telegraph messages to Tseng. He'd wired Tseng to meet him at Lashio on February 2, when he and Madame Chiang were passing through on their way to India. The Gissimo wanted to discuss new road projects with Tseng in case the Burma Road was closed, and wanted to have something concrete to talk over with British authorities in India. Of course, the telegram arrived too late, and Tseng was on his way down to Mandalay with Ausland and me when the Gissimo arrived. The Gissimo is never interested in excuses. He expects his men to be on the spot when he wants them. Tseng was feeling rather blue about things, and sore at the government which had taken his radio-telephone away. The reaction to his letter to Dorman-Smith was good, however, and that cheered him a bit. Rice was arriving for his coolies and Chinese refugees were no longer being pulled off trains. Other things were livened up too. A special house had been requisitioned for Chinese officers and they were being entertained on a scale, comparable to the reception accorded to British officials visiting Chungking.

The morning after I returned from Rangoon, another Australian journalist arrived, Tim Healy, correspondent for the London "Daily Mirror." Eve Curie, representing "New York Herald Tribune," and daughter and biographer of Madame Curie, the discoverer of radium, also turned up, fresh from Moscow. Dark, slim and very French, she was full of enthusiasm for the way the Russians were standing up to the Germans and was certain they'd hold out. She had reason to feel pleased with herself. She was the only journalist on the spot when the Russians recaptured Moznaisk and got a fine "scoop" for her paper. She and Tim Healy jointly hired a taxi for Mandalay and were soon on their way to Rangoon. I was still hanging on in the hope that the Chinese armies would start moving, but although there were plenty of rumours, and private trucks and cars were being requisitioned right and left, there was no date fixed for them to start. We had air alarms in Lashio fairly often, but nothing came except an odd reconnaissance plane. We expected Lashio to be bombed. There was an enormous aggregation of supplies there. Either the Japs were too busy elsewhere, or they wanted to capture the supplies.

Lashio was the most interesting town in the whole of the Far East during those last months in Burma. From a thatch village of a few years previously, it was now the bustling centre of a thousand and one activities. Chinese merchants, fearing the closure of the Burma Road were swarming down in their cars, loaded up with everything they could jam in, and tearing back up the Burma Road, hoping to wangle another trip or two before the Road closed. Until the military started requisitioning cars in Lashio, anybody that had a car to dump could drive it there and sell it for more than its new price to Chinese merchants. The latter would stock it with goods and drive it to Kunming or Chungking, sell the car for six times its new price and have the stock as extra profit. Dealers were scouring Rangoon and Mandalay for cars to sell in Lashio. Lines of American army trucks, originally destined for Greece and Yugoslavia, but despatched too late, were moving in convoys shifting petrol, bombs, ammunition, machinery, vast quantities of Lease-Lend material through to China. The place was alive with Jeeps. Every clerk in the multitudinous Chinese transportation organisations seemed to have a Jeep, in which they spent their spare time driving their girl friends round the Lashio golf course. A Chinese Commando Organisation financed by the British Government and comprising mainly of Scandinavians, headed by the gigantic red-bearded China born Swede—George Saudebaum—had its headquarters there. Saudebaum and his commandos were later transferred to Kweiyang in China, where they were disbanded, without ever entering action.

All the big British trading organisations in China had big godowns at Lashio Station and fleets of trucks collecting goods from the railhead, and hauling them up into China. Makeshift buildings and camps were pushing up wherever there was a few hundred square feet of space. Restaurants and cheap hotels were doing a roaring trade. The new aristocracy of China,—the Burma Road truck drivers—swaggered about with pistols and revolvers of every description ostentatiously bulging out of their hip-pockets. They were bewildered with their newly acquired riches, their salaries were nothing compared with the "squeeze" most of them made, or their profits from illicit trading. A single suitcase full of drugs, especially the new sulpha drugs for treating venereal diseases—Sulphanilimide, sulphathiassol, sulphapyridine—was worth a fortune in China. In Kunming there was little on which these drivers could spend money, only Chinese food and Chinese girls. In Lashio they had a Cinema, showing comparatively modern American films. There was a variety of food to be had, clothes to be bought, liquor to be swilled, and girls of various race and colour to be sampled. Lashio, to the Burma Road drivers, was a world metropolis, the nearest approach to the "bright lights" that many of them had, or would ever see.

As twilight closed over the rest of Burma, the tempo of Lashio's frenetic activity increased. An antiquated fleet of rattle-trap trucks, in which even the lynx-eyed car requisitioners weren't interested, maintained a passenger service between New Lashio—the commercial centre—and Old Lashio, where most of the transport firms and repair shops were established. The Sikh, Burmese and Chinese drivers of the passenger trucks contributed to the general uproar of Lashio by standing alongside their trucks all day long, pleading with and roaring at the tops of their voices to the public at large to patronise their trucks. They kept no schedule, but moved off when they had a good pay load.

At the very core of the roar and bustle of life in Lashio was the market-place. Here the tribes people from the Shan and Kachin hills came down once every five days as they'd done for generations past and exchanged their goods. Marus and Lashis, variations of Kachins, semi-nomad people of Tibetan origin were most in evidence there. The women wore colourful costumes, heavy red embroidered skirts or close-fitting red and black trousers and black jackets. Virgins were distinguished by having their lank black hair cropped off at shoulder level. Married women had the hair coiled at the back. All women wore a type of chastity girdle, ten or twenty thin black cane circlets worn round the waist, but which could be slipped down around their hips in case of emergency. Some of them wore black colour bolero-type jackets, elaborately decorated with silver coins. They carried huge loads of potatoes, chillies, ginger roots, tomatoes and other local fruits and vegetables in cone-shaped baskets, which rested on their backs and were supported by a wide band which passed round the front of their forehead. One saw long lines of them usually with their jackets opened in front and breasts bare trudging along the roads and across fields, heads bent forward and obviously labouring under the weight of their baskets. The Kachins of this area are a dirty, but industrious people, despised by Burmans because of their dirt and the fact that they eat dogs. Most of the women as they trudge along spin cotton thread from balls on to spindles, and they always work at some embroidery or other handicraft, while waiting for buyers at the market place. There were usually some Tibetans at the Lashio market, gentle-looking men with brown wondering eyes. They couldn't talk to anybody but did a good trade with aphrodysiacs, especially amongst the Chinese. Their stock-in-trade seemed mainly to consist of tigers' claws, teeth and beaks of various animals and birds, tufts of hair and dried bones. As love potions they looked inadequate, but found plenty of buyers. They were tall, brown fellows, with rounded features and long hair, incredibly dirty. There were Shans too at Lashio, mostly men with bulging mouthfuls of teeth blackened through betel-chewing and wispy drooping moustaches. The Shans usually came in thatch-covered cars with beautifully carved yokes for the unique trotting bullocks which drew them.

The open air market was the chief attraction for me at Lashio, but most visitors were more concerned with the soldier attractions at the roofed-in stalls nearby, where anything from a pound of dried fish to a grand piano could be bought. Cheerful Sikh tailors sat cross-legged at their sewing machines ready to measure you and make shirts and trousers with a smile while you waited. Incredibly slim Burmese girls smoking incredibly fat white cheroots, squatted behind piles of spices, eggs, fish, cheroots and matches, ready to enter a bargaining match with all and sundry. With their green, pink and mauve coloured skirts reaching to within a few inches of the ground and light blouses transparent enough to hint at shapeliness beneath; with their elaborate cone of jet black hair held in place with a large jewelled comb and their easy almost insolent grace, Burmese girls are easy to look at. Their loongyis cling so tightly round the nether parts, that the legs seem slightly bent forward at the knees. When they walk it loosens as if at the slightest provocation they might leap into a Cossack dance. Sikhs, Chinese, Burmese, Madrassis competed eagerly one with another for the passing trade in the closed-in market. There was not much competition, because there were plenty of customers to go round.

Lashio, a "Sleepy Hollow" had awakened to become the cross-roads of the Far Eastern Universe. Every day passenger planes called in at Lashio aerodrome with passengers from Chungking, Calcutta, Rangoon. Trains in increasing quantities dumped their quota to the steadily increasing dumps and puffed away for another load. New trucks arrived in their scores every day from Rangoon, making their baptismal trip along the Road. Old veterans poured in daily to take another dip from the pile and try their luck along the Road once again. As time grew short, stuff that couldn't be shifted along the Road was dumped in the surrounding hills by the Chinese. One hoped they knew where to find it again.

I had to make still another trip to Rangoon. The first time I went, I'd seen the Director of Post and Telegraph Services, about having my messages accepted "collect" from Lashio. He promised to give the necessary instructions but Lashio never received them. They sent message after message to their director, but never received a reply, and meanwhile I had to pay for every message I sent. As they were anything up to twelve hundred words long, I couldn't keep that up indefinitely, so in desperation I went to Rangoon again to get written permission to send "collect" messages from Lashio. Armed with this I returned to Lashio, but still they refused to accept messages until *they* received *direct* instructions at the office. For the rest of my stay in Lashio I sent messages to Rangoon by train. Slow as the train service was, it was almost as quick as the telegraph service.

There were raids every day at Rangoon and it was impossible to do anything in the way of shopping. Things were quiet on the front at this time, the Japs concentrating on tiring out our air force—pitiably reduced already—before pushing on to Pegu and so to Rangoon. David Maurice told me he'd been busy despatching explosives for demolition work around Rangoon, so despite General Hutton's brave words about holding the capital, things didn't look so bright. I took a trip out to the Mingaladoon area and saw the wreckage of several Jap planes. One had been brought down the day previously, and the body of a Jap flyer was lying not far away from where his plane crashed. He had no parachute on, was probably a rear gunner and had apparently leaped out shortly before the plane crashed. Like many other Jap airmen I've seen, this fellow was short and stocky but with a tremendous head. Maurice and I were inspecting the wreckage of one plane when there was a heavy explosion two hundred yards away, and a fountain of smoke and dust spouted into the air. We flung ourselves on the ground expecting a bombing raid, but could hear no planes. It was apparently a delayed action bomb, dropped in a previous raid.

If I were asked to write an article on "The Most Unforgettable Character I've Met," I think it would be about the English phoongyi Thea Prajnananda, who lived and probably still lives in a small patch of jungle near Rangoon. Few people know of him. He told me I was the first newspaperman—apart from one Rangoon journalist—ever to visit him. I found him seated cross-legged on a wooden floor in a thatch-hut, giving advice to some Burmans who were asking him whether or not they should leave Rangoon.

Begrimed with dirt, and with an unwashed smell about him, he rose up and welcomed me, inviting me to occupy the only chair in the room. He was clad in the saffron robes of the Buddhist monk. Above his hollow cheeks, his shaven pate showed a glisten of grey stubble. He turned from me, not curious to know why I'd come; and told the Burmans he didn't think they should bother leaving Rangoon, even if the Japs came.

While he talked with them I looked around the room. There was a small Buddhist shrine built in one end, with bits of tinsel and paper flowers in front of it. Opposite hanging on the split cane wall, was a framed certificate testifying that one Charles J. Fletcher had taken his degree in engineering. When the Burmans departed, the monk spoke to me, in a quiet and cultured voice.

"Well, my son, what can I do for you."

"I've only come to talk, really," I said, a little uncomfortably. "I'd heard about you and you must admit it's unusual to meet an Englishman in such surroundings."

"I'm delighted to see you, and delighted to talk with you," he assured me. "I'm only sorry I've no better chair to offer you. My monastic life doesn't allow much in the way of luxuries."

"I couldn't help being curious about the certificate on the wall," I said, still at a loss what to talk about. "Has it special significance?"

"It's all I keep to remind me of my past life. It's mine, of course. I was educated at Oxford. I studied theology at first, then took up and graduated in engineering."

"Forgive me for asking the one question that brought me over here, but what made you bury yourself in this?" waving my hand at the thatch hovel, and its jungle surroundings.

"Ah. That's a long story my boy," and he fingered his gaunt, grey cheeks, and his eyes momentarily lost their feverish brightness in a faraway expression.

"I was always interested in oriental religions, but I think it was mainly the war that finally turned me away from the west. I was through it from beginning to end. Finished up as a Major, and went back from France with my ideas of our civilisation and Christianity all topsy-turvy.

"Do you remember Annie Besant?" he asked me suddenly.

"By name only."

"Well, I was attracted by the idea of theosophy. If you remember, in 1922 Annie Besant collected a lot of money to send an expedition to Thibet with a casket of jewels to the Dalai Lama.. A man called MacGovern and myself with about fifty others set out, but all except MacGovern and myself dropped out and stayed in India.

The jewels were lost, and MacGovern, and I went alone for Lhassa. We were both stopped at Shigatse and warned not to go further. The Dalai Lama was not pleased to receive us, we were told. MacGovern disguised himself as a coolie and went right on to Lhassa; but was found out and thrown into gaol. I became friendly with some monks and entered a monastery at Shigatse. Stayed there a year, too."

His eyes and voice were both far away, and he spoke like a man in a trance.

"Might have been there still, if it hadn't been for riots breaking out in Lhassa, and trouble spreading south. But after 12 months the monks warned me I should go away.

"I'd learned much with those Shigatse monks, and was sorry to leave. My word, was that a terrible journey on foot over the Himalayas to Darjeeling? I stayed with (unfortunately, the name has been lost with most of my notes in Burma. WGB.) the greatest Hindu Yogi exponent of his day. With him, I learned principles which have governed my life since."

"In what way 'governed your life,' " I interrupted.

"Ah, governed my physical, and partly my spiritual life. Wonderful things they teach you. To sublimate the baser desires and gain greater mental powers. I've learned to treat my body as a plant. To roll in the dew in the early mornings. To let my body draw nourishment from the earth after its sleep. As vegetable life draws nourishment and strength from the earth, and early morning sun and dew, so do I. You can feel the sun drawing power from the base of the spine up to the brain. Pure physical sublimation. Living a purely natural life as a plant does, I can go for weeks without eating or drinking. Only thus am I strengthened for the intense mental concentration needed for true contemplation. I shall show you some Yogic poses afterwards, if you're interested," he offered.

"I'd like to see some Yogic exercises, naturally. When did you come to Burma?"

"Not exercises, my dear boy, poses. Ah, but I wasn't satisfied with the Yogi. Mind you, they do wonderful things. Shut themselves up in caves for weeks on end, living without air, light, food or water. But it seemed to me they were too remote from the world and their fellow-beings. After all, what good do they do to their fellow-men with their marvellous powers?

"I set out on a pilgrimage through India, studying various religions. With nothing but staff and begging bowl, I tramped from Darjeeling to Calcutta; from Calcutta to Bombay and right down to Ceylon. Three years, it took me. From 1923 to '26. Ah, what adventures I had, my son. I lived with the Shwetambar sect of the Jains for a time. You know they're similar to the Hindus, but fanatically strict vegetarians. No food must be partaken after dark, in case insects should be eaten by mistake. We could only drink filtered water and wore white cloths over noses and mouths so that the air we breathed should be free of any living organism. I left them and became a priest with the Digambar, also a Jain sect, and lived stark naked, my body smeared only with ashes. But all this fanaticism and asceticism seemed to me what Buddha described as a 'way to salvation over a dunghill.' I found the Buddhist creed more human and rational. In the Anagandasutta of the Sutta-Nipata, Buddha has written:

'Abstaining from fish or flesh, nakedness,
Shaving of the head, matted hair, covering with ashes, wearing
Rough deer skins, attending the sacrificial fire, nor
All the various penances in the world performed

For immortality, neither incantations, oblations,
Sacrifices nor seasonal observances, purifies a
Person who has not overcome his doubts.'

"I wanted peace and quiet, so I came to Burma and entered a Buddhist monastery in Mandalay. That was in 1926 and except for one brief visit to Europe and America I've been in the monasteries ever since."

"And are you satisfied with your life now? Have you found what you were looking for?"

He turned his grey, grimy face towards me.

"Does one ever find what one looks for in this life, my son? At least I have peace. That is more than most men can say. What has your Christian civilisation given you? Look at your poverty and misery and wars."

"It's true we've not got much to boast about, but I don't see that as Buddhists, you've done so well either. The Japanese are doing their fair share of bloodying, and so were the Siamese a little while ago against the French."

"The whole world has become corrupt and evil, my son. Just look at our monasteries here. Do you think the Lord Buddha ever intended them to degenerate to their present level? There is not one monk in ten who is not corrupt. Instead of spending their lives in fasting and teaching and meditation, they drink and gamble, and indulge in worldly pleasures. The phoongyi kyaungs have never stood at a lower level than today."

"It's true then, what one heard that the phoongyi kyaungs are full of thieves and swindlers? People who want an easy living or a refuge from the law?"

"I'm afraid it is partly true. There are many good and saintly monks who carry on the teaching throughout the land, but quite a number are spendthrift loafers, who use the monasteries for their own ends. Others want to turn them into political societies. It needs a Christ, my boy, to cleanse the Temple."

"One hears the monasteries are full of Japanese agents—even Japanese. Do you think that's true?"

"There have been Japanese monks, of course. But they weren't very popular. You see, Burmese Buddhism is the purest form of the purest branch of Buddhism practised on a national scale in the world today. We belong to the Hinayana or "Little Wheel" sect, which survives only in Ceylon, Siam and here in Burma. The Japanese Buddhists are bogus followers of the impurer Mahayana "Big Wheel" sect whose followers are found only in Thibet, China and Japan. As a matter of fact most of them are shintoists and trying to mix Shintoism and Buddhism, but it is like trying to mix oil with water. Shintoists claim that every Japanese is directly descended from a God, the Emperor himself directly descending from the Sun Goddess. How can their ancestor-worship be reconciled with Buddhism? We find they don't even understand Buddhism. An ordinary Japanese will tell you the only difference between Shintoism and Buddhism is that a Shintoist rubs his hands and a Buddhist claps his hands when saying his prayers. Actually the true Hinayana Buddhists don't clap their hands, but hold them together with finger-tips touching, under the chin. There is only one small sect in Japan—the Zens—who can claim to be Buddhist, and even their form of worship is foreign to us here in Burma. No. I don't think the Japs get much sympathy from the Burmans on account of their mutual belief in Buddhism. But it is quite possible, now that some of the kyaungs have become political hotbeds, that the Japanese have agents there. I know little what goes on in the kyaungs these days. I never leave this place, except sometimes, when I need food;

I take my begging bowl and staff and make my rounds. People near here are very good to me. I rarely have to go far before my bowl is filled."

"What sort of food do you get?"

"Rice. Almost always rice. Perhaps some beans or cabbage. I never take meat, you know, although contrary to what most people believe, Buddhists may eat meat. Bananas sometimes. It takes very little to keep this frame of mine going."

"What do you intend doing if the Japs come?"

"My son, I'm getting old. At my time of life I don't start running away. If the Japanese come, I stay here. If they kill me, they kill me. But I don't see why they should. I feel I no longer belong to the Western world. Perhaps they feel otherwise. When one's ties with this world are as light as mine, one no longer fears the prospect of death. What does it rob me of? My staff, bowl and parasol!"

His yellow robe had slipped down over his shoulders, revealing a hollow chest, and a few sparse grey hairs. His ribs stood out like steps on a ladder. I got up to go, and he stood up, wriggling back into his robes again and reaching for his parasol. At the bottom of the rough-cut steps, he shuffled into a pair of sandals and escorted me out through the overgrown paths. He allowed me to take some pictures of him squatting in his Yogic poses, in which every limb and muscle—even individual fingers—were kept rigid in position for several minutes. He demonstrated one position with his posterior in the air and head near the ground, which he told me was most beneficial, transferring sexual power up the spinal column to the brain.

I took a last picture of him standing with the sun streaming through his yellow parasol, illuminating his ascetic features, in front of a board which bore a roughly painted inscription:

Thea Prajnananda
English Monastery. Kokine Ave. Rangoon.

"Bless you my son. Bless you. Come back and see me when you can. You'll always be welcome," he said as we shook hands and I left.

That was the last I saw of Thea Prajnananda—one time Major Fletcher of the British Army. Friends have told me since that his interest switched to Astrology. I marvelled at the news. I had believed he had travelled enough through all the various sects and monasteries, and was at last content and tranquil within the Buddhist religion. And now I found he continued the journey, like a religious hitch-hiker, along the road that leads to nowhere. I hope the Japanese have left him in peace to work out his theory of the affinity between the prophesies of the stars and the tenets of Buddhism.

I met Leslie Smith, assistant Press Attaché at the British Embassy, Chungking. He'd been sent down to Rangoon to buy cars and station waggons and all the provisions he could lay hands on, for the Embassy. He was driving back to Lashio within a couple of days, and invited me to go back with him.

We drove back along the Prome road; there are two highways leading northwards from Rangoon, one swinging slightly West via Prome and Yenanyaung, the other bulging to the East via Pegu and Toungoo. They join at Meiktila 75 miles South of Mandalay, also the junction of the road leading East via Kalaw, Taunggyi and Loilem through the Southern Shan states to Kentung near the Thailand border. "Smithy," as he's affectionately known throughout China, still had his eyes open for provisions, and we inspected most worthwhile-looking stores on our way through. At Yenanyaung, the oil production centre, we discovered a gold mine.

A Sikh shop well stocked with just those delicacies most likely to tickle the palate of harrassed Embassy officials. Apart from tinned stuff—then at a premium in most parts of Burma—there was to be had Scotch whisky by the case, tins of Schlitz beer, good Dutch and French liqueurs, genuine sherry, Danish export lager, Gordon's gin, Roses's lime juice, and German Rheinberger and Kastelberger wine. We had to dump some things out of the car, to make room for these prizes, and Smithy threatened to send a truck down for the stuff we couldn't jam in.

It was a terribly hot day and we had a difficult drive. There are lots of semi-dry streams along the Prome road, difficult to negotiate. In one of these a crowd of youths were lounging about, ankle deep in water. Our car gently lowered its nose into the water, got half way across—and stopped. A shout of delight from the youths and half a dozen were all over the car in half a minute, bargaining to get us out. In the twinkling of an eye, one of them had the bonnet up, the distributor head off and the points cleaned. The motor started up and with five pushing behind, we were soon out on the other side, ten rupees poorer. The delighted youths took up their positions again waiting for the next sucker. They were good psychologists. They know that 'Burra Sahibs' don't like to take off shoes and socks and fool about in the water. The road was inches deep in dust, and with blacked out lights we went off the road a couple of times in the dark. We arrived at Meiktila about 9-30 p.m. with our throats coated with dust, exhausted, sweating, hungry and thirsty.

We found rooms in the Circuit House, specially provided for the convenience of officials on tour, beautifully situated on the edge of a small lake. After we washed and changed our shirts, Smithy, a man of few words, looked enquiringly across at me and I agreed. We ordered dinner and plenty of glasses. We started off with gin and lime juice. In retrospect I have such pleasant memories of that evening that I think we must have had crushed ice as well. We tried out the whisky too, one can't be too careful when one's buying for an Embassy. It was alright. So was the Danish export lager. The boy brought in the soup at that stage and the Embassy should have been very satisfied with the sherry we drank with it. Smithy thought it was hardly the correct thing to take German wine back to the British Embassy, so when the roast chicken arrived we disposed of one of the bottles of Kastelberger. We reckoned the other could wait till Lashio. We opened a can of cherries and a tin of cream for dessert, and after that a glass of Curacao seemed just right. We turned in that night with very easy consciences, feeling that we'd done a good job for the British Embassy. Everything we'd bought was first class. We were even more convinced of this by the time Smithy left Lashio.

CHAPTER X

On February 19 I was tipped off that the Chinese troops would start moving. I went to the welcoming arches at Old Lashio, where a great crowd of Chinese had gathered to cheer them on their way. Chinese, as a rule, are an undemonstrative people, and I've never before or since, inside or outside of China seen Chinese welcome other Chinese as the Lashio Chinese welcomed their compatriots in arms. A reception committee had been organised and each truck as it pulled through the welcoming arches stopped and cups of green tea and biscuits were handed up to the troops. I'd borrowed one of the cars Smithy had purchased for the Embassy, and with me was Leckie Thompson, photographer for the Public Relations Office. We had a job to get pictures because of the crowds pressing around the troops, but they thinned out as the long line of trucks moved on. Youthful, tough-looking lads, these troops were answering with clenched fists—the cheers of their fellow countrymen. They had banners on their trucks urging "Unity of the United Nations against Japanese Aggressors," "Arm, Work, Fight for Victory" "ABCD Front will destroy the Aggressor", "United we'll push Japanese from Asia." In New Lashio there were terrific scenes as we made our way through detonations and acrid smoke of thousands of exploding fire-crackers. Chinese merchants and Burma Road profiteers were cheering on the brave boys who were going to keep the Road open and their profits secure. "Wan Shwe. Jong kuo jen wan shawe", the cry rang out, "China ten thousand years." Back at the crossroads near the Lashio Post Office I met Dr. Seegrave, with part of his outfit. Behind his thick spectacles his eyes were gleaming with an unholy, joyful anticipation of action.

"Boy," he shouted to me, "at last we're off. At last they've got things shifting" and with a cheerful shout, "I'll see you down the line" he let in the clutch and was on his way, a bunch of demure but happy-looking girls in the back of the truck. We drove out to the Chinese bivouacking camp, sixteen miles past Lashio. Very simple bamboo shelters had been put up, and the troops jumped off their trucks, formed up and marched across to their quarters. Within a few minutes their cooks had their kitchens set up and fires lit. Mountains of cabbages—from Baptist Mission gardens—melted away as each unit took its quota. British observers, seeing Chinese troops for the first time, were impressed with the quietness and orderliness with which the troops moved into their barracks and prepared for the night. Some amusement was caused at the sight of a group of "hsiao kwei" (little devils), grinning, fresh-faced, yellow-clad cherubs who looked about ten years old, but were probably between thirteen and sixteen. They are used as orderlies and for any work whereby they can release able-bodied men for fighting. They're mighty fierce little fellows, and have often been known to seize weapons and jump into the fray when their "comrades" were in a tough spot.

It was going to take them several days to get down to their positions in the Southern Shan States, and it wasn't expected they'd enter action for some time. I'd been warned that the Gissimo was due to arrive any day from India and would stay overnight at Lashio. We guessed it must be true that he was coming, because a Jap observation plane came over Lashio daily, showing that something was in the wind. Eve Curie arrived back from Rangoon, looking very smart in her war correspondent uniform. While waiting for a plane to take her on to Chungking, she wanted to find out about Indo-Burma Road projects, so I took her along to Tseng Yang Fu. He talked to her about roads for an hour without telling her a word about what was being planned. Tseng was a master at talking without telling. I went with her to Major Ausland, who took only two minutes to tell her nothing about Indo-Burma Road projects. It was all very hush-hush in those days. Of course, if she'd really wanted the "low-down" she only had to listen in to Tokio Radio, which discussed nightly British and Chinese plans for opening up road communications with India.

General Magruder arrived from Chungking, and Tseng decided to throw a dinner party with General Magruder and Colonel Aldrich from the US Army Air Force, Major Ausland, a US Army captain, a British Major, Eve Curie and myself as guests. Tseng had a penchant for inviting people of varying view-points—and race if possible—to such parties and listening to their conversation with a benign smile of content, rarely contributing anything himself. I tried to memorise scraps that passed across the table, and noted them down before I went to bed.

"......it's a pity about France alright. Waai yer can't expect a country ter fight once it's lost its soul."

"My country has never lost its soul. It has been betrayed by people who are enemies of liberty and freedom. You have people like that in your country, too, Captain......"

"Why don't you Chinese take over Burma? You need a backdoor to the sea, and couldn't make a worse mess of the country than it's in now."

"My dear friend, we have enough to do to look after our own country. If we get all of China back again, we'll have enough to keep us busy. We don't want to buy anybody else's troubles. We say 'let the Burmans look after Burma, and we'll look after our own country'......"

"......Well, by Jeepers, we're certain after this lot we're not going to leave Britain and France to run things in Europe. Have the same thing all over again. You get yourselves into trouble, and then holler out for us to come and pull you out."

"But if you'd supported your own creation, old boy, the League, you'd have taken more of an interest in Europe after the last war and not left everything to us..."

"......of course, France will rise again. There's no question of talking of De Gaulle French, Vichy French after the war. There's only Frenchmen. France's collapse isn't something only of 1940. It has roots in treaties and non-fulfilment of treaties, in democratic powers' betrayal of Spain and Austria and Czechoslovakia. Of course, our governments were weak, but were we alone in that? Was Chamberlain a Frenchman? But the French people are suffering for it. And French people are fighting and dying for other people's mistakes......"

"No. I don't pretend China is democratic yet. But at least we've shown we prefer democracy. We fight on the democratic side. What do you think of, Major, when you talk of democracy? Political, social or economic? To a Russian, who lives under a sort of economic democracy your America with its extremes of rich and poor must seem the most undemocratic of lands. Yet, you have political democracy. To a Frenchman you are undemocratic because of your colour prejudices. What about your negroes? Do you think America has social democracy? Why, I love America, my friend, but we have a truer social democracy in China.

"......We had Japan bothering us then too, and we had to buy time in Europe I tell you. Was America prepared to come and help us if we'd got into holts over Czechoslovakia?"

"There wasn't a question of war then. Whose fault was it you were in trouble with Japan? D'yuh remember the Manchurian affair, and Stimson proposing joint British American action against Japan?

"I remember America *talking* a lot......"

"What does Australia think about the British Empire, anyway?"

"I'm only one Australian, so it's hard to say. There's a lot of sentimental affection for England. People making a trip there always say they're "going home." The Empire means England and Australia and to a lesser extent New Zealand—to most people. Few know or care anything about what happens in the other dominions, and still fewer could even name the colonies."

"But won't Australia break away after the war?"

"I doubt it. For one thing, a breakaway means a sentimental breakaway, as there's not much else holding us. Even the reddest 'leftists' don't agitate for a complete break from the Empire. What most progressives feel is that Australian Governments should make greater use of powers they already hold, under the Statutes of Westminster, to formulate their own economic and foreign policies. We don't like this attitude of immediate endorsement for everything Downing St. decided."

"......and after this war you'll do the same as last time, and repudiate your debts to us. That's what made most Americans so mad about England. Same with China. Look at all this stuff being poured along these roads—and most of it over the edges. Do yuh think we'll ever see a penny for it?"

"I always say there's nobody like an American for being hurt about how their government spends its money. One'd think every blooming dollar was being wrung out of his personal bank account. Cheaper to fight a war with gold than blood anyway. Where'd you be if we and the Chinese stopped fighting...... ?"

And so it went on, for the most part good humouredly. Tseng sat at the head of the table, with his button lips pursed and rosy, his hands resting on the table with finger-tips touching, his face beaming and eyes wrinkled with good humour, as he followed the discussions he'd set in motion.

After coffee was finished, Eve Curie was sworn in as a Burma Roadster—as far as I know the only person to hold that degree without actually having travelled the Burma Road. I think the idea of the "Burma Roadster" originated among the AVG and CAMCO boys at Loiwing. To qualify, one had to have travelled the Road between Lashio and Kunming. Initiation was simple. One paid two rupees each to all other Roadsters present at the ceremony—at least two witnesses were necessary—and had his or her name inscribed on a red ten-dollar Chinese bill, which the novitiate had to provide. Once a Roadster, you had to produce your ten-dollar bill on demand. If you failed to have it with you the penalty was to buy drinks for all other "Roadsters" present. With thirty signatures, one graduated to the rank of Burma "Highwayman." The idea was later adopted by people who'd crossed the Pacific by "Clipper." Signatures were collected on an American dollar bill, and graduates took the title of "Short Shorter." No doubt all very infantile, but in those days when we had to make our own entertainment, the Burma "Roadster" idea contributed its full share of amusement. In all parts of Burma and China since, I've seen people meeting for the first time and within a few minutes one or the other would say: "By the way, are you a Burma Roadster by any chance?" In a few seconds red dollar notes would be passed across and fountain pens got busy.

The photographer Thompson and I went out with Sir John Rowland to have a look at the work on the Burma section of the Yunnan-Burma railway. Sir John, middle-aged and with an explosive temper, was in charge of the construction. He'd lived long enough in Australia to acquire a vocabulary which would make a bullock-driver lean on his whip and sigh with envy. About ten miles of rails had been laid and we travelled out on rail motor, and listened with admiration while Sir John fluently and picturesquely cursed the British, Indian Burmese, American and Chinese governments and peoples. The British had let him down by not sending materials, the Indians by not sending sufficient coolies, the Chinese had wronged him by rounding up all the Chinese labour around the frontier districts, and worst of all, the Chinese with American connivance had offered to build a part of his section as well as their own, because of his slow progress. The crowning atrocity was that having in forthright terms spurned this insulting offer, in the end he'd had to ask the Chinese to do it. The Chinese and Americans had agreed immediately, but work was held up because sanction hadn't yet been given by the British Government. At the end of the ten-mile stretch we left the rail motor, and Sir John, clad in riding breeches and leggings, stumped along voicing his grievances as we went.

"See these b......girders. Do you think I got 'em from the British Government? No. I had to go and ask the Chinese for 'em. Hmm. Pa. What's this fellow Chiang Kai Shek gone to India for? Know what *I'd* do with him. Chinese? Huh. They're happy now. Got us in to fight their war for 'em. Indians? God, I hope I never see another Indian as long as I live after this's finished. If it ever *gets* finished. The dirtiest, laziest, most incompetent......Would I sooner have Chinese or Indian coolies? Give me Indians any time. If ever there was a despicable, thieving, lying bunch of.........it's Chinese coolies. When they're not smoking opium they're pinching things out of your tent. An Indian coolie'll do twice as much work in a day as a Chinese......What? Chinese have their section finished in six months? Who told you that? They'll never have it done in six years......Lot they know about building railways......They'll never build it......Yes, of course, people said it about the Burma Road, and they were right. What the hell is the Burma Road? A track scratched up and down over mountain tops. Ought never been built. Look at all the trouble it's got us into. Dragged us into this war with the Japs...... Well, (waving his riding crop down a valley where sweating Indian coolies were hacking a cutting out of a hillside) that's the way it goes for fifty miles......Now I s'pose you're satisfied. You'll go away and write some confounded nonsense about 'Romance of Railway Building in the Far East'" Poor Sir John. Later he was to be given the difficult task of keeping Burma railways running during the last stages of the Burma campaign. He achieved miracles; running trains without coal, keeping the rolling stock moving without repair facilities, stimulating the discontented railway staff to stick to their jobs till the last useful moment, and finally walking out of Burma with the staff he'd promised to stay with. He was offered a seat in one of the last evacuation planes, but refused it. He was offered a seat in General Alexander's staff car and the chance of evacuating with the Headquarters staff, but he refused. He'd promised his Indians and their families that he'd see them through, and he did. He had one of the most terrible journeys of any of the evacuees. From May till August the party was caught in the Naga Hills near the Chauxan Pass, with practically no food. An inch of mouldy rice in a cigarette tin per man, per day, sometimes eked out with stewed fern fronds and tadpoles. From a normal near hundred and eighty pounds, Sir John dropped down to nearly one hundred, by the time he and the remnants of his party staggered out of the steamy, leech-infested jungle into India. I've heard since that he cursed and swore, blustered and fulminated at every member of the party, was accused of callousness and brutality, but was the one man who never lost heart. He had a lot to put up with. I'm glad I wasn't one of his party when they finally had to pack up and walk hundreds of miles out to India through leech and mosquito infested jungle in the Naga Hills. I've heard since they subsisted partly on snakes, caught and cooked by Dr. Burgess Barnett—one time snake expert at Whipshade Zoo, London, and later chief malarialogist for the British section of the Yunnan-Burma railway.

On the 22nd of February I heard that the Gissimo was due to arrive in Lashio the following day. Tseng Yang Fu thought he could arrange for me to see either the Generalissimo or Madame or both. Eve Curie was the only other journalist on the spot and as she was working for American papers I didn't consider her a rival. Early next morning, to my horror, a serious rival—Roderick MacDonald—arrived. I sounded him out and learned he knew nothing of the Gissimo's visit. He was on his way through to Chungking. I had a brain wave and suggested that as Lesli Smith was setting out for Kunming that day by car, Mac. should go with him.

By dropping a hint that Smithy was carrying some good drinks, I sold Mac. on the idea and breathed a sigh of relief when I waved them good-bye a couple of hours later.

The Gissimo's plane wasn't expected in till evening, and as Eve Curie wanted to see something of the Burma Road, I took her for a run towards Kukai, about half-way between Lashio and the frontier. We had gone about thirty miles when she suddenly remembered that she was supposed to telephone to CNAC at 2 p.m. in case there was a plane to Chungking. It was already ten past one, so we had to turn round and tear back. As we got near Lashio, we could hear a plane and soon saw a CNAC passenger plane preparing to land. We both suffered acute mental agony. I was sure it was the Gissimo arriving ahead of schedule and Eve Curie became very excited and lapsing into rapid French urged "vite vite." She was certain it was her plane for Chungking, and was undecided whether to drive straight to the aerodrome and to travel to Chungking without baggage; or whether I should take her back to Porter's house. Porter, in whose house she was staying, was Superintendent of the Northern Shan States. There was an air raid alarm as we got into Lashio, so we went on to the aerodrome and found that it was a Calcutta-bound plane that had arrived. A Jap reconnaissance plane came over and leisurely flew away again. At the aerodrome they told Eve Curie that she would get a plane to Chungking that evening. We reckoned that she'd leave on the plane that brought the Gissimo and Madame, and if we came to the 'drome early, she'd have time for a few words with Madame before the plane left.

Mr. Porter had placed his home at the disposal of the Generalissimo and party during their overnight stay in Lashio. He was down at the aerodrome together with General Hutton—then still Commander-in-Chief, Burma, Col. Hobson, Tseng Yang Fu and other American, British and Chinese officials. Tseng didn't seem so sure about my interview with the Gissimo, as time drew near for the plane to arrive. He said he'd do his best, but "no doubt the Gissimo'd be very busy." I spoke to Porter about it, and he said he would mention it to Madame during the evening. Just casually say: "By the way, I've arranged for the "Daily Express" correspondent to be here at 8-30 in the morning," and I would turn up as if a definite appointment had been made. That seemed the best idea, in case I failed to button-hole Madame at the plane. Thompson introduced Eve Curie and me to Gen. Hutton, who'd just been involved in a plane crash. The Lysander in which he was flying to Lashio made a forced landing in the wild country near Hsipaw, and burst into flames. The General did a good job, beating out the flames with his great coat and pulled the unconscious pilot out of the cockpit. His ADC travelling in a second "Lazzie" parachuted down, and the two of them had about a forty-mile walk, before they got transport into Lashio. The pilot later died in hospital. The General was very formal and said he was convinced Rangoon would be held. He gave us the impression that the campaign was going fine.

We were told there'd be a plane within 20 minutes, and sure enough we soon heard the drone of a plane, and saw signals from its flash gun. The great black shape came quite low, before landing lights were switched on and it glided in, stirring up a great cloud of dust. We surged across as it taxied into position, and I steeled my nerves for button-holing Madame as soon as she stepped from the plane. The Gissimo is the hardest man in the world to interview and even if he said nothing but his famous "hao, ho-ho," it could still be turned into a "scoop" interview, by quoting negative or positive grunts to carefully prepared questions. I stuck close to Eve Curie as we waited for the plane doors to open, knowing she'd have a better technique than I for opening with Madame. But they were'nt there. A great disappointment for me, but not so great for Eve Curie who was pretty sure to see them in Chungking. Then word was passed around that they were following in another plane, due in an hour's time. I waved a triumphant good-bye to Mademoiselle Curie, as she was tucked into her seat, and the plane taxied off again. It looked as if I was going to have a completely exclusive story. The landing lights were switched on just long enough to allow the Chungking-bound plane to take off, and once again the 'drome was in darkness. They weren't taking any chances, in view of Jap curiosity during the previous few days. Exactly an hour after the first plane arrived we heard another plane. We saw it circling the 'drome, and its signal gun flickering. It circled round twice, then zoomed up, leaving us with the diminishing roar of its engines in our ears. An official came out and told us that was the Gissimo's plane alright, but the radio operator signalled that in view of Jap activity they were going straight on to Kunming without stopping. Sorry!

Generals and Colonels and officials politely tried to look as if they weren't in the least surprised or disappointed that they'd travelled 700 miles from Rangoon for nothing, and wasted days waiting for nothing.

CHAPTER XI

I wasn't certain what to do next. Whether to go down to the Chinese armies, where there didn't seem any prospect of action for some weeks, or to accept an invitation proposed by Tseng and Ausland.

The Gissimo was very interested in opening up an alternative trade route to China, once the Burma Road was closed. The first idea was to put a road through the extreme Northwest corner of Burma from Putao (Fort Hertz) to Sadiya the railhead of the Bengal-Assam railway in Northeast Assam. There was already a road of sorts, linking Fort Hertz with Myitkyina, on the Irrawaddy River and joined by rail with Mandalay. Myitkyina was also joined by river and road with Bhamo, from where a caravan trade route—the Old Silk Road —followed by Marco Polo—leads via Tengyueh through Yunnan and joins up with the Burma Road. Mr. Porter, who'd previously been stationed in the Hukwang Valley, which runs Southeast from Myitkyina towards Assam, had told Tseng Yang Fu he believed an easier route lay along the Hukwang Valley and over the Naga Hills to Ledo (also on the Assam-Bengal railway). There'd already been negotiations with Burma Government, and the Gissimo had doubtless taken up the question with the Indian Government during his visit to India. Matters had reached the stage where Ausland and Tseng were to go to Myitkyina and have a conference with Mr. MacDougall, secretary to Burma Government. They wanted to drive over to Myitkyina, and from there go as far as possible up the Hukwang Valley in Jeeps, and see what the existing trail was like. They expected the trip to last ten days, and I was invited to go along with them.

I had to make up my mind that night whether the story was worth ten days' time. Whether anything exciting was likely to happen in "my" area during the next ten or fourteen days. I decided I couldn't risk it and before turning-in that night I told Ausland I wouldn't go. After sleeping on it, however, I changed my mind. The Chinese were going to an inactive front and were moving in so slowly that I thought I could leave them for a fortnight. We spent the early part of the morning buying up provisions, and then had to tear out of town for an air raid alarm. It was late afternoon when we got started. Ausland and I in one car, Lt. Col. Haas and Tseng in the other. A fifth member of the party, Johnny Sharberg from Texaco Oil Company, had left by Jeep earlier in the day.

We made Loiwing that night. There were several AVG boys there, and we all made merry in the big common room at the hostel. I went to sleep in front of a huge fire, and when I woke up everybody had gone, except a red-moustached, red-haired AVG boy, who was bending over me with a whisky bottle in one hand and part of my shoulder in the other. It was 1-30 a.m. and I wanted to go to bed, but he had other ideas. He was certain I was "the smart guy" who'd "pinched" his girl in Rangoon. Now this was flattering, but very wrong. I'd never seen him, or his girl, in my life before. He was going to "do me in" right then and there, he said. I was just a "low heel limey bastard." I had a terrible time with him. Whenever I rose he shoved me back on to the sofa, and had another swig from his whisky bottle. It took me over an hour to get him to agree to postpone killing me till morning, when I promised to fight a duel with him. I saw to it that our party was roused out very early in the morning, and had a look to see who was at the breakfast table, before I went in. I suppose the AVGer was still sleeping off his whisky, because we got away without seeing him again. I guess if he remembered anything at all, he just wiped me off as another of those "yellow limey bastards" that had crossed his path.

We had to have special permission to travel the Loiwing Bhamo road in daytime. It was closed for repairs, steam-rollers were at work, and traffic was allowed only at night, 5 p.m. till midnight Bhamo-Loiwing, midnight till 7 a.m. Loiwing-Bhamo. It's a sixty-odd mile run, but the first forty miles from Loiwing consitute the twistiest road I've ever travelled. The Burma road is straight in comparison. I'll swear there's not one straight hundred yard stretch, and nearly all the corners are banked the wrong way. For most of the way there's no room for two cars to pass. We found a Chinese driving a YBR (Yunnan-Burma Railroad) jeep along the road, so he was instructed to bring it into Bhamo, where we would take charge of it. Bhamo, on the West bank of the Irrawaddy, owed its importance these days to being the chief distributing centre for gasoline, shipped up from Yenanyaung and passed across through Wanting into China. Tseng Yang Fu and Ausland had to wrest sufficient petrol out of the Bhamo agents, to shift the rice which had now arrived for the YBR coolies, up the road from Lashio. Lashio itself was out of petrol and so was Kyukok. After wasting two days in Bhamo, they persuaded Dick Frost and Jock Wilson of the APC to let them have sufficient to save the coolies. Johnny Sharberg had arrived with his Jeep and the Jeep we'd picked up in the road was overhauled. Another oil man, Calvert from Standard Oil decided to join us in the trip along the Hukwang Valley, so we laid in more supplies, cooking utensils, shovels, picks and axes and a good stout length of rope.

Just before we left, Tseng got a cable from Lashio, saying that the Gissimo wanted him to go to Kunming and meet him there as soon as possible. He decided to go on to Myitkyina first, so that he could report to the Gissimo the results of the conference with MacDougall, the Burma Government secretary. Col. Haas would then drive him back. We switched cars so's I could drive and Haas could have a sleep to fortify him for a non-stop drive back to Lashio after the conference. The Bhamo-Myitkyina road was very narrow and rarely used by cars. We met a couple of bullock carts, and the drivers had to unharness the bullocks, and drag the carts off the road to let us pass. Tseng meanwhile got friendly with the Shan ladies travelling in the cart and I had to take a picture of his fraternising with the Shans. He talked some Chinese dialect to them and they talked Shan back to him, and seemed to get along fine together. Not far from Myitkyina the road straightened out, and became much broader. We'd been warned that we had to get to Myitkyina before dark, otherwise they wouldn't ferry our car across the river—Myitkyina lies on the West bank of the Irrawaddy. So I was sending the big Army car along the good road at fifty without trouble. Some men were walking along about a quarter of a mile ahead, and tooted the horn. They looked round and kept on walking. There were two on the left and two on the right side. Just as the car was nearly on top of them, one man looked round and jumped straight in front of the car, apparently trying to cross to the other side of the road. I braked and hit him at the same time. He seemed to fly high in the air, and crashed down on the left light and mudguard, smashing the light to smithereens. The car was stopped by the time he landed, and Haas, first-aid bag in hand, was bending over him in a split second. I thought it was too late for a medical kit, but jumped out, feeling sick inside, and helped straighten the poor fellow out. He showed no signs of life, but Haas said his heart was beating alright. He tested him limb by limb for fractures, tapped him for broken ribs, felt his head and looked for blood, at nose and ears for skull fracture. The only thing he could find was a piece of skin rubbed off his behind. While he was cleaning this with spirit, the patient showed vigorous signs of life and tried to struggle up. His Shan companions reasoned with him and he lay quiet till the abrasion was dressed. In a minute he was on his feet, apparently demanding of the others what had happened; and they, with gesticulations and pointing to car tracks and the broken headlight, explained that he'd been slightly hit. Haas put his kit together and said:

"Well doggone it. If I hadn't seen that happen I wouldn't have believed it possible. There's not a thing the matter with that chap. He must be made of rubber. By the smell of him he's pretty drunk, but all the same, I'd never have believed a human being could take a knock like that and only get a bit of skin knocked off."

As the Shans were going our way, we put two in each car and pushed on. Before long the one that I'd knocked began singing away to himself most happily. We'd given him fifty rupees, and Haas reckoned he'd probably spend the rest of his life waiting on the side of the road for cars to knock him down. When we got to the village on the opposite side of the river from Myitkyina, we got hold of an interpreter and asked where the Shans wanted to go. After a long discussion the interpreter told us they'd just been to a Shan wedding and were all pretty drunk. They came from a village about six miles back along the road, but had continued on the car because they liked the ride—and had fifty rupees to spend.

We had to leave our cars on the West bank till next day and crossed the river by launch. Mr. and Mrs. Bathgate of Steel Bros.—one of the largest trading firms in Burma and China—gave us rooms for the night. The following day MacDougall arrived and Ausland was very satisfied with the speed with which decisions were reached. Full co-operation was offered by Burma Government in arranging rice supplies, preliminary labour in case they decided to build the road, and Tseng and Ausland were given a free hand to go ahead. After Ausland had had talks with political officers who knew the country, they decided to build a road somewhere near the Hukwang Valley, and Tseng went back to see the Gissimo, and also to start marching coolies over right away. Ausland was then cabled to return to wind up the YBR project while Chinese engineers were being sent over to survey routes etc. It seemed as if the expedition was disintegrating before it got properly started. The two oil men and myself decided we'd take the two Jeeps and go on alone. The oil men were supposed to report back to their companies the possibilities for an alternative oil supply route after the Burma refineries were blown up. For me the first trip over the projected road was still a good story and I knew our military people would be interested in a report on the route. People had been discussing the possibility of a road through the Hukwang Valley for years, but no one had been to have a look. A young British official of the Burma Frontier Service, Clive W. North, arrived in Myitkyina just at this time. Having just returned from an expedition a short way up the Valley, he was dead keen in coming with us. He could speak the dialect of the Kachins living in the Valley, and we were quite prepared to take him. His chief, Mr. Willkie, district superintendent, gave him the necessary permission.

North seemed a likeable chap, but very slow. If there was one thing the other three of us wanted, it was speed and hustle, and this threw North off his tracks for a while. He wanted to stay in Myitkyina buying more supplies, but we persuaded him we'd plenty for all, and hurried on with what he seemed to regard as indecent haste. We railed our Jeeps down to Mogaung, thirty odd miles South from Myitkyina, and from where the track led on to India—we hoped. No one knew. North had his wife in Mogaung—and he naturally wanted to stay the night there. But we told him remorselessly we had to push on. We allowed him an hour or two while we inspected the village, and saw a jade-cutting and polishing plant, run by Chinese. They had some magnificent jade necklaces for sale at a little over twenty pounds but we left them for the return journey. There are famous jade, ruby and amber mines along the Hukwang Valley, operated by Chinese, and Mogaung is the centre of the cutting and polishing industry.

By 2 p.m. we were on our way, two well-packed Jeeps with about sixty gallons of petrol each, provisions for four men for ten days, one .303 rifle, one .22 repeating rifle and one double barrelled shot gun. Small wonder with that arsenal poking out of the Jeep that word spread through Mogaung that we were the vanguard of the British army fleeing ahead of the Japs.

The first 25 miles were easy going along a regular road to Kamaing, the last outpost of British officialdom. We went along to the Assistant Superintendent's office but he was away on tour. There was a huge black-bearded figure in one of the rooms and when he saw us he let out a cheerful roar and invited us in. His name was Castens, and he was a forestry officer, on leave. As soon as he heard where we intended to go, he fished out maps—and several bottles of beer—and fingered over what he reckoned would be our route.

"You'll make it," he assured us. "You'll get right through to India. I've been trying for years to get someone to look at this route, and now to think I've run into a party that's actually trying to get through in Jeeps. Ho. Ho. Ho. Have a drink!"

Castens must be six and a half feet if he's an inch, and is huge in every dimension. His curling black beard suits him perfectly; one felt he ought to wear red shirts to complete the picture. When he laughed it started as a low volcanic rumble in the bottom of his stomach gradually working its way out and up gaining in intensity as it passed through his gigantic frame till it emerged as a mighty roar. He knew Burma's byways and paths thoroughly and offered himself to the army. He was, of course, turned down. I say "of course" because they turned down so many valuable men like him that one came to take it for granted. He was taken into the army *after* Burma was lost, and did valuable scout work along the frontiers before the first real counter-attacks against Burma started. We helped him along with some of his beer and got ready to leave. North pleaded: "Don't you chaps think we'd better wait till the A. S. (Assistant Superintendent) gets back? He'll be able to tell us lots about the track."

"Hell, no," said Calbert, "we'll go as fast as we can. We'll find the bad patches soon enough without being told about 'em first."

The track from Kamaing onward had only once previously been travelled by a motor vehicle, but it was hard and dry, and our Jeeps made good pace, with one wheel in a bullock-carts' ruts, the other on the top edge of the second wheel rut. The country here was fairly wild and hilly, timbered in the hills with lots of reed swamp on the level. Towards evening we approached a collection of thatch houses, which North recognised as the village of Shaduzup. We decided to camp for the night in a noble-looking hut, specially built—so North informed us—for touring government officials. It was at Shaduzup that we first appreciated the power of government. There was no need for us to rouse out the villagers. The noise and appearance of our Jeeps soon attracted the whole of the local population. North picked out the village headman, had an earnest ten minutes discussion and soon the whole village was at our disposal. Some commended to unload our gear and carry it into the hut. Others went searching for eggs. Small boys appeared carrying long bamboo tubes filled with washing and drinking water. They stood the tubes against the side of the hut and with their varying heights and thicknesses and their shaped ends for pouring, they looked like the facade of a pipe organ. Others brought firewood and started fires. We'd looked forward to doing these sort of things ourselves, but understood that it would give the natives wrong ideas; if we set a wrong example, the next government official that came along might have to draw his own water and light his own fire, so we sat down and looked tired and bored and felt like "Bearers of the White Man's Burden."

While all this activity was in progress, North—with maps and charts spread over the floor—was engaged in long and serious conversations with the headman. The Kachins here—in fact all along the Hukwang Valley—were much superior to those I'd seen around Lashio. They were much cleaner, and in better condition.

The women mostly wore long amber cylinders, shoved in the lobe of the ear. Those that stood round watching their husbands and sons attending to the comforts of the white sahibs nearly all had babies industriously sucking at their breasts. We greatly admired North's fluency of tongue and obvious understanding of the Kachins. What he found to talk about we never could understand, but the result always pleased him and the tribespeople immensely. At each stop he held these interminable discussions, sometimes till far on into the night. At the end he'd usually turn to us and say:

"That's grand. The headman says we probably won't have any difficulties making the next village tomorrow."

After dinner that first night we noticed some of the men had reed flutes, so asked North if they would play for us. One old man stepped forward and after some mild chaffing from his fellow villagers, he squatted down cross-legged and entertained us. He blew a few plaintive notes on the flute and then sang in a quavering voice, played on the flute again and sang. This went on for a long time, the old man alternatively playing and singing and then ended abruptly, with no apparent reason. North explained that the songs were ballads and the bard improvised as he sang. This particular bard—evidently wanting a handsome tip—extolled the benefits that British government had brought to his Valley. As a matter of fact these Hukwang Valley dwellers had reason to praise the government. Many of them had been slaves of the Nagas, the headhunting hill—dwellers at the top of the Valley. Until twenty or thirty years ago, the British government sent regular expeditions up the Valley to suppress the slave traffic and release the slaves, many of whom were settled along the Hukwang.

In the morning, the old headman came along, very excited to tell us that a tiger came quite close to our camp during the night. We were so tired we'd heard nothing. The next and last big village along the Valley was Maingkwan, another fifty odd miles from Shaduzup. We had no difficulties in cruising along at about twenty-five miles an hour till we reached Maingkwan just before midday. North was deeply shocked when we wanted to push on till dark.

"But chaps, Maingkwan is the base. It's the last stop. We'll have to make all our preparations from here. I'll have to talk with the villagers and find out what the track's like; whether we can get help along the road; which is the best track......"

We relented to the extent of allowing him to have a chat with the headman. After an hour's palaver, during which lunch was prepared, he came to us with a long face.

"Well, I've had a good talk with him. He knows the route alright and says we can get to the next stage—12 miles away—in a Jeep, but it'll take four days."

We laughed and said we'd just carry on and go as far as we could. If it meant wasting four days' time to go further, we'd turn round and go back. North decided to have another talk with the headman, and after half an hour, during which time we reloaded the Jeeps, he came back with his face wreathed in smiles.

"Now that's grand. I've explained to him what marvellous cars these Jeeps are, and he says we might get through in two days."

"Okay," said Johnny Sharberg. "Hop in. We gotta get goin'". And protesting at our slap-dash methods, North jumped in. The headman decided he'd come too, so he hopped on top of the baggage of one of the Jeeps. Maingkwan was the ultimate limit to which any wheeled vehicle had reached. Bullock waggons and just one truck—containing District Commissioner Willkie—had penetrated as far as Maingkwan, but no further. The trail narrowed down to a path along which humans, elephants and occasionally mules had passed.

The first few miles were not bad going; the track was not bad, but after we passed a turn off to the amber mines, we ran into trouble almost immediately. Every few hundred yards there were small streams across the track, and although they were bridged, the bridges were too light and too narrow to take a Jeep. We set to work with axes and hoes, and North and the headman rounded up some Kachins to help us. They came along with razor-sharp dahs, carried in a wooden sheath, which was attached to a cane girdle—slung bandolier-fashion over one shoulder and under the other arm. They wore turbans, a sort of scarf wrapped round the head and usually with the fringe dropping down to their shoulders. Most of them carried opium pipes. They laughed at my efforts with an axe. They'd never seen an axe before, and after examining it with wonder made signs that we should have a log-cutting competition—axe versus dah. They picked a six-inch log, and I'd have sworn that their champion dah-man wouldn't have a chance with his light dah, against a sharp axe; but he hacked through and beat me by seconds, to the great delight of his compatriots. Later I had my revenge, when we came to a place where logs had to be split into planks wide enough to carry Jeep tyres. It was beautiful splitting timber, and with one blow of the axe I could lay a nine-inch log into two halves as like one another as two sides of a pea-pod. I wasn't reared among Australia's tall timber for nothing, and our party gained great prestige from that log-splitting. We were in a hurry and because we all worked like Trojans —especially North—with axes and picks, the Kachins worked well. It was like a marvellous picnic for them. They dashed off into the jungle, and returned dragging great poles. They slit bamboos and stripped off the outer skin to make strings for tying poles together; cut forks to support them; split one side of a thick bamboo and put slits in all the way round so that it spread out flat; and laying this across the poles, threw dirt on top. They were very quick in catching on to what we wanted. As soon as one bridge was finished, they'd help us across, pushing if necessary and as many as could would pile on to the Jeeps, the rest scamper on ahead shouting and yelling, till they came to another difficult place. We had two knee boots filled with silver rupees brought specially for the purpose, but I'm sure the excitement of watching the Jeeps, and the fact that we all joined in the work, prompted their enthusiasm more effectively than the promise of cash rewards. They divided themselves into teams. After the first bridge or two we picked out half a dozen who seemed the best and most intelligent workers, and they always travelled on the Jeeps. One team had measured the width of the Jeep wheels with a stick and these pranced on, and wherever a tree or log lay across the track, they hacked a path through it just the width of the Jeep. Another concentrated on bridges, a third on cuttings. By the first evening out of Maingkwan we'd covered the stage which the headman assured us would take four days— "perhaps two in a Jeep." He was greatly astounded at the powers of the Jeeps.

The Jeeps created an enormous sensation in the valleys. As we got away from Maingkwan we met tribesmen who'd never even seen a wheeled vehicle of any description. Not a bullock cart nor wheel-barrow.

This first night, out of Maingkwan, the villagers kept a respectful distance from the Jeeps, until some of those who'd been helping us, and thus felt superior, came over and touched it and leaned against it. Then they came closer. I got my pencil and asked North to translate some of the remarks he heard. Johnny Sharberg started up the engine of one. There was a terror-stricken stampede. They kept at a distance, men in front, naked children with fingers in their mouths hanging close to their mothers' skirts in the rear. Johnny drove slowly around, bringing the Jeep to a standstill near the hut again, but left the engine running. There was a diversion while the village headman arrived—a superior-looking fellow with an aristocratic-drooping Mongol moustache—with his two wives and daughter. He made a wide detour of the cars, and went to a door on the opposite side of the Jeeps, and offered North a chicken and some eggs. North led him round to the Jeep, while his two wives and the daughters joined the other villagers—still keeping their distance. North sat on the bonnet and after feeling it carefully, the headman—demonstrating his superior attributes as chief—sat alongside him, holding tightly on to the windscreen. The rest of the villagers gradually came over, and walked round, examining everything with their eyes, but not yet daring to touch. The engine was still running quietly, and North passed on some of the comments.

"It's tired. Hear how heavily it breathes."

Johnny Sharberg shifted North and the headman off the bonnet, lifted it up, and unscrewing the radiator cap, filled up with water.

"See how thirsty it is! It drinks more than a buffalo!"

One had walked to the far side of the Jeep and felt

the hot air from the exhaust, and excitedly called the others.

"It's sick. Feel how hot is its breath." Others weren't so certain.

"It must have run a long way to be so hot."

Some had wandered over to the other Jeep and were timidly touching it.

"Ayeee. It has no more life. It doesn't breathe. It's cold."

Then someone touched the horn and there were yells of terror and everyone rushed away. The headman, only made an involuntary short dash, and came back with a sheepish grin. He decided it was time to dispel all these silly ideas of the common villagers, and he made a thorough examination of the monster. When he had finished he announced with great deliberation:

"It's a steam boat. My father has told me of such things."

Everybody was satisfied then, because the headman's father in his youth had travelled to the ends of the world —even as far as Mandalay, some said. North invited him to get in and have a ride, but he decided to try it out on his wives and daughter first. He called them over, one fairly shrivelled old lady, the others young, round-faced and very attractive. They were in mortal fear at first, but eventually were shoved in by willing hands. They clung grimly to the sides of the seat. There was another scatter as the engine revived up, but shouts of admiration as it slowly moved off and gathered speed, circling round and round in the open field. At one point the Jeep leaped forward at an alarming pace. The younger wife, feeling herself insecure, had fastened on to one of the knobs and pulled the hand throttle wide open. Johnny had to switch off the engine and gently release the trembling hand. They all looked very fearful until the Jeep stopped, and then were very blasé and cheerful.

The headman had a ride then, and after that, fear of the Jeeps was largely banished. There was some excitement, however, when the lights were switched on.

"See how angry it is. Look how its eyes glare. They're fiercer than tigers' eyes."

Although they paid polite attention to the headman's pronouncement that it was a "steamboat," they were all convinced that it was some new and wonderful animal that the white man had discovered and tamed. They were out early next morning to watch us pour "medicine" into the gasoline tank of the second Jeep, and marvelled to watch both animals "wake up from their sleep" after we'd "pressed them in the stomach" several times. They observed that the strange creatures "groaned" for a while before they were properly awake.

My Leica camera was a source of great fear at first and I found it almost impossible to get any pictures. I had the other boys doing all sorts of antics while I pointed the camera at them and pretended to snap the shutter. I pointed it at myself and after a while North persuaded the headman to stand with him while I took their pictures. Then things got easier. The best pictures, of course, were made while North and the other two distracted the villagers' attention and I took some unobserved and natural shots. They'd seen white man's firearms before and thought the Leica—especially when I had on the long lelefot lens—was another variation of a pistol.

After that first village we had no difficulty in getting labour. We usually had upwards of fifty men with us. One of our biggest obstacles on the third day was a stretch of swamp about a hundred yards long. The mud seemed bottomless and even the multi-purpose

Jeep can't swim through mud. The Kachins worked like Trojans, cutting long Y-shaped forks and driving them deep into the mud, placing six inch diameter tree trunks along between the forks. The trunks were laid in very carefully, because they had to be exactly wide enough apart to take the Jeep wheels. In some places several smaller logs were bound together with bamboo "hide." It was a test for steady nerves and good driving to take a Jeep over those smooth round logs for a hundred yards, with a four feet drop each side and in between into a soupy morass.. Sharberg and Calvert were both splendid drivers, but sometimes a slight spreading of the logs, or a curve in a tree trunk would throw the tracking out of gear and we would be in trouble. It was in such cases we appreciated the qualities of the Jeep. With back and front wheels both engaged in the lowest gear, you could move back or forth by fractions of an inch on the steepest of grades. It took us four hours to negotiate that swamp and that was the longest delay we had over any operation. Every two or three hours, the Kachins used to stop what they were doing, drop their dahs and hoes if working, halt if marching, squat in the shade and have a pull at their opium pipes. I hardly ever saw them eating, but every man and woman seemed to smoke opium. There was very little rice cultivation, the land was poor and in many parts swampy, but apparently suitable for growing the opium poppy. The brown, sticky preparation more precious to the Kachins than food, was the commonest form of currency along the Hukwang Valley. During daytime I never saw any of them sleeping after their pipes. They just resumed work as we would after a meal or a cigarette.

We expected to strike our biggest snag in crossing the wide Tarung and Tanai Rivers, which join further

South to form the Chindwin River. To reach the Tanai we had to cross some opium fields, where the poppies were in full bloom.

There were lots of Kachins—mainly women—living in make-shift huts on the field and North explained that during cultivation and harvest time the natives leave their villages and camp at their work. The light green of the poppy stems and leaves; the purple flowers; the bronzed bodies of the Kachins; the blue of the river in the background made me sigh for a few feet of colour film. After a little negotiation, most of the poppy-harvesters came along with us to the river's edge, to assist in the crossing. The Tanai is about a hundred and fifty yards wide at this spot, and we were relieved to see a large bamboo raft on the opposite bank. Lusty shouts produced a wizened old chap, who yelled and waved back and disappeared. Soon he and several others came back and jumped on to the raft, paddling it across. We estimated, after inspection, that with a little reinforcing, it would carry a Jeep. It was made of two tiers of bamboo poles lashed crossways and covered with bamboo matting. We had several wooden poles cut, about the same diameter as the bamboos, and pushed under the matting alongside the top layer of the bamboo poles, so that they would take the direct weight off the wheels. We had to measure the raft and adjust the poles so that the weight of the Jeeps would be centred. Driving the cars on was something of a problem, because at the first touch of the wheels, the raft naturally pushed away, out into the stream. We drove stakes into the bank, and with our rope round one end, and a pleated bamboo rope tied round the other end of the raft, we "anchored" it back on to the stakes, and pressed close to the bank. Half a dozen Kachins waded into the river and with sharpened stakes thrust into the river bed, levered against the far side, and with much bending and crackling of matting and bamboo poles we got the first Jeep on board. The raft sagged sadly in the middle till it was under water. We had to balance the rowers carefully, because a pound or two weight on the wrong side would have tipped the thing up. Sharberg and I made the first crossing and we watched anxiously as the middle sagged deeper and deeper under water. Two rowers jumped off and swam alongside and that eased things a little, but we were relieved when we touched shore. We sent a note back to North that the middle should be further strengthened, and sent the contraption back with two rowers, while we started putting a cutting into the river bank. It was clayey cliff about fifteen feet high.

We hacked and hewed, while Calvert and North brought the other Jeep across. The raft was sent across once more, to bring our workers over. The wizened old man who was in charge of the raft, was one of the most villainous-looking individuals I've ever seen. He'd a chin and nose that almost met, no teeth, and chewed gum when he wasn't talking. He had a vile temper and cursed and shouted till he frothed at the mouth; but he was splendid engineer. We got on fine together. I called him "Grandpa" and we seemed mutually to agree and disagree on all important points. We had a lot of excavation to do, and he scorned to use a hoe, but sharpened a big stake with which he alternatively levered off huge chunks of the bank, and prodded or belaboured some malingering workman. It was at his suggestion that we made a bamboo fence—a retaining wall—to prevent the edges of the cutting crumbling away under pressure from the Jeeps. "Grandpa" rounded up all the able-bodied souls from his village, and we must have had nearly a hundred people frantically digging, carting rocks, chopping trees and pleating bamboo poles for our fence. It took something less than two hours to put that cutting in, and we were very proud of it when we'd finished. That was our finest piece of work for the whole trip, levelled, graded, banked at the turn on to the level bank, and paved with flat beach pebbles.

"I dunno about *finding* a road to India," commented Sharberg. "Seems to me we're building one."

When everything was ready, we tied the rope to the front of the Jeep and everyone lent a hand. We didn't want to use the engine because wheels roll lighter when they're pulled than when they're driven. We wanted our track to be in good order for the return journey. There was much merriment when the rope broke and everybody including North and myself tumbled into a heap. At the next try, the Jeep sailed up without difficulty. It quickly pulled up its twin brother.

With our best efforts we couldn't manage more than about twenty miles a day, and at that were pretty exhausted by the time we arrived at Shinbwiyang, at the very tip of the Hukwang Valley, and the foot of the Naga Hills. We were disappointed with Shinbwiyang. It had been a name to us for so long. We'd seen it marked on the maps and expected a decent-sized village. North explained it was only on the map because it was the last recognised point in that part of Burma. Beyond lay the Naga Hills, unadministered territory, however, of reputedly savage headhunters. Shinbwiyang consisted of four huts—as well as one for the convenience of the visiting Frontier Service Officer. It was late in the evening when we arrived. The Naga Hills were practically blotted out under heavy black clouds. By 4 p.m. it was almost pitch dark in the jungle. We had to use our headlights. Everything was perfectly still with a flat stillness which made the normal quiet of the leaf-carpeted jungle raucous by comparison. We bogged the first Jeep in a stream a mile distant from Shinbwiyang, and it took us over an hour to get it out and up the mushy, sandy riverbank on to hard ground from where it could tow the second one through. Rumbling thunder and lightning flashes became more frequent and nearer, and rain drops, heavy as treacle, began to fall. By the time we got to the village we were driving through a solid sheet of rain. It stopped as suddenly as it had started—giving us time to have dinner outside—but the air hung heavy and thick, and lowering blue black cloud masses closed in on us.

It must have been nearly midnight when I woke to feel a faint icy breeze and heard a rushing roaring sound in the distance. The others were awake soon after, and we huddled together, sitting on the floor with our backs against the wall. The roar quickly grew in intensity, until it filled the whole atmosphere with the most frightening sound one can imagine. One could have fired off a shot gun in the hut, and not heard the report. We were shouting at each other, but could only see lips moving. There was an earth-shaking, ear-splitting explosion and a zig-zag of lightning hovered winking from the sky to the ground, seemingly just in front of us, then flamed into blinding brilliance which lit up the whole landscape. In a brief glimpse we could see tree-tops bent flat and great ragged balls of clouds racing past them. The hut was not shaking, but seemed to be leaning forward, held there by gigantic pressure. Then it swayed back gently and the great wind had passed us by. I wondered if my face showed such a ghastly green as the others in the forked lightning flashes. The rain banged down steadily after the wind passed. We could hear the roaring gradually fade away as the hurricane moved on up the valley, until the sound of its breath was drowned in the beating rain. We didn't sleep much that night and were glad when morning came. Some of the village outbuildings had lost walls and roofs but otherwise little harm was done in Shingbwiyang.

We reckoned we must have just caught the tail-end of the hurricane. Nearly two months later, George Rodger, "Life" photographer and I trekked out of Burma to India over Naga Hills. About thirty miles further West than Shinbwiyang, we came to a patch of jungle that looked as if it had been trampled down by a herd of mammoths. Trees, up to six feet in diameter, had been broken off only a few feet from the ground. Forest giants had their tops twisted off, great limbs split off and smaller trees completely flattened. When we got to a nearby height, as far as we could see in both directions, there was a half mile swathe of flattened jungle, and snapped-off trees. The leaves on some of the broken branches were still green, but limp, so I reckoned that the "destruction belt" that we could see must have been the core of the path of the hurricane which just missed us earlier at Shinbwiyang.

We stayed a whole day at Shinbwiyang, drying our clothes and overhauling the Jeeps. With Shingbwiyang Du Hkawng, the fine old Naga chief of the village, we made a tentative drive along the track leading out towards the Naga Hills in the later afternoon. After all the rain we weren't feeling very enthusiastic. The Jeeps were slipping and sliding all over the place, and when we stopped at the first stream and got out, we were covered with leeches within a few minutes. We left the Jeeps and went on by foot for a mile or two, with brown leeches from the leaves underneath our feet, crawling up our legs, and green leeches dropping on to arms and necks from the shrubs we brushed in passing. According to the map we'd come 160 miles from Mogaung, more than half of it over a road we'd had to make as we went along. There was still sixty miles to be covered between Shingbwiyang and the Indian railhead at Ledo. Sixty miles if one measured in a straight line, but there were six thousand feet high mountains to be negotiated. The trail was covered with undergrowth and the chief said there were no villages for labourers.

We decided to return with a report on what we'd seen to date. After the storm of the previous night, we were worried about the state the track would be in, whether our bridges were still standing. It had taken us four days from Mogaung to Shingbwiyang and we hoped to get back in less. We checked over our provisions and reckoned we had plenty, so had an immense dinner that night and turned in early, ready for a good homeward start next day.

There's little of interest to write about the return journey. The track was sticky for the first few miles but after that dry as a bone. The brown leaves which carpeted the paths stood on end and danced behind us as we sped along. Once a herd of elephants, trunks waving wildly, swayed across our path and crashed away into the jungle. A Himalayan black bear was the only other "wild" animal we saw. There were plenty of jungle fowl—slightly larger than bantams and with the same colouring—but we were not successful in shooting them. Our bridges were all in good order and at the Tanai River crossing old "Grandpa" had been at work. He'd vastly improved the cutting and so strengthened the raft that we took both Jeeps across at once. We reached Mogaung in two and a half days. Before we left Shaduzup on the last stage North invited us to stay with him a night or two at Mogaung.

"What time's the train leave for Myitkyina?" asked Calvert.

"Around two in the afternoon," North replied.

"Well, I guess we'll get to Mogaung around midday an' better shove straight on."

"But even if we make Mogaung by midday—and I doubt it," said North, "you won't have time to load your Jeeps. Haven't got a chance"

"Sure. We'll gettem on, you see if we don't."

"That's impossible chaps. It simply can't be done. They won't have trucks for your Jeeps for one thing, and even if they did they couldn't shove them on at such short notice." And North shook his head mournfully.

We arrived in Mogaung and drove the Jeeps almost into the stationmaster's office. A sleepy, but startled looking stationmaster swung round as four bewhiskered, begrimed and bepistolled wayfarers strode in.

"We've gotta put these Jeeps on the afternoon train to Myitkyina. We'll be back in half an hour to load them. Okay?"

The stationmaster pulled his specs down from his forehead and fingered his beard, murmuring something about "no trucks," "insufficient time," and "trains can't be delayed."

"These cars have got to go on 'poppa.' You have a man ready to help us in half an hour. All right?"

"All right. Better give me an hour though, and I'll get a truck shunted up."

"Well, you did it," North said as we left, "but you know, you have no authority to order the people about like that."

"I tell you what, North," Sharberg said. "We all admire very much the way you got on with the Kachins. Don't know what we'd have done without you. We appreciate, too, the way you slogged in when there was hard work about; but a man gets nowhere if he starts off by figuring everything's impossible. You gotta make things possible. Think that old "geeser" would've done anything for us if we hadn't bullied him a bit ?' There's only one test of what's right what's not right. Theat's which works best. And the only way to find out which works best is to take a crack at it. We could've frigged about for months talking to people about what this Hukawng track's like, and not been much wiser. In seven days we've been and found what there is to it. We've driven a Jeep to the foot of the Naga Hills. That's a solid fact that couldn't a been established in years of argument."

That evening we were in Myitkyina. We'd made careful notes all along the route, type of soil, where rock and timber was available, width of streams, state of bridges on existing road, where labour available, where road would be under in wet season, etc. We drew up a report the evening we arrived, pointing out that the Hukwang Valley was largely under water in the rainy season, but in dry weather a Jeep road could be put through as far as we had gone, in a few weeks. We'd left North at Mogaung with his wife and Willkie the D. C. told us that if the road was built North would probably be sent to Shingbwiyang to arrange labour and build godowns for rice supplies for the Chinese coolies. We gave a good account of North's excellent relations with the Kachins.

CHAPTER XII

I left by train for Mandalay, the morning after arriving at Myitkyina, on March 3rd. The news was not so good. Orders had been given to the civilian population on February 20th, to evacuate Rangoon by noon the 21st. No one seemed to know where GHQ was situated. People in Myitkyina and on the train had all sorts of wild stories of reinforcements arriving; new squadrons of planes in action; that Rangoon was evacuated because the military wished to defend it street by street; the Burmans were rising against us; etc. etc. My immediate concern was to find Public Relations and get my Road Story censored and despatched.

Mandalay, to most Burmans, the capital of Burma; the former seat of their Kings and the home of most of Burma's phoongyis, is a city without a hotel. An Anglo-Indian with whom I shared a compartment on the train, offered to take me to his sister's home, where we could both get a bed for the night. Many other people had apparently thought of the same idea, for the house was packed with relatives, bedrolls spread over every inch of floor space. Everybody shouting at the top of their voices, their experiences of leaving Rangoon. How they'd had to leave this and that behind. Everybody blamed the government for not having given them proper warning, though anybody that followed the army communiques with a map should have seen the writing on the wall for Rangoon. The Anglo-Indian and I hired a tonga and made a tour of the places in which one can normally stay in Burma—

the Circuit House, Dak Bungalow, PWD House—but these were all overcrammed with evacuees. Tired and hungry, we ate in the "V" tea-rooms—just established by an evacuee, and after the inevitable chicken dinner, we pleaded with the proprietor to let us sleep there. Eventually he took us upstairs and allowed us to unfold our bedrolls on the concrete floor of a verandah. Next morning I learned that Army Headquarters had been established at Maymyo, so I reckoned Public Relations would also be there. At lunch-time—eating again in the V-restaurant— I received a great whack on the back and—there was my old friend David Maurice. As a practising Buddhist he didn't drink, so we just pumped each other's hands for a while.

"My God," he said, doffing his topee and wiping the sweat from his forehead, "when this war's over I'm going to sit down and write a book. I'll call it 'I also Ran!' Jesu! did they run? And the 'burrah sahibs' led the race."

While he plodded away at a salad and lime juice, I asked him what the devil he was talking about. Then he told me something of the evacuation of Rangoon. Of officials dropping their work and clambering over each other to get away; of one of his colleagues who tried to take all his furniture with him, including a billiard table. Others who buried their valuables, hoping to come back soon and dig them up. Nurses and doctors ordered to leave their patients and "scram." He happened to be passing the lunatic asylum when the inmates were being set free, with warders beating them with sticks to make them hurry and get away.

"I wake up at nights and see the faces of those poor bastards. Vacant; crazed faces. Terror printed on idiocy, cowering under blows of warders, chasing them out into a world they'd been cut off from for years.

Not knowing where to go, what to do, impelled forward with a sudden, terrible urgency of action. Then the lepers and the criminals out. I met three Burmese brothers let out of gaol. They asked me for a lift in my launch. Bits of kids they were. Howling they wanted to go back to their mother. Some of the poor fools started looting straight away. Everybody had left their shops and houses. The police and military had great fun shooting them at the rate of twenty a day. Much better to let the Japanese have the stuff, no doubt," he said bitterly, "than have it looted by our own people. Fires were going everywhere. Some started by bombings, others by our own demolition gangs, some by fifth columnists and plenty more by the idiots. It was a grand "free for all." One idiot seemed to be enjoying himself best of all. With a maniacal grin on his face he stood on Pagod Intersection (one of Rangoon's busiest cross-streets) directing military traffic. No one stopped him. The convicts had done a wonderful job unloading stuff at the wharves. When the coolies fled after the first two raids, convicts were used as wharf labourers. They were well disciplined, and never used their position to try and escape. Several times during raids, their supervisors left them, but the convicts always turned up again and carried on with their work, entirely off their own bat.

"The whole thing was terrible mess. Fielding-Hall, the Welfare department officer took the blame for prematurely releasing the lunatics and convicts. He committed suicide afterwards."

"What happened to the coolies and people without cars? The trains couldn't get them all away in two days?"

"They left them to walk. After all 'ole bhoy' its only four hundred and thirty-two miles to Mandalay, and another thousand miles or so to India, dammit. Haw-Haw. Do the beggahs good, donchemo?"

"What's all the 'haw-haw' accent about?" I asked.

"Because I'm fed up to the teeth with the whole bloody thing. I got my coolies to work with me till the last hour. They risked their necks time and again down at the explosive dump. They carried that stuff off the wharves because I stayed with them. They stayed on because they thought I would see them through. Now I've been ordered to get out, and they have to walk. Who's going to feed them? If the others get to Mandalay, what then? We've let them all down, and we expect them to find their own way back to India, and no doubt tell their relatives over there how generous and benevolent is British Government. Like bluddy hell they will! They were taught to jeer at those who ran away at the first bombings. Now who's going to do the jeering? They believed in us and we've let them down so completely that they'll never believe in us again. And if they do, they'd be crazy!"

"There's only one thing I'm personally pleased about in all this. A couple of weeks before the evacuation order, Indians in the bazaar were asking me whether they should start clearing out of Rangoon. I told them no, that they'd be evacuated in plenty of time by the Government. Afterwards I told this to the Assistant Food Controller, adding: 'of course, you *are* making plans to evacuate them, aren't you?' To my amazement he said: 'Of course, we're not. They have to take a chance. We can't do anything for them'. I said, 'Do you mean to say, after pleading with these people to stay behind and help keep things going, after abusing all those that have fled, you're not going to help those that have stayed? Well, if you're not, I promise you there'll be very few left in the bazaar tomorrow, because I'm going right back to tell them now.' And I did. I went straight back to the bazaar and told my friends that I'd made a mistake in advising them to stay. The time to go was now, because no one was going to help them when the time came for general evacuation. And so they went. Thousands of them started out and were well on their way before the final panic set in."

"What's happening down there now?"

"They're getting ready to blow the place up. My last days were spent in delivering explosives for the demolition experts. I wanted to stay and watch the show go up, but was ordered out a few days after the civilian evacuation. I lent my launch to a bunch of Indians who used it to evacuate themselves and their families to Mandalay. I drove out along the Prome Road with some Burmese friends."

"Is there much stuff still left round the wharves?"

"Of course, there is. Hundreds of tons of it. They're destroying it as fast as they can. All unnecessary. You know, there was an Australian, Ross Neil, who volunteered to form a labour battalion to work on the wharves and get the stuff away. They didn't accept his offer. He wrote to the paper about it several times, and the Rangoon Gazette, backed him up, but nothing was ever done about it. As a result tons and tons of valuable supplies are going up in smoke now."

Maurice had been given three months leave on full pay by ICI. but was looking for something to do. He'd again applied to the Oriental Mission but there was still nothing doing. He supposed he'd stay in Mandalay for a while. Maurice lent me his car to drive on up to Maymyo. I left that afternoon and discovered Public Relations just in time to hear that Rangoon was being evacuated by the military. Demolition work was in full swing and the Syrium oil refineries were due to go up that night. I shared a room that night with Maurice Ford, newsreel cameraman for "Paramount News". For the first time in nearly three weeks I slept in a bed, or rather, I lay in a bed. I didn't sleep because my body had to get used to softness again. W. O. Gallagher and Leland Stowe rolled up next morning. Leland Stowe, whom I'd last seen in Chungking, was clearing out of Burma and going to Moscow and Gallagher told me he was leaving next day for India, so I'd have the whole Burma show to myself in future. That suited me. After telephoning Ausland in Lashio and confirming that they were going to build the road, and a railway as well, I despatched my Burma-India Road story. Chinese coolies a hundred thousand or so, were already being marched over from the YBR project now temporarily abandoned. My Burma-India Road story got to London at the same time as the news that Rangoon was evacuated by our forces and the Burma Road definitely closed. The "Express" got a decent scoop, which partly compensated them for the long delay in getting a story from me.

I thought I was exhausted when I reached Maymo, but hearing there was a possibility of a "show" on the Sittaung River, I left for the front the day after my arrival, with George Rodger of "Life and Time" magazine and Alec. Tozer, "Movietone News" newsreel man. They each had a Jeep. During the last days in Rangoon, when the American Technical Group—comprising of forty mechanics brought out as part of Major Wilson's scheme for introducing a little efficiency on the Burma Road—were working without eating and sleep, feverishly assembling Jeeps and trucks; and British demolition experts were feverishly and efficiently going round truck assembling yards, dynamiting and firing every Jeep and truck they could find, and just as efficiently American demolition experts were patrolling the roads blowing up and firing those trucks which had escaped from Rangoon. During those wild and woolly days anybody could take a Jeep and drive it away. One only had to sign a paper promising to deliver it within an unspecified time to the Chinese authorities at Lashio. I regretted having been one of the few correspondents who missed out on the Jeeps.

Also destroyed at that time was much Lease-Lend material that was later sorely needed by the Chinese armies in Burma. The first Japanese bombs on Rangoon and resultant flight of labour from the docks and railways was mainly responsible, although everything could have been cleared if the Chinese offer to despatch coolies and train crews had been accepted.

I travelled in George Rodger's car, the Public Relations Conducting Officer with Tozer. We had a chit entitling us to draw petrol, when we wanted it, and rations from Army stores at Mandalay. The SSO (Station Staff Officer) who exchanged our petrol chit for an order on the petrol supply station, had his office inside the Mandalay Palace grounds. He was away at lunch. We went back into Mandalay and bought some cooking utensils and had something to eat ourselves. Back to the SSO's office. He would be back in half an hour. We waited and got our chit exchanged and explicit instructions as to where we drew our petrol and rations. We went to the petrol dump—still inside the Palace Grounds, and found it had been shifted. We found the new station and joined a line of trucks and cars being filled by hand out of two gallon tins. The attendants had a tiny funnel with a half inch pipe, and unless a truck had its own funnel, about half the petrol splashed out on to the ground. We didn't feel like waiting till all the trucks were filled, so went up and grabbed three tins, and carried them down to the Jeeps. There was a row about that.

"A nice thing it'd be if everybody came along and 'elped theirselves wouldn't it be?" said an indignant sergeant.

"And a nice thing it'd be if the bloody army had to wait while you filled up its transport out of two gallon tins," said Tozer, a cheerful Londoner. "Here's our chit. You get on with your job. We'll look after this. Get it?"

We went to draw our rations from the office to which the SSO had sent us, and were directed to another depot. We went to the other depot and produced our chit. An NCO carefully wrote down particulars, and then looked up. "I'm sorry sir, but you've come to the wrong depot. This is really for bulk supplies."

"Well, we've been sent here by the SSO and want to get some rations quickly. We have to get away this afternoon."

"Tell you what I'll do, sir. I'll send my man over. He'll fix you up in no time. Four men for seven days, is it, sir? Won't be a jiffy."

After half an hour an orderly came back with a few biscuits and a couple of tins of cheese. A flurried argument and the NCO turned to us.

"I'm very sorry. They've made a mistake and sent rations for four men for one day. You wanted for seven days, now didn't you? I'm sending him right back. Won't be long."

We groaned and Rodger suggested going off with what we had, and try to buy a bit of extra food in Mandalay. But tinned food was getting scarce and we thought we'd better get what we could. We had to wait a long time and the NCO explained that it was very awkward for the quartermaster's staff, working out the correct proportions for four men for seven days.

"You see, it means breaking into pounds and working out percentages of tins and making out the correct proportion of substitutes for things we're out of. For instance, a man gets a tin of bully a day, but when we can only give him half a tin of bully that doesn't mean we can make it up with half a tin of cheese. Makes it awkward like, doesn't it?"

The orderly returned again, this time with slightly more than before and the NCO very red in the face had to tell us that he'd brought back rations for one man for seven days. Again he was sent back. Two and a half hours after we exchanged our chit at the SSO's office, we drove out of the palace gates, with petrol, a big bag of army biscuits and several tins of cheese "......in lieu of." Several items were listed on the chit we signed, tins of sausages, bully beef, tinned fruit, but these were crossed out and against each item was written" ......tins of cheese in lieu of tins of bully beef," etc., etc.

It was dark by the time we reached Meiktila 75 miles South of Mandalay, and we slept on the ground alongside our Jeeps. We wanted to leave early next morning, but had to wait till 9 a.m. for the SSO to come and give us a petrol chit. The front was still about 250 miles away and we were told to fill up our tanks and take as much as possible in tins, because nearer the front petrol was getting scarce. We had 5 two-gallon tins for each Jeep and we joined in another long line of trucks at the filling station. The station attendant had a tiny funnel, the type one uses for filling a kerosene lantern, and was trying to fill two-gallon tins from the petrol pump with petrol running all over the place. The funnel couldn't possibly cope with the flow from a two inch nozzle, and he kept switching the release on and off to try and reduce the quantity of petrol bubbling over the funnel top, while British Tommie truck drivers fumed and cursed at the delay. They were taking supplies down to the front. We had to wait our turn here, and it was late in the morning before we got away. The road from Mandalay to Rangoon is flat and straight. On both sides almost as far as one could see were level rice-fields for the most part covered with brown stubble. The only variations were small villages dotted here and there, and usually surrounded by groves of palmyras and other varieties of palms. In between centres such as Meiktila, Pyinmana and Toungoo, where we usually had to stop for petrol, the Jeeps hummed along at a steady fifty miles per hour, for hours on end.

At Toungoo—174 miles North of Rangoon—we went to H/Q of 1st Burma Division, where Gen. Bruce-Scott received us, and gave us the "low-down" on the situation. The Chinese 5th Army, part of whom we'd seen moving down past Mandalay, were taking over from us at Toungoo, and at Pyu, a village 30 miles further South. The 17th Div., commanded by Maj. Gen. Cowan, had been battered about since the beginning of the Burma offensive, and following the evacuation of Rangoon, was going to withdraw over to the Prome Road. The 1st Burma Div. had just put in a counter-attack the previous night to try and drive the Japs out of Daik-U, just south of Nyaunglebin (rail junction 101 miles north of Rangoon) and Shwegyin, (on the Sittaung river, 20 miles east of Myaunglebin.)

It was then March 12th. Scott had been out of touch with headquarters for nearly a week and was still carrying out a plan formulated weeks before. He said he wouldn't have attacked if he'd known the true position, but at least he'd given the Chinese a chance to consolidate their positions.

The attack against Shwegyin was successful, that against Daik-U not successful because the Japs had more men there than we expected. The General said we could go on down to Nyaunglebin to Brigade H/Q and across to Shwegyin. We drove on till dark and camped out in the open. We each took a two hour turn at sentry duty, not so much because we were near enemy occupied territory, but because of possible hostile Burmans. We'd heard of too many truck-drivers found in the early mornings with their throats cut, and truck tyres slashed, to take any chances. We drove the Jeeps well off the road and parked them under a wide spreading tree, their noses pointed to the road in case we wanted to make a quick get-away. Nobody came near us, though the sound of voices during my 2-4 a.m. shift made me reach for my revolver. I was about to waken the others, when I saw some Indian coolie refugees, filing across the fields towards the road evidently making an early start to fulfil their daily quota on the thousand mile trek to India. George Rodger had the 4-6 a.m. shift, and by the time we'd wakened he had brewed a fine pot of hot coffee, which helped us swallow our concrete biscuits and cheese.

On the way to Nyaunglebin we passed the burnt out remains of twenty-two Lease-Lend trucks, some of them the latest ten-wheeler type. They represented one of several fully-laden convoys, prematurely destroyed by enthusiastic American demolition experts.

At headquarters we were advised to hang around for a while as the new CIC Burma was due to arrive that morning. He came after lunch and scowled heavily at us when he saw we were War Correspondents. We were taken aback with his first remark, made with some bitterness, after we'd snapped a couple of pictures of him.

"Well, I suppose you're going to label them 'The Defender of Rangoon.'" I missed the point of that remark, until Rodger explained later that he'd been appointed to the command shortly before Rangoon fell, and at a Press Conference, some correspondents hopefully dubbed him the "Defender of Rangoon.'

It was General Harold Alexander and he had reason to feel bitter, I suppose, having been handed a situation impossible to retrieve. With Rangoon lost, and all possibilities of reinforcements—except Chinese—gone; with no replacements of equipment possible, he had to try and create a "legend" that Burma would be held, at the same time making plans to extricate his army in as good order as possible. A soldier can never make a reputation with retreats, no matter how successful they are. Alexander "of the tanks" had already done a great job in the "Miracle of Dunkirk," and was probably sore that he was supposed to perform another "miracle" in Burma. His day came later when his organising ability and aggressive spirit had full play in the Middle East, and in ten weeks pushed Rommel's dour Afrika Corps 1,400 miles across Egypt and Libya into Tunisia and drove the Italians out of the last corner of the Mediterranean Empire.

He looked tired that day at Nyaunglebin and his eyes were red-rimmed through lack of sleep. We asked him if the Shwegyin offensive was the beginning of a full scale counter-attack.

"We'll shove the Japs back wherever we can shove them back. That's all I can say." And with that we had to be content. He was in a hurry, and paused only long enough to let us get a picture of him, poring over a map with Major Gen. Bruce-Scott who'd accompanied him. We hoped to see him later in the evening, and left him to his conference with Brigade H/Q staff.

There were half a dozen Burmans including several phoongyis enclosed in barbed wire fenced pen. We took some pictures and asked what they'd been doing and what would happen to them.

"Any Burmans moving about near the front lines don't stand much of a chance if the troops see them. Some of these were just rounded up near the village. Others were caught with rifles at Shwegyin."

"What happens to Burmese prisoners who are known to have fought with the Japs ?" we asked the Brigadier later.

He smiled wryly. "We don't take many prisoners you know. We don't mind killing them in battle, but it's not so good killing in cold blood. We question these chaps. If there's nothing against them, we boot them in the backside and tell them to clear out of the district. If they've been fighting with the Japs they're sent back for civilian authorities to deal with."

We went on to the Sittaung River opposite Shwegyin, but it was too late to get any pictures. There was a bit of a village on the East bank of the river, to which our troops had advanced during the night preceding the attack. For several days beforehand, Burmese Intelligence officers, disguised in loongyis had been in Shwegyin itself and actually worked on Japanese fortifications. They brought back reports of the exact strength and disposition of the Japs. Our troops crossed the river before dawn and the boats had almost reached the shore before the Japs knew what was happening. The Sikhs went in with their bayonets, yelling their fearsome battle-cries, smashing in doorways and buildings with rifle butts, impaling Japs and Burmans and firing timber and thatch houses. Burmans firing from windows with .22 rifles and shot guns, soon fled. In three hours' fierce hand to hand fighting the village was cleared.

We came back next morning, and the battalion commander repeated the action for the benefit of the photographers. Houses and shops were still burning, and with a realistic background the Sikhs put on a terrific bayonet charge, that gave the photographers all the action they wanted. As we drove back through the village, I saw an immense bald-headed, ragged-feathered vulture, judicially perched on one leg and with the other turning over the blackened upper remains of a human corpse, red-rimmed where the lower half had been eaten away. It followed us with its beady eye as we rolled past, but didn't move from its meal.

As we drove back lorry loads of Chinese troops, their trucks festooned with green branches for camouflage, passed us heading for Toungoo.

Long lines of skinny, weary-looking Indian evacuees, averted their heads from the clouds of dust which was raised as we passed. The younger men, armed with knobbly sticks, and sometimes long, roughly-shaped steel-pointed spears, marched in front, their baskets on their heads. Women, usually with one, sometimes two babies on their hips and surrounded by several younger children marched in the centre, of the column, followed by older men and women and young men at the back. Usually there were stragglers, limping along behind no doubt hoping they'd catch up with the main band before nightfall. If they dropped too far back, they knew the dacoits—Burmese robbers—would kill them, for the little money and goods they carried. The groups were mainly small—30 to 50, and the younger men took turns in sentry duty at nights. We picked up those stragglers we could carry, but they always wanted to be dropped off when they'd caught up with their group. In some cases Burmese villagers took pity on them, giving them water and cocoanuts, perhaps a handful of rice. Usually they had to pay exorbitant prices for food—and even water. There was a long-standing animosity between Burmese and Indians.

For generations Indian money-lenders had been acquiring the Burmans' land and renting it out to them at high rental rates. The Indians, if not cleverer, at least were more industrious, and the easy-going Burman found himself displaced right and left by Indian craftsmen, Indian technicians, Indian clerks, and even Indian professional men. He couldn't even compete with Indian businessmen. He saw himself displaced, his country gradually dominated by Indians. Certainly the fault was his own and the remedy lay in his own hands; but it's always far too easy to blame one's woes on the "foreigner" than search for the cause in ourselves. So the Indians became hated, and *so* the Burmans took it out of the unfortunate coolies, who daily trudged along the roads past their villages. The coolies were doubly wronged. Firstly by the firms—often Indian firms—which brought them into the country and did not assume any responsibility for their evacuation; secondly because they became scape-goats for the sins of their money-lending and commercial compatriots. Coolies had never harmed or competed with the Burmans who would never demean themselves to perform such menial work as the coolies did.

During the weeks that followed, as we rushed up and down the road between Maymyo and the Front, we began greatly to admire the stout-heartedness and community spirit of these coolies. They plugged away, day after day, leaving hours before daybreak, resting during the heat of the day and continuing in the evening.

We reckoned after checking the progress of one particular group that they averaged about twenty miles daily, and allowing for loads they carried, the children, the sick and the aged, that's not bad with the temperature around the country for most of the day. Often emaciated forms were left under trees, dying of cholera; in the interest of the community group they had to be abandoned. Four hundred and thirty-two miles to Mandalay from Rangoon—and that was only the beginning. Every now and again they'd be caught in bombing raids and the family group again reduced. Many of the ricksha coolies had brought their rickshas and pulled in them their goods—and the aged and sick. Others had heavy handcarts requiring two men harnessed in front and two pushing behind. Bathed in sweat by day, shivering in their cotton loin cloths at night, they shoved these clumsy contraptions for hundreds of miles, until the group's manpower was so cut down, that they had to be abandoned.

Our greatest difficulty along the road lay in getting petrol. Not on account of the shortage, but because the technique of obtaining it was so complicated. At Pyinmana, returning from the Sittaung Front, we drove to the petrol pump: the attendant looked at our chit and said:

"You'll have to go to the station staff officer and get a voucher."

"Look here. There's our chit entitling us to draw eight gallons of petrol at Pyinmana. There's the authority. Give us the petrol and we'll sign for it."

"Sorry sir, I can't give you petrol without a voucher."

We went over to the Station Staff Officer. He was feeling very pleased with himself, having salvaged some of the last beer from Pyinmana. He naturally wasn't concerned with the fact that I wanted to rush back and send off a despatch. He looked at the chit, put it on the table with a book on top to stop it blowing away and asked about the front. How things were going? If we'd seen any abandoned Jeeps along the road, because he wanted a spare fan-belt.

"Say look here. We're in a bit of a hurry. What about that petrol?"

"Oh, sorry old boy. Look here, I can't do anything for you here, you know. You'll have to see the chap that runs the station he's in Pyinmana main street, where the Taxaco office is."

We drove around Pyinmana's much-bombed streets until we found a Texaco sign. An Anglo-Indian came out and looked at our chit.

"Oh. You've come to the wrong place. Sure, I run the petrol station, but you'll have to have a chit from the AS (Assistant Superintendent)."

"Where does he hang out?"

"I don't know. He should be at the Club by now. Maybe the SSO will know. No need to come back here when you get a chit. Go straight to the pump."

Back to the SSO. It was quite dark by this time. Our tempers were still holding. The AS wasn't there, but the SSO was coming over to the Club in a few minutes and he'd take us round to find the AS. The AS wasn't in the Club. No one knew where he was. We took the SSO in one of the Jeeps with Rodger and I, and went to the AS's house. No one at home. We were getting wild by this time.

"How do military trucks get on, obtaining supplies? Is this the only supply in Pyinmana?"

"Yes, but you must admit, old boy, it's a bit late to come looking for petrol at this time of day." (It was about 8-30 p.m.)

"I'm going to make a report about this when I get to headquarters. It's an appalling disgrace. My God, no wonder things in this country are the way they are. On the principal trunk road in Burma, within a hundred odd miles of the front, at half past eight in the evening we can't get a drop of petrol, because somebody that should give us a chit isn't to be found."

The SSO was indignant at this outburst.

"You fellows running about the country, expect us to be at your beck and call any hour of the day and night. It's not my fault the regulations are the way they are. What can I do about it?"

What indeed? It was true it wasn't his fault and we recognised it.

"You come down to the filling station and order the fellow to give us petrol. Surely you can do that."

"Alright I'll do what I can. If he refuses I can't force him, though".

We went back to the station and a sleepy guard told us the attendant had gone and taken the keys with him.

"Tell you what I'll do," said the SSO. "How much petrol do you want?"

"We want to drive all night, and get through to Maymyo. We've got some in tins, but our tanks are empty. If you fill them up, we'll be okay."

"Well, I'll give you some out of my private stock. I won't see you stuck."

CHAPTER XIII

I slept most of that day, and left for the front again—this time headed for Toungoo, which the Chinese had now taken over, establishing their front line at Pyu a largish village 30 miles further south. Toungoo itself was a big centre, one of our chief air bases in Burma and site of a large military hospital.

General Stillwell—the Generalissimo's Chief of Staff and Commander of Chinese Armies in Burma—had established headquarters in Maymyo, and an advanced headquarters of the Fifth Army at Pyawcwe twenty-three miles south of Meiktila. I had to get a chit from Capt. Eldridge, the American Public Relations Officer, to General Tu, commanding the "mechanised" Fifth Army. From General Tu, I received an impressive-looking document, covered with Chinese characters and large red Chinese seals, which with my photograph pinned in one corner was to serve as a pass.

I was a bit doubtful about the car I'd borrowed for the journey, and wondered whether it would stand the strain of almost non-stop driving for seven or eight hundred miles—which is what a trip to the front at that time entailed. There was much the same trouble as on the previous occasion in trying to find the correct people to issue petrol chits—and trying to get petrol once we had the chits. I had a Public Relation Conducting Officer with me and when we got to Toungoo we went first to British headquarters and found only a handful of officers left. They had already handed over to the Chinese and were only remaining to superintend removal of supplies. The PRCO being an old soldier was a born scrounger. He smelt that where a headquarters was evacuating, there must be whisky, and perhaps foodstuffs that night be left behind. He immediately got busy to see what he could collar. I was loth to waste time and we had a bit of a row.

"Well, we don't want to leave things like that here, for the bloody Chinks, do we?" he argued.

"You mean for the Japs?"

"No. The Chinks. They're taking over here aren't they?"

Toungoo had been badly smashed by Jap bombers and the Chinese seemed intent on completing its destruction. Homes were being blown up, the remains of the railway station demolished, even Buddhist temples flattened. Gardens, shrubs, trees were being cleared and burnt. The PRCO was very critical about all this,

"Blooming good cheek they've got, destroying our property like this. Mighty funny way to defend a place I must say. Start by tearing it to pieces."

He wasn't even satisfied at headquarters, when some of our officers assured him that the Chinese were doing a good job, digging themselves in, and clearing a line of fire.

"Dunno what the Empire's coming to, when we have to have Americans and Chinks to fight for us," was his comment..

Toungoo was the first place I'd seen in Burma where any preparations were made for defence. The only place where troops dug themselves in as if they meant to stay. In the few days that had elapsed since, we passed through Toungoo, there was a tremendous change. The Chinese had decently built machine gun nests, and make-shifts, but solid pill boxes. At every street corner and crossroads there were barricades and machine gun nests. A clean line of fire was cleared, and any buildings or shrubbery likely to afford cover for Japs, snipers and infiltrators were ruthlessly removed.

We picked up a Chinese soldier as we headed back to Chinese divisional headquarters. He was tremendously pleased at my few words of Chinese, and rattled away at a great rate, quite satisfied if I said "Hao" (Good) now and again, that I understood everything he said. We were just going through Toungoo's main street when we picked up a nail in the front tyre and had to change the wheel. While we were doing that we heard planes, and in a few minutes nine Jap bombers, came over, flying low. The PRCO and I jumped for the ditch. The Chinese soldier turned the corners of his mouth down, and waved his hand deprecatingly, pointing up at the planes and shaking his head as if they weren't worth worrying about. He stayed on the road and started jacking up the car. We yelled at him. He just pulled off his cloth cap, ran his hand across his stubbly, shaven head, looked up at the planes and spat contemptuously and expressively. I felt the most miserable coward, and clambered out to help him, reckoning I could land back in the ditch in one jump if I heard the swish of bombs. They didn't drop any that time.

We didn't know exactly where headquarters was and after we'd changed the wheel the Conducting Officer drove slowly along while I waved my pass and yelled out: "Su Ling Po" (headquarters) to every Chinese I saw. At one place a fierce-looking fellow waved at us to stop. The PRCO thought he must want a ride and went to pass on, and the soldier levelled a Tommy gun so smartly that the car pulled up with a jerk. I waved my pass. The sentry took no notice of that, but imperiously motioned the PRCO to get the car off the road, under the trees. The PRCO objected to being ordered about by a "Chink" and wasn't inclined to take much notice until the "Chink" jumped on the running board and shoved his Tommy gun into the PRCO's armpit. I took the wheel and shoved the car under the trees. Only when we shut off the engine, could we hear planes about again, and the crump crump, ...crump......of falling bombs a few seconds later. We were at the headquarters and the sentry rightly felt that the flashing windscreen of our car might attract the enemy's attention. After the car was parked to his satisfaction, he sent another soldier for an officer, who read the pass and escorted us to the Commander of the 200th division of the 5th Army.

General Thai en Lai reminded me of Jan Kiepura, the Polish screen star and singer. Clad in a light silk khaki shirt, and belted brown trousers with a sensitive and intelligent face, he looked more like an orchestral conductor than a soldier. He read my pass gravely, looked sharply at the photograph and across at me. Then his face lit up with a welcoming smile, and he took us over to a timber-reinforced trench, where he had his headquarters. He was busy on the phone for several minutes and we stayed in the trench till the planes went away. It was nearly six o'clock and the General was just about to eat. He invited us to eat with him. The PRCO looked at the food, smirked, and said, "We'd be eating later on up the road." I translated in slow, simple English to the interpreter that we'd both be delighted to dine with the General. General Thai and his interpreter both spoke a little English, and understood the simplest words spoken very slowly.

We'd just started to eat when a British officer arrived. He told the interpreter with great haste that in fifteen minutes the RAF were sending over six Blenheims to bomb Japanese positions in a village, just forward of the Chinese line at Pyu. He wanted the General to know, so that he could order his troops to attack as soon as the bombing was finished. The interpreter thanked him gravely and said something to the General, and by the latter's reaction we knew the interpreter hadn't understood a word of the message, except the words "planes and bombs." I tried again with the interpreter.

"6 o'clock eh ?" Switching the hands of my watch round to 6 o'clock with interpreter and general watching me intently.

"Our planes bomb Japanese."

"Ah, Ah, Ah, Japanese planes coming 6 o'clock? Very bad. Very bad,"

"Not Japanese planes. Our planes. British planes."

"Ah, ha, eh. British planes. Good. Good. Where British planes ?"

"British planes in ten minutes time, (holding up both hands), bomb Japanese near Pyu."

Their brows were deeply furrowed, and they still couldn't understand what we meant. In desperation I pulled out my map and marked Jap. positions and Chinese positions at Pyu, and we staged an elaborate pantomime of bombs from British planes dropping on Jap positions.

"Seven minutes time." I again pointing to 6 o'clock on the watch, and holding up seven fingers.

This time he understood. We didn't have to make the suggestion that he might like to attack the Jap positions. He jumped for the telephone and with his eyes on his wrist watch, shouted orders into the mouthpiece. Punctually at 6.00 p.m. we heard bombs dropping, and shortly after that the whooom...whooom...whooom of trench mortars, and the heavy rattle of machine guns, so we gathered the attack had gone in. I was beginning to despair of having any sort of a talk with General Thai, when a British liaison officer came along.

He was one of several Chinese-speaking Englishmen commissioned for liaison work between the Chinese and British armies. Those I met were good at their job, speaking Chinese much better than the Chinese interpreters spoke English. General Thai told us that that morning, March 19, Chinese troops had had their first brush with the Japs—the first contact between Chinese and Japanese forces in Burma. He demonstrated with his chop-sticks the dispositions of the Japs and his own troops. He'd sent a small force down to Pyu to act as a sort of antennae for his main forces established is Toungoo. He was sorry the Japs had attacked so soon. He'd have liked a bit more time to prepare. He showed us, with his rice bowl, representing Toungoo, how the Japs were working round his flanks in a wide encircling movement. It would weaken Chinese forces in Toungoo too much, he said to put out a sufficiently strong screen to stop the Jap infiltration. The Japs had used mounted infantry for this first attack, which the Chinese had thrown back. "No," he didn't think, his troops would hold Pyu. They had orders to resist, but gradually to fall back on Toungoo.

"What are you going to do when the Japs get round the back of you?"

He rubbed a slim hand up and down the back of his neck and grinned.

"We stop here. Our troops hold Toungoo and the area across the Sittaung River. (At Toungoo the Sittaung flows parallel to the main road only a mile or two east of Toungoo itself). The Japanese can cut us off. Yes. But they can't advance as long as we hold out here. We have road, railway and river supply lines and he can't move far forward while we hold those. Let you people keep the Jap air force away and we'll hold out here, and maybe give the Japs some surprises."

"What's the main difference fighting the Japs here and in China?"

"It's too early to say much yet. We only met him this morning," and he smiled apologetically. An orderly brought us hot towels, and toothpicks and we wiped faces and hands, and the General meditatively selected a toothpick before continuing.

"We have difficulties, of course. The heat is very bad. Much worse than in China. We're used to picking our positions in China, and try and fight our battles in mountainous country where there's plenty of cover from air attacks, and the Japs can't make the best use of his artillery. Again in China we have good co-operation from the local people. They're friendly to us. They know we're fighting for them. They bring us food and water. Bring us information about the enemy. Even come up to the front lines and help with the wounded. Here, we're in a strange land. People resent us being here. Some of my men have been murdered at night. At best we get no co-operation from the Burmans and worst we get open hostility."

Before the light failed I wanted to get a picture of him, and he led us over first to a shed, and had a wounded Chinese soldier carried out on a stretcher, and had himself photographed talking to the soldier. He lapsed into infantile English. "This soldier......" and he searched for the word screwing up his eyes and looking heavenward for inspiration, smiled and said hesitatingly: "hero. All Chinese soldiers heroes."

Turning to the interpreter again he explained that

in a fierce hand to hand combat, this soldier had killed four Japanese horsemen, and when a Jap officer was about to pistol a wounded Chinese colonel, the soldier flung himself on the Jap, clinging to him despite the fact that the latter repeatedly plunged his short sword into his arm and shoulder. He hung on till another soldier came up and bayoneted the Jap officer.

As we drove away, the CO commented.

"Didn't see much like a general, did he? Couldn't even tell he was a blinking officer. They're queer alright, these Chinks. I s'pose we'll get dysentery or something after that meal. God, what a lot of muck they eat. I s'pose they wouldn't know what to do with a decent meal of bully and biscuit."

I wanted to drive through the night, and hoped to cover the four hundred miles to Maymyo by daylight. The story of the first clash between Chinese and Japs, was something I wanted to get away the earliest possible. It was news for which the Allied press had been waiting a long time. The 6 cylinder Austin wasn't used to being driven at a high speed for hours on end, and began to chew up oil. We had another battle for petrol and oil at Pyinmina, and after a long delay only got enough gas to take us on to Meiktila. We were both very sleepy by 11 p.m. and only spirited arguments kept us going.

The PRCO was very worried about the ills of Empire and some of his ideas, provided plenty of fuel for discussion.

"Don't you think it's a pity the way the colonies are drifting away from the Old Country?"

"What do you mean exactly?"

"Well this business of places like Australia and Canada sending out their own,—with a fatuous smirk—what they call diplomats, to places like America and China and so on?"

"If you're so worried about the Empire you might at least have taken the trouble to find out that Australia, New Zealand, Canada and South Africa are Dominions and not Colonies. You know some people from the Dominions are very sensitive about being called Colonials?"

"Of course. I forgot you're Australian. But Dominions and Colonies, it's the same thing really. Any way don't you think it *is* a pity; this business of setting up their own Legations and things. Why can't Australia, for instance, be satisfied to let the British Embassy in Chungking and Washington handle its affairs. They could have an Australian representative at the Embassy. Why wouldn't that do them?"

"Did you ever have a father?"

"Hey. What are you getting at? Of course, I have a father, and he's still alive."

"Well, when you were a small boy, you were quite content for him to look after you. Buy your clothes, and feed you, and if the teacher slammed you too hard, it was alright to have the 'old man' go up and have a word with him. While you were growing up you were satisfied to let him decide what was best for you. But when you came of age, and got married maybe, did you still want your 'old man' bossing you, and deciding what you should do; what friends you should have? What you should do with your life? Of course, you didn't. And if he was sensible he realised it and let you go your own way. You'd sooner make mistakes of your own making than never make a mistake and take orders from someone else for the rest of your life. Even if *they* were good orders. Did you never realise that after the last war, even the British Government realised that the Dominions had come of age? Did you never hear of the statute of Westminster...... ?"

"I can't help feeling all the same that it'd be better if we all stuck closer together. The 'old dart' had been running the show for a long time now, and with their experience they can make a better job of things for all of us, than every little farthing dominion trying to run things on its own."

"But you see," I continued, "a lot of us in Australia think you've made a pretty bloody mess of 'running the show,' especially in the last twenty years. Why should we allow you to say what we're going to do in the Pacific, for instance? Or, what our relations with Japan and China and America should be? We've got to live and trade with those countries, now you and Britain sensibly realise that......"

We got too tired even to argue after a few hours, and shortly after midnight, we spread our bed rolls on the ground alongside the car and went to sleep.

One bug-bear of motorists in Burma were the convoy of covered ox-carts which stuck to the middle of the roads, despite the special cart tracks, on either side. Strung out in batches of forty or fifty, they never heard the klaxon until a car was almost on top of them, and then the startled bullocks were liable to plunge across the road, in any direction. If one driver heard or saw a car in time, he would roar a warning to the rest and they would get their carts on to the side very smartly. With only one set of wheels and rigid shaft, and the bullocks usually plodding along slowly, they could turn on the proverbial three-penny bit. To see a long line of them split up—alternate carts swerving to right and left—was like watching some nicely-executed military manoeuvre. Between Meiktila and Mandalay, I had to swerve off the road to avoid some ox-carts, and the car wheels sunk deep into dust-filled ruts cut by the cart wheels. We felt a bit of a bump at one stage and thought we'd blown another tyre, but on inspection tyres were alright, so we hoped for the best and sped on. Near Mandalay, I noticed the oil pump wasn't working. I stopped and tested the oil level, but although I'd filled up at Meiktila, ninety miles away, the pump showed dry. We shoved the car off the road and saw a black patch of oil on the road where the pump had been. Crawling underneath I found a big dent in the pump, and two bolts sheared off. The last of the oil was trickling out of the bolts' holes in the pump-plate. It must have been a big rock I'd hit when I swerved off the road.

We had to send in to Mandalay and get a truck to tow us into a garage. An Anglo-Indian mechanic, after I promised him double ordinary charges, promised to have the pump repaired by evening—it was noon then—and I left the PRCO in Mandalay while I tried to get a car to take me on to Maymyo. There were no taxis about, so I took a tonga (horse-drawn cab) to the outskirts of Mandalay and started to walk along the road, determined to stop the first car that passed. After half an hour's walking I saw a big blue limousine coming and stood in the middle of the road till it stopped. There was a Chinese chauffeur driving and the occupant was a fat commercial-looking Chinese who looked fearfully at me at first. I was covered with grease and had two days stubble on my face but he willingly gave me a lift and drove out of his way to drop me at the door of the Press Hostel. He was a bank manager from Rangoon, and with a car full of water-melons was on his way back to China. He must have been very wealthy to have resisted the temptation of taking goods more profitable than water-melons into China. I cleared off the grease, typed my story and went to bed.

A few hours later I had a shave and something to eat, drove David Maurice's car down to Mandalay, and despatched my censored story about the Chinese Army.

Sending out stories after Rangoon fell and GHQ was shifted five hundred miles north to Maymyo was a strenuous business. Correspondents for individual newspapers, try and get exclusive stories; that is, stories not covered by the Agencies. They also have to try and "scoop" each other. The agencies in Burma very sensibly decided to co-operate. Dan de Luce and Darrel Berrigan, from Associated and United Press, the two biggest American agencies, always travelled together and often Ian Munro of Reuters went with them. For the rest of us, it was a matter of trying to race each other backwards and forwards to the front, hoping that luck would be with us when we got there, and something important happening. Communications were so bad that headquarters were usually unable to give an up-to-date picture of the front, at any given time. (Headquarters in fact relied a good deal on correspondents' reports, in building up their own picture of the frontline situation. Commanders at the front found that we could give them much later news of the general situation that they could get elsewhere).

Getting a story entailed a wild drive of upwards of four hundred miles; the minimum of time at the front; a dash of four hundred miles back to get the story censored, then a 45-mile drive down to the telegraph office at Mandalay for despatch and back again to Maymyo—to get ready for the next trip. Once a correspondent has a story, he can't eat or rest, till he's fought it through the Censor's and knows it's despatched. At Maymyo we used to take it in turns to take all the despatches down to Mandalay—usually about 11 a.m. Stories that came in after that, were the individual responsibility of the correspondent concerned. Once at Mandalay we found our stories delayed in the telegraph office, with operators passing them round the room for everybody to read and enjoy. After that we felt like standing over the operators till our messages were actually despatched.

I met the PRCO with the repaired Austin, and he chuckled as he told me he'd beaten the Anglo-Indian mechanic down from our agreed price of twenty to fifteen rupees. Of course, the Anglo-Indian yelled, "Blue murder" but I told him he was lucky to get anything at all, and drove off and left him."

I felt pretty sick about that, because he'd only done a rush job as a favour, and because I'd offered him double money. It was Saturday afternoon and his day off. I asked the PRCO to go back and give him the extra money, but he wouldn't, and didn't even know the name of the fellow or the address. The mechanic had delivered the car to an agreed rendezvous in Mandalay. I cursed him thoroughly and swore I'd never travel with him again, even if it meant I couldn't go to the front again. I stayed the night with David Maurice and he told me that cholera had broken out in the refugee camps round Mandalay, with deaths averaging seventy daily.

"Of course, it's mainly the Indians walking along the roads that've brought the cholera. And that's just one more reason why the Burmans are hating them. Those poor bloody coolies have to suffer for their own troubles and everybody else's as well."

I asked him if he'd heard any of the Bazaar gossip lately, about how things were going. How the Burmans were reacting to the Chinese troops? What they thought about the Japs chances? How they liked the idea of a change of British for Japanese masters?

He didn't think they minded Chinese troops much, because they were quiet and well behaved. There was, he said, an organised whispering campaign in the bazaar that the British were handing over the whole country to the Chinese, but he thought the Burmese didn't pay much attention to that.

"The most dangerous thing is this talk about the Burma Independence Army," he added. "I remember about two years ago, that thirty odd Burmans, including Hla Pe and Aung San—both well-known Thakins—went to Japan. The Jap Consul-General at Rangoon arranged it, and no one thought much about it. The story going about now is that they were given a military training with special emphasis on sabotage and then sent to organise the nucleus of an army from Burmans and Shans living along the Thai frontier. They're supposed to have raised a thousand men, armed by the Japs, and—so the story goes—they formed the main part of the force which first entered Burma, down at Tavoy and Mergui. The locals here, claim they're advancing with the Japs, enrolling volunteers as they go."

"Do you think the story's right?"

"I don't know. Might be", and he bit his fingernails speculatively.

"I think there's at least a grain of truth in it. It would pay the Japs well to use them. The 'Burma Independence Army' fighting for the 'freedom' for Burma, with the kindly Japs just giving them a helping hand. That's the line. Burmans are nationalistic as any other people, and what would appeal to their vanity more than to kid themselves, that they're the ones that are kicking the British in the pants?"

"But surely to God, they're not naive enough to think the Japs'll clear out and hand Burma over to the Burmese once they've booted us out."

"Ha. But that's just it. The Burmans are realistic enough to know the Japs won't want to leave Burma, but if they believe this story of the 'Burma Independence Army' they'll reckon it's their guarantee of independence. Don't you see? They think they'll be devilish clever. Accepting Jap help and quietly building an army, which they believe—once we're out—will be strong enough to oust the Japs by force if they won't go quietly. It's probably true they're helping the Japs now. Not that they like them. Every Burman I talk to says he hates Japanese. If he had to choose, he'd sooner have British ruling him than the Nips, but he thinks he's a better chance of getting rid of us right now, by using the Japs, and then getting rid of the Japs."

"The question is how far the Japs will allow this Burma Army to grow. I guess they've got no illusions about what the Burmans want."

"You'll see what happens. If the Japs push us out of Burma, the first thing they'll do will be to liquidate the Burma Independence Army. The trouble is there's nothing being done in the way of propaganda to tell the Burmans what's happening to them and what's going to happen. Why don't you fellows do something about it?"

"We're not allowed to suggest there's such a thing as organised Burmans hostility. We're not even allowed to talk of a fifth column. Now, they occasionally allow us to refer to "Traitor Burmans."

"Traitors! To whom are they traitors? From *their* point of view those that collaborate with the Nips or with the British are 'traitors.' If only we'd face up the thing. Forestall the Japs, and give them something ourselves and show them what the Japs have done in other countries. What the Germans did to their collaborators in Austria, Czechoslovakia, Rumania and other places. The Burmans trust us more than they do the Japs. They'd rather believe us if we offered them something, than believe the Japs promises. But we are so hard-necked and aloof. We refuse to see what's under our noses. Because, it would mean 'loss of face' to back down one inch, and give the Burmans any promise of independence now or in the future we'd sooner loose the whole bloody caboose and we will do. We appeal to them with abstract cries for 'discipline, patriotism' and promise them 'victory, freedom, democracy,' while the Japs offer them, 'finish of British rule,' 'Burman land to be owned by Burmans, 'end of foreign exploitation.' Concrete things that they all understand and want. Of course, they're phoney promises, but they go down when there's nothing else being offered them."

CHAPTER XIV

Learning that Tseng Yang Fu had returned to Lashio, I jumped on a goods train and shared an open platform on the end of a guard's van with a King's Messenger, also bound for Lashio. It was bitterly cold and we slept huddled together with his escort. Early next morning the train stopped for an hour at an unimportant-looking station, where nothing seemed to be loaded. The train was loaded with supplies for the RAF at Lashio and for the Chinese 6th Army, and we wondered what the hold-up was. The King's Messenger and I walked up to the engine-driver's cab. A grimy fireman explained that there'd been a robbery the previous evening in the railway men's hut at this station. The Burma Police had arrived and as the engine-driver lived here, they'd taken him off the train for questioning. We went over to where we could see some police and the KM called them a variety of names. We ordered the engine-driver back into the cab and told him to get the train going as quick as he could for Lashio.

If the police had only known they could have arrested us for "interference," but they probably noticed we had superior fire-power—the only thing that counted in Burma then. The train was hours late, getting in to Lashio and there were no taxis or tongas at the station—which is several miles from Lashio town. I phoned Lt. Col. Maas and he came and collected us from the station.

Tseng had promised to try and get me a Jeep, and that was the main reason I'd gone to Lashio, but I was disappointed. Most of the YBR Jeeps had been destroyed in Rangoon and there were no spares.

Following on the report we'd submitted about the road project in the Hukwang Valley, they'd decided to go right ahead and establish rice dumps along the route we'd taken. Coolies were marching across, engineers and health experts were already established at Mogaung. The idea was to open up a Jeep track for hauling in supplies, while the engineers found all-weather route in the hills slightly to the south. The Gissimo had got on well in India and Indian Government had agreed to supply coolies and start building a track from Ledo in towards the Burma Assam frontier. The road built through the foothills, would be built according to railway grades, and later, rails would be laid. The American Government had agreed to supply rails and locomotives etc. Lease-Lend supplies already on the water for the YBR, would be diverted to this project instead. Tseng was willing to put 200,000 coolies on the job. A road in 3 months, a railway in 9 months was Tseng's goal, and Ausland reckoned it could be done.

Tseng had maps spread all over his bed, and his podgy fingers were tracing out routes and lingering on spots where he was likely to strike trouble. Rice was already being stored at Mogaung. Bullock carts and drivers were being requisitioned by the hundreds to shift rice up the Valley. Everything had to be done with feverish haste. The monsoon was only about 3 months away, and the Jeep road to India had to be completed before then. Work on the YBR was being wound up, engineers and malariologists recalled. Chinese engineers were crawling over the hills south of the route we'd taken. Geologists were searching for suitable rock. Things were moving.

"The Generalissimo's worried, Burchett," his high

pitched voice crackled on as he folded up his maps, "about relations between Burmans and Chinese. Army reports show there's been difficulties down at the front. You've been down there. What's the matter ?"

"Didn't seem much trouble where I was. There's talk, of course, that the British are going to hand over Burma to the Chinese, and maybe the Burmans are sore about that. Why don't you tell them over the radio, that you don't want to stop in Burma ? That you're interested in fighting Japs where you can find them. Japs attacked China four years ago......"

"Nearly five years, Burchett."

"......and now she's attacking Burma and attacking China again through Burma. Tell them you want to stop the Japs and then go home again."

"I think you're right. That's just what we're going to do. You know Burchett, I think we should try and do something with the Burmans. Maybe for an organisation of some sort."

"I thought your job was building roads and railways. What have you got on your mind now ?"

"In the old days, my friend, we had to be ready to do all sorts of things. When the Generalissimo wanted me to go to the front and fight battles, I went and fought battles. When he asked me to publish a newspaper I published a newspaper. When he told me to build roads or railways, I built roads and railways. When he asked me to negotiate between the Kuomintang and the communists, I negotiated. Now he's worried about the political situation in Burma and he wants me to do something about it. And I want you to help me," and he laughed fatly and patted me on the back, out of his room and round to the hostel bar.

"Now just a minute. You tell me what's it all about."

"We think there's one thing we share in common with the Burmese. That we're both victims of Japanese aggression. Whatever other differences there are that one point's clear. It's the Japanese in both cases that have done the attacking. The Burmans are Buddhists like us and therefore pacifist. I think the term, Anti-Aggression Front, should appeal to them, don't you? We want to form an anti-aggression front."

"Why not call it an anti-Fascist front?"

Tseng shut his eyes so tightly that little wrinkles formed at the corner.

"Now you know, old friend, that 'anti-fascist front' is a communist term. We want as wide a basis as possible for our organisation."

"The best people among the Burmans for such an organisation are in jail and not likely to be let out", I told him.

"Now let me talk for a while, Burchett. We know who's in jail, and who isn't. Those that we think can be useful, we can have, when we're ready. While you've been running round the countryside, I've been working. I've seen many of the Shan sawbahs (princes) and they want to co-operate with us. You wait for a while. We're going to have a big meeting here with the Shan sawbahs taking the main part, and we're going to get our anti-aggression movement started in a big way. Burma Government are going to give us time over the air for broadcasts. We're going to publish propaganda sheets......"

"Be more useful to have whispers in the bazaars and hpoongyi kyaungs", I mumbled.

"And who said we wouldn't?" Tseng smiled fatly, "......or haven't", he added.

"My God. It's a pity someone didn't start something like this a few months ago. It's a bit late now, isn't it?"

"Well, we do what we can. Isn't it the English that say 'where there's life there's hope'?"

"What do you want me to do? Seems to me you've got everything you want now. Except the enthusiasm of the Burmese."

First we want propaganda. You can bring correspondents up to our inaugural meeting and set it off with a bang. Send us up any ideas you have for propaganda. You hear the sort of things Burmese are talking about. Let us know. Above all try and persuade your army that all the Burmans in this country aren't traitors. We have to try and get their co-operation and we can't get that if we start shooting them up everywhere. Let's have any ideas you've got for improving our relations with the locals."

"The first thing you ought to do is to start some free feeding booths for Burman and Indian refugees at Mandalay and other centres. Maybe have mobile kitchens patrolling the roads giving evacuees at least something to eat and drink. Stick up big posters, "Chinese Relief Committee" or "Madame Chiang's Evacuee Relief." People listen to propaganda much easier when they've full bellies."

He thumbed me over the back and said, "I'll wire Madame Chiang today. That's a great idea you've given me. In fact I can get things going without waiting for a reply from Chungking. I'll send a few thousand rupees down to Mandalay immediately and get the YBR agents there to get moving." He grabbed the phone and got through to his office and then and there gave necessary instructions.

I met Doc. Seagrave that evening, just on his way to his ambulance unit at Loilem in the Southern Shan States. He was making arrangements to shift a Mobile Dressing Station across to Pyinmana to take care of the

Toungoo casualties. Dr. Robert "Bobbie" Lim, China's most famous medical man, well known abroad as an authority on biochemistry and at that time Secretary of the Chinese Red Cross was also at Lashio, on his way to Toungoo. I left next day with Van Shapard, a six feet tall, bronzed, AVG instructor at the Chinese aviation school at Yunnan-Yi. He was taking a truck from Yunnan-Yi down to Taunggyi in the Southern Shan States and gave me a lift as far as Maymyo.

CHAPTER XV

George Rodger and I had planned a tour of the Southern Shan States, taking in the Chinese 6th Army, Seagrave's Hospital, and we also wanted to go down and take a look at the Giraffe-necked women around Loikaw, and the leg-rowers at Lake Inle. George had been commissioned to do a special coverage of General Stilwell, but grim, gum-chewing, "Uncle Joe" wasn't having any. "You wait till I've done something, young man, before you go splashing my mug around your pages." Clare Luce, wife of Harry Luce, editor and owner of "Life" Magazine and herself a writer, was due across from India at any time. As Rodger didn't want to go away for too long, we decided to have another quick look at the Toungoo front.

As we approached Pyinmana, we heard planes about and a fairly solid bombing taking place. The place was well ablaze when we arrived and Chinese soldiers were doing their best, cutting and burning breaks and stopping the flames from spreading. We were worried about Seagrave's outfit, but had no idea where it was located. Then I saw one of the boys, I'd seen when I first met Seagrave at Namkham. He told us the hospital was alright, so we went on down to Pyuwbwe, to Fifth Army HQ. Stilwell was there, and we asked him it it was worth while going down to the front. He said he thought it was. We stayed the night at headquarters, and I did a late night trip with two officers, who wanted to find out if their reinforcements were getting through. They checked up on the numbers of trains that had gone down, and seemed to think things were going alright. Truck-loads of troops were speeding down by road, also light horse-drawn artillery and mountain batteries.

General Thai en Lai as he had prophesied was cut off. And also as he had prophesied he was staying put in Toungoo. The Japs had come around his right flank, bypassed Toungoo and established themselves along a twelve-mile section of the main road, between Toungoo and Yedashe 17 miles to the North. Another Chinese division—the 22nd—had been pushed down the road as quickly as transport permitted, and were due—in two days' time—to start a drive down from Yedashe in an attempt to sandwich the Jap forces and cut a way through to the besieged division at Toungoo.

Rodger and I went on down to Yedashe, and met bespectacled General Liao, the Belgian trained Commander of the 22nd division. He was busy making final preparation for his attack, due to start in the early hours of the morning. We were given floor space in an old Burmese mansion, which we shared with Col. Sliney and Lt. Laybourne, two American artillery officers, advisers to the Chinese Army. It was midday when we arrived and we spent most of that day buzzing up and down the road, watching Chinese troops moving into positions. They were excellently camouflaged with pieces of shrubbery tucked into their belts and caps. When they stood still it was difficult to pick them out against the green scrubby jungle lining the road. We had dinner with General Liao and were relieved to be able to dispense with an interpreter's service. The General who was trained in St. Cyr. Military Academy spoke excellent French. We were on good terms immediately, partly because George and I were both used to eating with chopsticks, partly because I'd been in China and at the third victory of Changsha. Discussing his prospects for the morrow's battle, he said with a touch of cynicism:

"Avant la bataille on est toujours confiant, hein? Mais après......Alors! C'est autre chose."

We both had the impression he wasn't very optimistic about things. We asked if Gen. Thai couldn't evacuate Toungoo by river.

"Certainement. Mais il a recu l'ordre de rester là. Et il y restera." Handing the communal rice bowl across to George, he continued: "You know my friends, the success of great battles is often not some big spectacular movement of armies. It's usually a few men holding out at a given point. Being able to hold out an instant longer than the opponents can maintain their attacks." He took off his thick lensed glasses, wiped them, and set them back on his nose. His chopsticks hovered over a bowl of boiled cabbage.

"General Thai has already gained us valuable time. He's held up the Japs long enough for me to get my division here. And there's more of our troops on the way. Maybe the Japs will get a surprise here. Qui sait?"

We were awakened shortly after midnight with the explosion of artillery. Lt. Laybourne said, "That sounds like our 75's opening up. I wonder what the Japs think about that?"

"They seem to be firing off a whale of a lot of shells. Hope they know what they're shooting at," Col. Sliney said pessimistically.

"Sounds like they're firing because they like the sound of it."

I didn't sleep after the artillery started up. I thought it was probably the Japs firing at the Yedashe railway station, about a quarter of a mile away. Machine-guns soon joined in the fray, the chatter of

Brens and a slower duller pap-pap-pap of Jap heavy machine-guns. The front line was less than two miles down the road, and we could plainly hear the shouts of the combatants. Rodger's nerves were better than mine. He woke once or twice, and I whispered across to him.

"Hear those machine-guns? Don't you think the noise is getting closer?"

"For Christ's sake let me sleep. We'll know soon enough," and he turned over and went to sleep again.

Just before dawn, Chinese light tanks rumbled past, their caterpillar tracks making a thunderous racket on the tarmac road.

"If they keep rattling those tanks along the asphalt at full speed like that, they'll tear the tracks off in no time," grumbled Sliney.

George brewed a good strong pot of coffee, and we didn't wait for breakfast, but pushed on down towards the front. We hadn't gone far when we saw the first casualty coming back, staggering along supporting himself with a bamboo stick. He had been shot through the thigh, and had a bayonet thrust through the fleshy part of his shoulder. We turned the Jeep round and spread a tarpaulin over the stuff we had packed in the back. We wanted to lift him on but he stood with one hand on the car and jerked the other over his shoulder, trying painfully to turn his head round. Then we saw another chap lying on the roadside a hundred yards further down the road. We had a liaison officer with us, so he got out and held the wounded chap, while we backed down to the other one. His arm was limp and covered in dried blood, with a gaping hole above the elbow. His boot was oozing blood and there was a bloody trail leading from the bushes at the side of the road. We picked him up as carefully as we could and laid him on the canvas and collected the other one. They didn't murmur, except one who asked for "Kai Shwe" (hot water).

We gave him some cold water from one of our water bottles and he seemed satisfied. We drove back to a field dressing station, and passed the first stretcher bearers we'd seen, loping down towards the front. The artillery was kicking up a great noise by this time. We spent a few hours ferrying wounded back, and then joined a British liaison officer—a former Shanghai policeman—and set out to see how the Chinese batteries were doing. We drove as far as we reckoned safe, and parked the Jeep under some bushes. Continuing on foot, we met some Chinese officers walking back along the road. Fearing if they found our Jeep they might drive it away—abandoned cars at that time were fair game for anybody that found them—George went back to the car. The LO and I went on down till we met more Chinese soldiers, rifles at the ready, crouching low as they pushed on down the road. We hugged the bushes pretty closely. We came to a line of gun tenders and ammunition trucks, covered with green branches; and Chinese in yellow overalls, armfuls of shells and ammunition boxes suspended on poles slung between two men. Following the shell-bearers, we crossed a small dry stream and saw a battery of three rubber-tyred howitzers, in a clump of trees to the left of the road. On the road itself was a big barricade of trunks, branches and barbed wire.

Col. Sliney and his Lieutenant were there arguing with some Chinese officers. One of the latter roared a command, the three guns banged hard and I jumped in the air. Sliney and the Chinese officer who'd ordered the guns fired, had another argument. Sliney seemed trying to prove something from calculations he was pencilling in his notebook. Every few seconds the Chinese officer would turn away from him, shout at the gunners and "bang" went the guns. In a little hollow nearby another officer at a telephone was yelling away into the mouthpiece and then yelling at the officer giving the commands. Sliney and Laybourne walked over to us, and Sliney said mounfully: "They just won't listen. These guns are built so's they can fire high trajectory, and they keep firing too low, just skimming the tree-tops."

"Who's the guy with the telephone?"

"They say they've got a spotter on the other end of the telephone right up near the Japs' lines, giving this chap the range."

I got out my camera to get a few shots of the Chinese artillery in action. I'd just got the shutter set when they fired and the shutter clicked before I was ready. I wound it up again, when there was a low "whoom" from the direction of the Jap lines, and a high pitched "whirr" that made us duck instinctively. There was a sharp-crackling explosion and a fountain of dust— spouted up twenty paces away from us. Whoom. Whoom. Whoom. Shells landed all round us. For the second burst, I huddled in the hollow with the telephonist, who didn't stop shouting down the mouthpiece. By the fourth salvo I'd hugged my way across the ground to the stream-bed. The lieutenant with bulging eyes and red face appeared to be swimming his way through the grass. I felt ashamed of myself to see the artillery officers and the telephonist, still on the job and laughing like hell at us. I went back and took some pictures and tried to walk casually away, but the next "whoom" sent me scurrying into the stream bed again. I had great respect for the accuracy of Jap mortar fire after that, but not for its destructive power.

They landed fifteen or twenty shells in a semi-circle round us, from twenty to fifty paces away, but though we were covered with dust, no one was hit.

I heard Rodger yelling out to ask if I was alright, and found him under the bridge which carried the road over the stream bed. The Japs had stopped shelling and we went up to get some more pictures, but they soon started up again. We went back, throwing ourselves in a ditch every time the Japs fired. I'd always been told that when you hear a shell scream it's already past you, but we heard these screaming seconds before they landed. And they always burst quite close to us.

The Chinese were shifting the battery out to another position, and were leaving it to their machine-gunners to silence the Jap mortar battery. Col. Sliney was feeling sore about the way the Chinese were using his beloved howitzers.

"Afraid we're useless down here. They just don't give a good Goddam for anything we say about using these guns. At the rate they're going they'll soon use up all the ammunition without hitting anything. They just play with 'em like new toys."

We started off back the road, and heard tanks rumbling along behind us. Standing up in one, with fist clenched in greeting to us, was General Liao, his spectacles winking in the sun-light. He rattled past us, with his chubby chin thrust out, and arm extended looking like Mussolini taking the salute at the Palazzio Venezia. He'd been on an inspection tour. The stretcher-bearers were busy now, carrying the most desperate cases, leaving those who could move at all, to stagger along on their own. We picked up a couple more, when we got to the Jeep. The Japs had been pushed back a few miles, but the going was heavy and the Chinese had plenty of casualties already. Later in the day we went back to get our pictures of a Chinese battery. We parked our car under a group of trees opposite the guns just as they fired. We dropped flat, and leaves and twigs showered down on us. One of the shells had tipped the trees only a couple of hundred yards ahead of the battery. After that we kept well out of the line of fire of the Chinese guns.

That afternoon, the Chinese rounded six Burmans whom they'd caught near the front—they said, signalling to the Japs with mirrors. Two of them had driven cattle across to the Japanese lines. Three of them were yellow-robed hpoongyis. They were squatting on the ground when we saw them, their hands tied behind their backs, and all roped together. They looked at us imploringly, but didn't speak as we passed them. Their usually orange-coloured skin was grey. They were shot an hour afterwards. The Chinese had announced to all and sundry that any Burmans found near the front lines would be suspect and liable to execution. I made a mental note to write to Tseng Yang Fu about ways and means of increasing Sino-Burmese co-operation.

General Liao was too busy to see us during the day, but after dinner he came over to our quarters. We asked him how things were going.

"La situation est très grave. La lutte continue. Ce soir peut-être sera l'heure la plus critique." (The situation was very serious, he warned us the battle would probably carry on all night). On the west side of the road, he explained, the railway line ran towards Toungoo, crossing the road about two miles north of Yedashe. The Chinese had pushed down the line a few miles and captured a small railway siding. The Japanese had counter-attacked several times so far unsuccessfully. He expected the Japs would try that night to retake the station and push up the line to where it crossed the road at the back of us. We would be cut off, and have to wait till the 96th division got down to try and break through to us, as we were trying to break through to the 200th in Toungoo. I had visions of Chinese divisions strung out like sausages all along the Burma road, each sausage trying to squirm along to join up with the one ahead of it. Before he left us to return to his staff, Gen. Liao wished us "Bonne nuit" and paused at the door—a trifle dramatically, I considered.

"Alors, j'espère que vous dormirez bien, mais......" Then he shrugged his shoulder in true French style "Alors, bonne nuit, méssieurs." We looked at each other uncomfortably at that.

"I don't much fancy staying here if we're going to be cut off," I said to George. "I don't like the idea of having a Jap bayonet shoved through my entrails, and I doubt if they'll stop to read our shoulder badges and see we're non-combatants."

"There is no way of getting back......now", opined George. "You know what Chinese sentries are. You wouldn't travel twenty yards without being shot. We wouldn't be able to pronounce the password recognisably even if we could remember it. Anyway, I think that comrade Liao was piling it on a bit."

We agreed hopefully that he'd been a bit theatrical, and as there was nothing else to do, we tried to sleep. The artillery started up again about midnight, but not so constant as the previous night. The machine-guns were much more active. At first, I thought it was my imagination that the noise of machine-guns seemed to be shifting round to the side, instead of ahead. I listened for a long while, and was soon convinced that the Japs were pushing round our flanks, along the railway line as Liao had prophesied. I wakened

Rodger, and he agreed. The firing was much closer and seemed very close to Yedashe station.

"Looks like we're for it 'cocky'," Rodger said. "We can't do anything now, anyway, so we might as well get some sleep. If we're still alive at daybreak we'll have to hoof it across to the river."

I marvelled at his nerves that he could turn over and fall asleep with the noise of a grim battle only about three quarters of a mile away. I couldn't sleep at all. About 4 a.m. I heard the tanks rolling back again, and thought that ominous. The sound of firing didn't get any closer, however, and I fell asleep. Just before daybreak I woke up with the appetising smell of George's coffee.

General Liao wasn't at headquarters and we began to fear the worst, till we went on down the road, and met him coming back in an armoured car. His face was wreathed in smiles as he shook his fist at us in greeting. The machine-gun fire seemed a lot further away, and the batteries were in about the same position down the road. We went back up the road past the railroad crossing and found the tanks being refuelled there. Some of them headed round and went back down towards the front. Back at headquarters Liao told us it had been a very tense night. The Japs had recaptured the railway station and pushed right up nearly to Yedashe, when the Chinese counter-attacked with bayonets and pushed them right back to where they'd started from.

The Chinese had also attacked an enemy artillery post and wiped it out in hand to hand fighting. There were three dead Japs back at the dressing station and an interpreter told us the Japs had tried to rescue the bodies after the Chinese picked them up.

Casualties were given field dressings a mile or two

behind the front line, and at night ambulances—actually ordinary transport lorries—driven by members of the Friends Ambulance Unit, collected them, and took them back to Seagrave's Hospital at Pyinmana. We drove back to American headquarters, just missing another heavy bombing of Pyinmana. The Japs were trying to hit Chinese troops trains there, but hit almost everything in the town except the station. We felt our way round to Seagrave's Hospital and found it undamaged, although flames were ringing it round. Indian evacuees had suffered casualties, and there were frightful scenes as families, collected their dead and wounded, and howling at the tops of their voices carried them away to a depression near the petrol station where most of the evacuees were sheltering. There was no one to help them. They just had to take what was coming to them, and keep on marching. Chinese battle casualties were scattered all round the verandah and courtyard at Seagrave's Hospital. Burmese and Shan nurses were cleansing, swabbing, dressing and bandaging out of doors. Inside 'Doc' was busy operating. The sisters told us he'd been going non-stop for eighteen hours. We didn't interrupt him. They wanted more trucks, fitted up with bamboo racks to carry wounded, and more coolies to help with hospital work. We promised to take a message back to Stilwell's headquarters.

Chinese were still battling with the flames as we drove through Pyinmana back to Pyuawhwe. We intended just calling in at Pyawbwe and then going right back to Maymyo, but when we found that Stilwell and General Tu were going down to the front next day; we decided to wait and go down with them. I wrote my despatches and sent them back to Maymyo with an American officer, and next day we tore on down to the front again. Stilwell was riding in an ordinary staff car, but General Tu had a hefty armoured car, full of steel-helmeted guards and a lorry load of guards in front. We called in at Seagrave's Hospital again while Stilwell carried out an inspection and found out what Seagrave needed. The old 'Doc' had been taken into the army with the rank of Major. He was doing the work of three men and was loved by everyone who met him. Once again the Japs bombed Pyinmana just before we got there.

The situation down at the front hadn't changed much. Liao's troops were still swaying backwards and forwards with the Japs. He'd improved his position a little, but not enough to do any good. More troops were being rushed down the road and mountain and field guns, anti-tanks and more howitzers, and we thought something big might be coming off. We knew that Stilwell was all in favour of having a good solid crack at the Japs and there were rumours of the British having a smack at them over on the Prome Road.

Stilwell didn't want Rodger to take any pictures, but Col. "Pinky" Dorne, Stilwell's aide, said if he liked to play about with his camera while Stilwell was working, he didn't think "Uncle Joe" would object. General Liao had his headquarters in a clump of trees further down the road, and the Generals met in conference there. They were just getting busy over maps, when a Jap fighter plane came overhead, just skimming the tree tops. It went backwards and forwards, and we jumped into slit trenches changing from side to side of the trenches as it went past and turned back. Then a second one came. Stilwell's lantern jaws were still champing away at his gum, and discussions didn't stop for a minute. Both the planes were swooping up and down, and we held our breaths, expecting bombs to drop or machine-guns to clatter at any minute. They both zoomed off, however, after several minutes, and we reckoned it wouldn't be long before the bombers came over.

I guess the Japs don't know what they missed in that hundred yard long stretch of trees. Maybe they had no bullets left for their machine-guns, but they had a wonderful chance of picking off General Stilwell and the two Chinese generals.

While we were having a "picnic" lunch with Stilwell, Dan. de Luce and Darrell Berrigan arrived, and my exclusive run with the Chinese Army stopped. They were just starting to give us the "low-down" on the Prome Road front, when we heard the heavy drone of Jap bombers. There seemed to be plenty of them, and we scattered out into the bushes, flopping down into hollows, where we could find them. They came right across, wheeled round twice and, as we held our breaths waiting for the "swoosh" of bombs, they veered off to the north. I'm certain they were after the generals and their staffs, but weren't certain which one of half a dozen similar copses they were in, so decided to bomb a more obvious target. Pyinmana got it again.

There wasn't much to do but return to Maymyo. It would be several days before enough of the 96th Chinese division got down to reinforce the 22nd so's they could make a complete breakthrough. Liao was gloomy when we went to say good-bye to him.

"Ca va mal. Maintenant les Japonais emploient des chars blindées. Ca sera mauvais pour nos camarades a Toungoo."

The Japs were using tanks. It was certain Gen. Thai couldn't hold out against tanks, plus the Jap air force which was ceaselessly pounding them from the air. We were supposed to have rendered Rangoon harbour useless to the Japs, for six months, yet they were unloading tanks within one month. Thai was still in wireless communication with headquarters, and seemed cheerful enough about things. He'd still got plenty of ammunition and stores, and his men were not only defying all Jap attempts to drive them out, but were making sorties against their attackers, and causing them heavy casualties. Thai already had held the Japs for a record time in the Burma campaign.

Over on the Prome Road Battle, wearied British troops who'd fought their way back for hundreds of miles were still repeating the same old manuoevres. Bound by motor transport, they stuck to the roads and could not send out wide enough screens to prevent Jap outflanking movements. The Japs sent pincers round our forward troops, closing in behind them on the road. With tree trunks and branches flung across the road, they blocked them as they raced back in trucks to establish another line "somewhere in the rear." While green-painted snipers strapped to trees alongside the road picked off truck drivers and stragglers, mortars which had previously registered on the road block, picked off trucks with deadly regularity as they dashed through. The Japs didn't make a frontal attack, only moving up the road after we'd gone back. Plenty of our troops had fought—and fought well for months—without seeing a single Jap. Without sleep, without food, in terrible heat, they kept going day after day, mile after mile, always backwards. We hoped a halt might be called at Prome, almost opposite Toungoo with only the spiny Pegu Yomas mountain range separating the two centres. If only Prome and Toungoo could be held for a few weeks, more Chinese troops could come down and reinforce not only their own comrades, at Toungoo, but also the exhausted British and Indian troops at Prome.

As we drove back to Maymyo, we decided to have a

couple of days' spell. We wanted to have a few decent nights' sleep, and then do our trip to the Southern Shan States. Rodger wanted to have a look at the Shan States, and then if nothing much was happening he was going back to India. We hoped that Tseng's road project would have advanced far enough to allow us to drive the first Jeep through to India. I could arrange for someone to cover the Burma Front for me for a couple of weeks and drive Rodger's Jeep back to Burma. We took a run up to Lashio and saw Tseng. He said things were going alright and he promised us that no one should get in ahead of us driving over the road. He didn't reckon it would be ready before the middle of May.

CHAPTER XVI

We had another look at the Toungoo front, before setting out for the Shan States. We heard bombings as we approached Pyinmana, and the small town of Lewe, 35 miles North of Yedashe, was ablaze when we arrived. Houses on both sides of the road were burning steadily and the road itself was a mess of twisted corrugated iron. Rodger thought we could get through, but we drove gingerly over the white-hot iron. We saw a blazing wall swaying towards us. He stepped hard on the accelerator and the wall shattered into sparks just behind us.

Liao's headquarters had shifted back a little, but the position was about the same. Both sides piling up reinforcements for a bigger effort. Jap planes were pounding Toungoo, while we were talking to Liao. Berrigan and De Luce arrived while we were there, and they took my message back to headquarters for me, while Rodger and I made back to Meiktila, where we passed the night. Early next morning we branched off East for Loilem and Taungyi.

It was a great relief to leave the burning Irrawaddy plains behind and climb up into the Shan Hills. From dirty greys and browns, the landscape changed to restful greens and mauves and purples. Instead of stunted scrub there were firs and pines on the hills, bamboos and willows in the valleys. There were peasants and ploughs instead of soldiers and guns. We lunched like Emperors at the beautiful Hotel at Kalaw, one of Burma's most popular Hill Stations. There was nothing there to show that the bitter fighting was raging less than a hundred miles away. There were probably fewer diners than usual in the huge dining hall, but otherwise everything was as in peacetime. Beautiful cuisine, well-stocked cellar. We enjoyed the first beer we'd had for weeks—and it came off the ice too. We would have liked to stay, but had to shove on. There was golf, fishing and riding to be had. The woods were full of jungle fowl and pheasants.

We turned off the Loilem road, to Yawnghee village, and parked our Jeeps on the edge of a canal leading into Lake Inle, home of the Inthas. These Intha tribes people are the most interesting of all Burma's medley of races. Their origin is obscure, but most Burmans believe they are descended from the remnants of a band of Tavoyans, who invaded Siam in the Middle Ages. On their return they are supposed to have been captured by the Shans of the Inle district, and kept by them as slaves. So that they could not escape, the Inthas (the name meant "Lake Men") were marooned on the large floating islands for which the lake is famous. Their chief task seems to have been to provide their Shan masters with fish. The Inthas were an ingenious and adaptable people. They built homes on poles high out of the water, and made cultivation patches by packing the matted reed islands together, and anchoring them with bamboo stakes. They cut up the reed patches into convenient sizes and turned them up-side down, planting rice in the muddy bottoms. The Lake is a large one—about fourteen miles long—and fierce storms quickly whip up the water into dangerously large waves, so the Inthas dragged islands together and formed breakwaters and fences with them. They use these latter for their burial grounds, pushing the bodies into the water and underneath the islands. The language used by the

Inthas is not spoken elsewhere in Burma, but has a slight similarity to the Tavoyan dialect. Hence, the legend of their Tavoyan descent.

Sir George Scott in his authoritative work on Burma makes the following reference to the Inthas:

"The Inthas, who live round the Yawnghee lake have a direct tradition that their original home was in Tavoy. Their name has no more special significance than the *Chaungtha*. The latter name means 'Sons of the Stream' and Intha means 'Sons of the Lake.' But they are often called Dawe (Burmese for Tavoy), though perhaps more in formal lists than in conversation. Their own tradition is that they were artificiers who were brought up by Prince Mani Sihtu when he visited the lake district in 715 B. E. (1353 A. D.) and built pagodas and left images there, among them the famous 'Hpaungdaw-u' —so called because it was carried in the bows of the Prince's barge. (Every October there is a very big festival and the Buddha's image is taken round the lake in the bows of a barge).

"The Intha language is undoubtedly Burmese in the main, but instead of having a Tavoyan accent, the people pronounce it as a Shan would pronounce Burmese in reading it from a book, without a knowledge of the language beyond the written characters. They dress as Shans, both men and women, but the latter wear black lacquered string garters to show off the whiteness of leg. Neither Shans nor Burmans understand them unless they know both languages. In the census of 1901 they numbered 5851 and as they are a conceited self-assertive race, it does not seem probable that they will drop out of future census tables like the Tavoyans, Yaws and Yabeins."

We hired a gondola-shaped boat to take us out along a hyacinth-lined canal to a rest-house built in the centre of the lake. The Inthas are unique in their rowing methods. Balancing on one leg in the bow or stern of the boat, they row with the other leg wrapped round the oar. Through generations, they've evolved a perfect sense of poise and balance, and the chap that rowed us a couple of miles along the channel and across the lake, rarely touched his hand to the oar. Occasionally —specially when large clumps of hyacinths floated too near—he steadied the oar with one hand, but most of the time he stood, his left leg perfectly straight, the rest of his body pivoting on his left hip and the right leg wrapped round the oar, dipping, pulling and lifting the oar, rowing as efficiently as we would with our arms. Standing that way they can better see the fish, and if necessary throw net or spear without unnecessary motion. We were told they can row forty miles a day with ease. They seemed a happy crowd of people, and boatloads of them who passed us on their way to and from the villages on the far side of the lake, waved and grinned at us most cheerfully.

We stripped off and had a swim at the rest-house, our shaven-headed rowers discreetly turning their backs on our nudity. They posed for some photographs and we went back to the village and on to Taunggyi.

Next day we continued on to Loilem, where we visited General Kang of Chinese 6th Army Headquarters. We wanted to see Major Seagrave's establishment, then go down to Loikaw and Mong Pai, to have a look at the giraffe-necked women, and their beehive-shaped homes. On our way across to Seagrave's Hospital we met a British officer, who at first was very tight-lipped and secretive, but obviously bursting to tell us important news. We found out later he was a newly commissioned Liaison Officer. After making sure we were "responsible" people, he told us that the Chinese had just broken through to Toungoo, cleared the Japs right out of the area, and were pushing right ahead. We sighed, and began to work out how quickly we could get back to Toungoo.

We went on up to the Ambulance Unit, where Dr. Graham and his wife, both of whom I'd met at Namkham with 'Doc.' Seagrave, gave us a slap-up lunch and told us what there was to tell about their set-up. They hadn't much to do as there was only patrol activity on that front. They were keen to get down with 'Doc.' at Pyinmana. When they heard we were going back, they brought us some letters and telegrams to take back to the hospital. A beautiful luscious-eyed Burmese girl came over and begged us to take her down to help at Pyinmana. She'd been left behind because she'd been sick. Graham told me the day before she'd performed a minor operation at one of their advanced stations, and driven a wounded Chinese officer back to Loilem in a Jeep—working the controls and steering according to the officer's instructions. She'd neither performed an operation nor driven a car before. She wept when Mrs. Graham thought she'd better not go to the front until 'Doc' agreed she was fit again. Rodger got his pictures and we turned reluctantly back and made for Kalaw late that night. We got some drinks, a bath and a good dinner. More drinks a soft bed. Before we went to bed that night, the hotel manager told us he couldn't understand why the Chinese were only guarding the main Loikaw-Loilem Road when there was another road quite good enough for trucks and armoured cars, leading from Jap-occupied territory to the Taungyi-Loilem Road, with not a soldier guarding it. We remembered that later when the Japs cut through the Southern Shan States without opposition.

We'd just crossed the railway into Thazi next morning, fortunately easing up a little over the tracks, when there was a blinding explosion ahead of us. Our Jeep seemed to lift high up from the road and a tornado of wind struck us. We were both lying face down in the gutter within a split second. The earth was vibrating with explosions and debris flying everywhere over our bodies. The noise cleared and we gingerly raised our heads. Fifty yards ahead of us was a blazing ammunition truck, cartridges popping merrily. There were pieces of the driver scattered alongside the cab. Further ahead a petrol bowser was lying drunkenly on its side. A bomb had landed squarely between the bowser and the station. Fortunately there was no petrol there. Flames were licking up through the dust all over the town. We'd heard no planes, and hadn't noticed the absence of people as we neared the town. We rushed over to the station, where a troop train had been hit. A dusty boot and part of a trousered leg lay near the platform entrance. Several mules in trucks were bleeding and lashing out, and pieces of another were scattered between the rails and the platform. Most of the mules were still standing quietly in their trucks. A couple of officers and some railway people came along and someone said he'd try to get a message through to Meiktila for an ambulance train.

We tried to drive through to the outskirts and look for cars and trucks that could get through and help pick up the injured, but there was no way past the blazing streets. Fresh fires were starting up every second. We saw some Indians frantically digging with their fingers at a collapsed shelter. A bomb had landed a few feet away. We had a hoe in the Jeep and helped to drag the dirt away until we cleared the entrance. Some Indians and Burmans staggered out uninjured, but said there were wounded inside. George climbed in with our water tin, while I walked on and, keeping to the open field, came to the main road. There were Chinese soldiers lying about in the fields and two on the road vainly tried to get up as I approached. One was only a boy, and cried, "Mama, Mama." His legs were covered with blood. The other asked for water. I left them my bottle and ran across to a truck, and asked the driver to go straight into Meiktila—12 miles distant—and get help, trucks, ambulances and doctors. A British officer arrived and with some Chinese soldiers began carrying wounded Chinese and laid them out under nearby trees. The Chinese had been waiting for a train to take them South to reinforce the 5th Army at the Toungoo Front.

Back in the town George had got all the wounded out of the shelter, except two who, he thought, shouldn't be shifted, they were so badly knocked about. Just where we'd stopped the Jeep when the bombs landed, a hundred or two Indians had gathered and women and children were shrieking and wringing their hands as the whole of the tenements and shops opposite went up in flames. Some of them had dragged out bundles and suitcases. Shopkeepers had rescued what stock they could. Underneath one of the verandahs we saw a dusty bundle moving, and a bearded Sikh, tried to crawl over to us. He raised himself up, but slumped down again. We backed the Jeep as close as we dared and got some Indians to help us lift him up and carry him on to the back of the Jeep. He'd been hit in the backside and didn't seem too badly hurt.

The Indian women were still yelling and screaming, and we tried to shut them up. A young Burmese woman was lying under a tree, her arms caked with blood. Her black hair streamed back into the dust, and she had a comb clenched in her fingers. There seemed to be holes through both her ankles. She moaned for "pani" and we lifted her head so that she could drink better and gave some water from my bottle. Huge billows of smoke were sweeping across the road and red and orange flames licking up the two storied buildings opposite. Cartridges in the munition truck were still popping like chestnuts in the coals. The Burmese woman watched the flames apathetically and lay back again in the dust. George was haranguing the crowd of Indians in his best Hindustani, trying to clear them out or shut them up. He found a Hindu who spoke English and ordered him to take charge of them and keep them quiet. He drove the Jeep round the corner out of danger of the flames. Just as the heat became unbearable we got the Burmese woman out and putting her alongside the Sikh, drove them away under some trees, till we could decide what to do with them.

A medical officer had appeared from somewhere and set up a dressing station at the station-master's house, so we drove our wounded round there. An assistant gave everybody a jab of morphia as we brought them in. While we were unloading our first two, a Colonel rushed along shouting: "Where's a doctor? Confound it all; Where's a doctor?"

AMO came out of the emergency dressing station. The Colonel very red of face, and with his topee pushed well back on his head, grabbed him by the arm.

"Want you. I want you. Have to do something for my mules. There's one there had to be shot. Two more only slashed in hips. Valuable animals. Have to do something for 'em."

The MO looked disgusted, murmured......"Sorry. I'm busy with casualties here."

"My mules more important than these locals, dammit. Can't leave them in the state."

The MO didn't say anything, but walked back into his improvised dressing station and we went with him.

"What sort of a man does he call himself? Trying to drag me away from these unfortunate people. As if I care for his bloody mules. Fellow like that ought to be court-martialled," and the MO continued applying field dressing.

A Burman rushed in. "Sir, sir. You must come. My brother. Both his legs gone and he's bleeding to death. Oh, sir, come quick."

The MO handed a syringe to an orderly and said, "Go and give him a squirt of morphia. It's all we can do. Why the hell doesn't that hospital train arrive."

We went out looking for more casualties and a fat Burman lying on the ground clutched at my trousers.

"Excuse me, sir. I'm a police officer at Thazi. I must be taken to Meiktila immediately, to make a report. I must be the first to be taken away."

He was wounded in the buttock, and we told him the MO would decide who went first, and in any case there was no transport yet.

There was no attempt made to save the town. It was well ablaze by this time and nothing could be done about it. We hoped it would burn out quickly, so trucks could get through to take back the wounded.

The Chinese were running about, dragging boxes of ammunition out of reach of the flames and collecting the wounded as they came to them. Burmese and Indians were streaming both ways; East along the road leading towards Kalaw and West to Meiktila, with bundles and cases on their heads and under their arms.

Thazi is the junction of the main North-South Rangoon-Mandalay line and the East-West Meiktila-Taungyi line. Apart from a direct hit on the mule train, the Japs hadn't touched the station, but by the time the fires had finished the town would be wiped right out. We saw some trucks coming along the road from Meiktila direction and walked across to help load Chinese wounded. There were about a dozen laid out under the trees, most of them not seriously hurt. A couple of trucks started right back to Meiktila Hospital, while others waited till the fires had burned down to get through to the other wounded. We heard the welcome whistle of the hospital train and went back to our Jeep, to cart people from the dressing station down to the train. A Punjabi was trying to get wounded mules out of a car, and was sobbing as he worked. Whether for his wounded mules or the remains of one of his comrades lying about, we didn't know.

Laid out on a stretcher alongside the train was a two years' old Burmese child, its body swathed in bandages, its face marble white. It had evidently been given a good shot of morphia, but it slept uneasily. Its tiny lips puckered and blew out protestingly with each breath expelled. Stretcher-bearers were on the job now, and trucks had driven through to the dressing station. It was a matter of luck who was taken to the train and who went by truck. We saw the Burmese woman we'd picked up earlier and the fat Burmese policeman jolting away on the bottom of a truck, with half a dozen other Indians and Burmese. It was nearing midday and the sun was beating down at full strength, but nothing was available for covering them up. They just had to lie with the sun shining full on their faces, and we felt sick as we watched them bumping along, trying to turn on their sides away from the light and heat. The truck drivers were used to hauling munition or rice, but not wounded people, and they bolted along at full speed.

We only realised after it was all over, that we hadn't taken a single picture, so we went back and George shot a few rolls of film of people being lugged across to the train and loaded into trucks. There wasn't much for us to do after that, so we drove out across the corrugated iron and telegraph wires, back to Meiktila. I typed out a story at the Meiktila barracks and left it with a courier to take back to Maymyo. We filled up with petrol again for a dash down to the Toungoo front. They were still trying to fill two gallon tins with tiny funnels from the petrol bowser and losing half of it on the ground at Meiktila. We had our own funnel by this time. Just as we were leaving the filling station, a Jeep with a couple of American officers drew up and we asked them how things were going "down the road."

"Just the same. Old Liao's still trying to squeeze the Japs off that road South of Yedashe."

"You mean it's not true that they've cleared the Japs out and are pushing down South of Toungoo?"

"Hell, no. Unless it's happened within the last few hours. We've just come right back from there and there wasn't anything happening then. They're waiting for the 96th Division to come down."

"Well, they might have to wait a bit. The Japs have just bombed Thazi to hell, and got some of the 96th there."

"The hell they have. Many of our chaps knocked out?"

We told them all we knew about it, and cursed that Liaison Officer at Loilem, for giving us wrong information and sending us scuttling back on a wild goose chase. There was no point on going back to the front. So we headed back for Mandalay and Maymyo once again.

A couple of days later on April 3, Dan de Luce and I left Maymyo with the day's despatches for Mandalay. We heard some bumps shortly after we left, and when we got past the hill section on the seventeen-mile straight stretch of road which leads into Mandalay, we saw the tell-tale geyser spouts of smoke reaching high into the air. People were already streaming out along the road from Mandalay in cars, tongas, on bicycles and on foot. We went in by a back route and tried to get through to the telegraph office, in the main business street. It was impossible. Big shops on the opposite side of the street were ablaze. The main business section of the city was in flames, and also the poorer residential section along both sides of the railway junction. Twenty-seven planes had come over. There was no air raid warning.

I was worried about my friend Maurice. It looked as if the section where he lived was badly hit. We manouvred round back streets, taking the Jeep as far as we could. Near where Maurice lived the whole area was flattened. There was no way of distinguishing streets. We walked back to the main road, and I counted the rows of telegraph poles till I found what I reckoned was Maurice's street. The roads were covered with red-hot corrugated iron, smouldering telegraph and electric poles lying in a tangle of wires, bricks and slates and fronts of houses. It was difficult walking. Eventually I found where Maurice's house had been, identifying it easily because it was next to a corner block. His burned out Baby Ford had settled down on to the wheel rims. There were three blackened smouldering human bodies, one lying cross the open doorway of the car, two more near where the front door of the house had been. There was a big bomb crater at the back of the house.

I went back to Dan and we drove round to a Baptist Mission schoolroom that had been turned over to a hospital. In front of the entrance, was an ox-cart, with the bullock out of the shafts and tied up nearby. Lying on top, waxen and stiff was a young Burmese woman, and a young Burman was sitting in front between the shafts with his head in his hands, sobbing. As we went in, an Anglo-Indian in blue overalls stopped me and asked if he could speak to me.

"I want to know, sir, why our ambulances were not allowed to be kept in readiness stocked up with petrol, instead of empty and useless as they were this morning."

"Look here," I said, "It's no good speaking to me about things like that. It's nothing to do with me. I'm not a military, I'm a newspaperman."

"I know, sir. I saw your badge. That's why I spoke to you. Why don't you write something about it ?" He looked up at me, his face smeared with black, his eyelids scorched, his eyes red-rimmed. I thought, how little he knew to think I could get such a story past censorship. He went on brokenly......

"My wife's out in that,......" pointing with his chin in the direction of the smouldering waste "......and my child......I don't care for anything now. They weren't killed by bombs. They were hardly hurt, but hurt enough not to get away from the flames. I'm an ambulance driver and left them there, wounded as they were. I left to do my duty, which included picking them up and taking them to hospital......I drove ambulances in Rangoon and know how things are in an emergency. We'd asked, and asked again that all ambulances here be kept ready with their gas tanks filled......While I was trying to get petrol for my ambulance, houses in my block caught fire......My wife would be telling the kiddy: 'Don't cry Daddy's coming for us in a nice ambulance.' I was still looking for petrol. 'Daddy's coming for us.' Think of it, eh ? Flames getting nearer and nearer and people rushing past screaming, and them lying there. No. It's no concern of yours. It's no concern of anybody's. It wasn't nobody's concern to sound those bloody sirens. Or, to have ambulances ready. And how many more d'you think got caught in those flames?"

Dan was alongside me, his face very white under the tan, his hands trembling as he took down what the chap told us. We muttered some words of sympathy and moved away.

"You don't think that can be right? No petrol for those ambulances, do you?" he whispered, as we went on into the dressing station.

"Why not? It would be just about on a par with everything else that happens round here. No warning. No Ack-ack, no planes. Why not no petrol for ambulances?"

We drove round and had a look at the station. It had been hit, but not badly. One set of points was knocked out, and a goods train hit, but the damage there was slight. The Queen Victoria Hospital near the station had a direct hit each end. We went in to make sure. When we mentioned in our stories that this hospital had been hit, the Censor wanted to cut it out.

"An Intelligence Officer's just come back and reported several hospitals damaged by fire, but none hit," said the censor. After I'd described and Dan confirmed the hits on the Queen Victoria, he passed the message.

We sought out the Director of Posts and Telegraphs before we left Mandalay, but he could give us no indication of how we could send out messages in future. We asked if no alternative arrangements had been made for despatching and receiving cables, but he said not.

"How would we know they'd bomb Mandalay and knock out our telegraph system?" How, indeed.

"As a matter of fact," turning on us severely, "you

know you fellows have made things very difficult for us. Caused a tremendous amount of defeatism, with our messages piling up the way they have been, on our overworked staff."

So we drove back to Maymyo, still with ours and other correspondents' despatches, wondering how they'd ever go out, and how we were going to work in future.

I was surprised and delighted to see Jack Belden sitting in the Press Hostel when we got back. He'd just arrived from Chungking, and had dropped International News Service and was now Special Correspondent for "Life and Time" Magazine and the London "Daily Mail." Clare Luce had also arrived from India, and George Rodger brought her over after dinner and introduced her to the correspondents. She didn't have much to say, except—jokingly—that we should all go across to India.

"The slogan over there is 'Come to India and forget the war,'" she said, and by what she described, it seemed that the atmosphere in Calcutta was the same as in Singapore and Rangoon and in Honolulu—before the bombs fell. Dressing for dinner, races, bridge, cocktail parties—all the hooh-ha without which life becomes unbearable for conscientious bearer of the "White man's burden."

CHAPTER XVII

Wally Crabbe, Public Relations Officer and I went up to Lashio next day to take all our despatches, including those describing Mandalay bombing to the aerodrome. We had with us an RAF security officer who was flying to India and would send our stories direct from Delhi. As soon as we got to Lashio, Tseng Yang Fu whispered in my ear that the Generalissimo and Madame Chiang Kai Chek (Gissimo and Gissima as the Americans had dubbed them) had arrived a few hours before us, and were continuing on to Maymyo next day. The Gissimo was apparently very dissatisfied with the way things were going, both as regards British, American, Chinese co-operation, and relations between his own generals and General Stilwell. He'd brought down with him General Lo Tso Yin, former commander of the Nineteenth Group Army, which had fought very well in the Hunan campaigns. General Lo was to be commander of all Chinese armies in Burma, under Stilwell. Stilwell had also come to Maymyo and discussions were to take place that night.

Maurice Ford of Paramount had driven his Jeep to Lashio, and we were going to drive it back to Maymyo. General Stilwell had agreed that the Press were to use those Jeeps in their possessions, until such time as the Chinese Army had to requisition them. He didn't think such an occasion would arrive. We collected the Jeep and drove round to the SSO's office to get a petrol chit. The SSO wasn't there. He would be back in half an hour. We went back in Wally Crabbe's staff car several times, but he was never there. A captain, who worked in the office, seemed very uncomfortable each time we returned. Eventually we created such a noise that the captain said he'd give us a chit.

"But I don't think it will do you any good," he added.

We got petrol for the staff car that evening. Next morning I took the Jeep round several times, but the SSO was never there. The captain refused to give me a chit. "No, No. I've already exceeded my authority once. I couldn't do it again."

I waited for an hour, and the SSO came along. He was chary about giving me a petrol chit. Asked me what type of car I had.

"A Jeep, eh? Let me have a look at that. Hmmm. You know I've instructions to requisition these, I suppose?"

"You'll have a job to requisition this one, Colonel. It's already been requisitioned by the Americans. I'm just driving it back to Lashio to Stilwell's headquarters."

"Another one they've pinched from us. My God, what do they expect *us* to do for transport?"

"I thought these were brought out for the Chinese Army originally. Look here, what about my petrol chit. I've been waiting here for petrol ever since yesterday afternoon. Sq. Leader Wallace Crabbe from headquarters is waiting for me to get this Jeep filled up so that we can get back to Maymyo. It's the same thing everywhere one goes in Burma, this inexcusable delay in getting 'chits.' If you're not going to give me any petrol, say so. If you want to take this Jeep, take it. And take the responsibility that goes with it."

"How many gallons do you want?"

"Two will take me to Maymyo, but we've been told to fill up here, to save supplies further down the road."

I got a chit for eight gallons, and drove round to the CNAC Hostel to see Tseng before we left. As I stepped out of the Jeep, an American Colonel walked across......

"Well, now. Are you going to give me that Jeep now?"

"You too, eh? Have you got an order for it?"

"I received instructions from General Stilwell last night, to requisition all Jeeps here and that includes this one."

"This Jeep has been requisitioned for the use of correspondents. I'm not entitled to hand it over to anybody."

"I'm a busy man," he roared, and waving his arm at a couple of staff cars, "see those cars? They represent the total transport of the American Army in Lashio. Now will you give me the key and let me get on with my job"

"Well, I'll have to report this matter to General Stilwell, you know, Colonel?"

"You'll report to no one. Now get outta here."

So I got out, I thought the emergency provided for in the understanding General Stilwell had given us, may have arisen. I walked back, to the RAF mess very humbly and told Wally Crabbe what had happened. We both went back, but the fiery Colonel was adamant in hanging on to the Jeep.

The poor Colonel fairly danced with rage next day when another correspondent arrived from Maymyo with a signed order from Stilwell that he—the Colonel—had wrongly requisitioned the Jeep, which was to be handed over immediately to the "bearer of this order."

We set off back to Maymyo, taking the RAF security officer back with us. He wanted to see Hollington Tong, who was accompanying the Gissimo to Maymyo, so had postponed his departure. He'd promised to send the despatches on by plane, but when we'd just about got to Maymyo, he remembered they were still in his attaché case. He stayed another three days in Maymyo, and the despatches stayed with him. There was no other way of getting them out. Alfred Wagg of "Allied Newspapers, London, and "Liberty" Magazine, New York, scooped us all by flying to Chungking, and sending an account of the Mandalay bombing from there.

Only a portion of the road from Lashio to Maymyo was bitumenised, the rest was a dirt-road hidden under several inches of red dust which drifted in through windows and doors. Even if one endured terrible heat and kept the windows closed, the red dust still found its way in. We passed a line of cars stopped along the road from Maymyo, and in one was Madame Chiang, with the door open trying to rid herself of the worst of the dust, before reaching Maymyo—and official receptions.

The day after the Gissimo arrived on April 8, Maymyo was heavily bombed. It was the first bombing it had had, except for one small raid when the invasion of Burma started. It was, I think, aimed at the Gissimo and Madame, and the Japs succeeded in landing one bomb in the compound of the house in which they were staying. Several bombs landed near Stilwell's headquarters, and when George Rodger and I dashed across there, U. S. officers were trying to clear out a shelter which had collapsed. Clare Lucc, her fair curly bobbed hair flying in the wind, was dashing about in slacks, snapping Leica shots as the officers worked. One young and one old Anglo-Indian lady were inside the shelter. After much careful digging we caught sight of the younger woman's arm. She called out that she was alright, that they were both alright. She was white but cheerful as they gradually released her, and ran across to a house opposite. A small boy threw himself into her arms, and she promptly collapsed. A bunch of tonga horses, released by a fire, cavorted round, kicking up their heels, uncertain what to do with their new-found liberty. They delayed the rescue work until they were chased off.

We drove round to have a look at the damage. Driving back to the Press Hostel, we found a little Indian boy, his leg wrapped in bandages, manfully carrying his little sister who was bandaged round the arms and head. We picked them up and drove them to where the little boy said they lived. There was a burned out gap in a row of houses. Some Indians who spoke English came over and told us every one in the houses had been killed. We asked them not to say anything to the children, and took them back to the Press Hostel. The Indian servants and their wives did everything possible for the children, tenderly washed the blood and dirt from their limbs, and gave them food. The little girl was put to sleep, and her brother stood alongside her, finger in mouth. Every few minutes she turned restlessly and screamed, and he patted and spoke soothingly to her.

Flotsam of war. Who would feed them? clothe them, house them? dress their wounds even?

In this case the problem was solved by one of the servants who went off making enquiries and eventually discovered some of their relatives for them. So they were handed over to them, together with some money readily subscribed by the Press Hostel.

We heard there was plain speaking between the Gissimo, Stilwell and Alexander at their conferences. Maybe, it was already recognised there that Burma was lost. That it was a question of gaining time for the defence of India and salvaging what was possible of our armies. We've been told since that that was the object of the Burma campaign—to fight a delaying action.

The Press certainly weren't told that. We were told confidentially that another Chinese Army was coming down, and we would start a drive through to Bangkok and cut off all Jap land communications. Planes were being sent—British planes, American planes. We might possibly lose Lower Burma, but Northern Burma would be held, through the monsoon, and then we would build up our counter-attacking force and shove the Japs into the sea. Reinforcements were being flown into Shwebo—the Iniskillings—veteran troops of the East who'd been in Hong Kong and Malaya. Heavy stuff would soon be coming down the new roads which is being rushed to completion.

There wasn't much point in going to the front those days, because there was no way of getting messages out. The Chinese pushing south from Yedashe and General Thai pushing north from Toungoo had given the Japs a good "squeezing." The 22nd couldn't fight its way through to Toungoo, so the 200th division fought its way through to the 22nd on March 30 (twelve days after the first clash at Pyu) killing plenty of Japanese on the way. The Japs suffered more casualties at Toungoo, than at any other point in the Burma campaign. The Chinese were steadily being pushed back up the Toungoo Road, the British along the Prome Road. Demolition experts were on the job at Yenanyaung, the main oil production centre in Burma. Drills were dropped down the shafts and concrete poured down after them. Oxy-acetylene flames cut teeth out of gear wheels. Machinery which could be removed was shifted, vital parts removed, gelignite laid for the day when further defence was impossible, and the whole show had to be blown up.

The Jap Air Force had caught Americans and British on the ground at Magwe in two attacks on March

21 and 22, and knocked out most of both air forces. There was talk of shifting Army headquarters across to Myitkyina, and we were told that communications wouldn't be established again till we got over there.

George wanted to get "cracking" on the trip to India. Although Tseng had warned us that as far as the Chinese were concerned work on the road hadn't really started, he told us he'd information that local labour had cut a track from Shinbwiyang—the furthest point to which we'd penetrated during the previous trip—to the Pangsao Pass, the summit of the dividing range between Burma and Assam. On the other side tea planters with coolie labour were building a "Jeep Road" from Ledo, the Assam railhead, to the Pangsao.

CHAPTER XVIII

We made preparations to leave. I packed all my gear, intending to leave most of it at Myitkyina on the way through. We'd collected provisions here and there on our trips through the country saving them for our trip to India, and were well stocked with everything except solid food. We had plenty of bottles of cocktail cherries, olives, tins of herrings, Chinese packed tinned fish, peeled tomatoes, beetroot, cream, grapefruit and pineapple juice, mandarins, and most important of all plenty of coffee and tinned milk.

Tseng Yang Fu promised me a Jeep, on condition we left it "somewhere" along the road, so that his road-builders could use it. We'd changed our plans. Once we got to India, George was going to drive right down to Calcutta, if possible, while I intended to fly back from Dinjan—an airfield not far from Ledo—to Myitkyina. There was a regular service at that time of American Army transports evacuating refugees from Myitkyina to Dinjan. I hoped by the time I got back, that headquarters would be established at Myitkyina and normal communications working again.

Just before we left Maymyo, I was relieved to get a note from David Maurice. He'd left his house a few minutes before the bombs started dropping. He didn't remember hearing planes, bombs or anything else. Just picked himself up out of the gutter, after it was all over and managed to get away from the flames. His servants were all killed. All he had vanished with his house and car. He'd offered to take a convoy of boats up to Myitkyina and expected to be there within three weeks' time. I hoped to see him there.

We felt a trifle sentimental leaving the Press Hostel at Maymyo. Although neither of us had spent much time there, it had been a "home from home"—place to come back to after the front, and always some friends there to talk to. The "home" was beginning to break up. Vic. Thompson of "Daily Herald," Cedric Salter, playwright correspondent for "Daily Mail", had gone to India. Rotund, cheerful Alfred Wagg, (Waggie to his friends), was in Chungking, "Tim" Healy of "Daily Mirror" was packing up, Maurice Ford already gone. We hadn't talked about our plans, because we wanted our road story exclusive. No one knew, until the morning we left, where we were going. We said good-bye and casually—and super-optimistically—announced we were driving across to India. There were good-humoured jeers and sallies round the breakfast table that morning. They all thought we were pulling their legs. So we were, pulling their legs and our own too—but we didn't know it then.

Lashio had been bombed the day before we got there, and there'd been alarms twice a day for nearly a week. People came to work with their lunch wrapped up. Punctually at 11 a.m. the alarm went and everybody who had cars drove out of town, and took his lunch with him. We passed lines of cars, under the trees near Lashio. Chinese merchants had tables and chairs set out and were taking life easy, eating and sleeping and drinking tea. People were sprawled out on the grass, no one seemed worried about enemy planes. We pulled in for a while, then the "all clear" sounded, and we could see the two bamboo balls, which served as warnings, being taken down. We started off in, but no one else moved. We learned afterwards, there was usually another alarm about 2 p.m. so people just stayed out.

We went to the CNAC Hostel, and found a notice pinned to the door, intimating there was no accommodation, no meals or drinks would be served to outsiders, only two meals a day to inmates, no drinks served in rooms, and "prices would be just the same." We hunted around for a place to eat but found none. The sirens sounded again and we started off for the road, but could hear planes coming, so dumped down in a small creek, alongside the golf course opposite the power house. Two planes came over and skimmed the tree-tops, so low we could see the pilots. They weren't interested in us, thank God, and sheered off without firing.

Haas, the malariologist, gave us his blessings and quantities of Atebrin to keep malaria away. He was going over to the road in a few days' time to get anti-malarial works started before the main batch of Chinese coolies arrived. He reckoned that the Hukwang Valley with two hundred inches of rain in a season would be the biggest problem he'd yet had to tackle.

Tseng was very happy about his anti-aggression War Campaign Association. It had been successfully launched and he'd been made president. He took us across to meet one of the men who direct China's intelligence and propaganda services, General P. S. Wang, better known in China as Wang Pun Shen, adviser to the Generalissimo on Japanese affairs, and member of the Military Affairs Council. When he lets his moustache grow, Wang Pan Shen looks like Warner Oland's representation of Charlie Chan, but this time he had his moustache clipped, and looked very trim and severe in his New Life uniforms. He has a massive head, with plenty of hair brushed straight back in front and bristling down his fat neck. His rather piggy eyes peer out through horn-rimmed spectacles. He's one of China's big men, and he probably knows more of what's going on in Japan, than any man in the world—outside of Japan. He invited us to share a Chinese meal with him, and—as we hadn't then found accommodation—he offered us a room each for the night.

It's unfortunate that most of things PS told us that night still can't be published, for to publish them might endanger some of his sources and contacts in Japan. PS knew of me in China, and Tseng knew enough about us both to believe he could guarantee our discretion; so Wang "let his hair down." He'd come down to help with Tseng's anti-aggression campaign amongst other things. His agents were already in the bazaars, hpoongyi kyaungs, evacuee camps, wherever gossip was to be picked up and rumours combated. Some of his agents were there that night, and told us the sort of things David Maurice had told me weeks earlier. Wang had his finger on the pulse of Burmese life soon after he arrived—but he arrived too late. He'd visited anti-Fascist Burmans in Mandalay jail—genuine intellectuals who'd been locked up for anti-Fascist, anti-war activities. Men who were strongly anti-Japanese and had influence with the Burmese people. Wang had got the British authorities—I think through the Oriental Mission—to agree to release these men, who'd pledged themselves to work for the Chinese and United Nations in anti-Fascist work. (Later, several of them—including Kyaw Sein, Mya Thwin and others—were actually released and were being escorted up to Lashio, when the Japs cut the Lashio Maymyo road. The major escorting them took them back to the jail and locked them up again). PS also had "roped in" Daw Mya Sein, brilliant and charming Burmese lady,

Oxford graduate, Burma representative at the Round Table Conference. The "Anti-Aggression War Campaign Association" had been given a festive birth, at a dinner in Lashio attended by the Burmese Prime Minister, Sir Paw Tun, several of his Ministers, leading Sawbahs of the Shan States, and representative Burmans. The programme for future activity was divided into three parts. Publicity—to tell Burmans what the war was about and why they should want to defend themselves. Organisation—to organise and train the people for active participation in defence—guerilla activity. Aid and Comfort—to help evacuees, and care for soldiers at the front and assist those fighting behind the lines. It was a grand scheme, and a pity that it was formed only a month before Burma fell.

In between dishes, at dinner, I asked PS what he thought the Japs would do next. He wiped his fat face and podgy hands with a hot towel, brought in by a smiling Cantonese woman, and said:

"In China we think it a poor compliment to our cooks to mix politics with eating. We'll talk afterwards."

And after the table was wiped down, and bowls of tea and melon seeds set round, Wang seated himself at the head of the table, laid his glasses down and started to talk. His knowledge of English is good, but he spoke haltingly and preferred to use an interpreter. Several times he stopped the latter and corrected his translation. His voice is heavy and hoarse as if it has a difficult time forcing its way through the rolls of fat in his throat.

"What will Japan do next, eh? We're not the only ones to worry about that. Japan wonders too what she'll do next. Siberia. South Seas and Australia. Hawaii. India. They are the possibilities. Either of the first four would have to be tackled separately. Siberia, Australia and Hawaii, each require a full-scale military effort, but India Japan expects to take with a small military but large political effort. Japan counts on the apathy of the great majority of Indians—the open hostility to Britain of a minority—to take India. Therefore a campaign against India may be undertaken simultaneously with a campaign against Siberia, Australia or Hawaii. The Black Dragon Society, Japan's religious foreign espionage service is operating in India now, as it operated successfully in Malaya, Burma and Java. Japan expects India to fall like a ripe apple when the tree is shaken. With raids, broadcasts, and its 'Indian Independence Army' formed from Indian units captured in Malaya, and Indian police from Shanghai, Hong Kong and Singapore, Japan is getting ready to shake the tree. Siberia—Japan will not attack until Russian resistance, potential there, reaches its minimum. Perhaps this will happen at any time. If the Germans press hard, and the Russians have to transfer so much material from Siberia that her defences are weakened, Japan will attack. Maybe this won't happen. That leaves Hawaii and Australia. Japan fears Australia most because it's being built up as a base for attacks against Japan itself. If she could secure New Guinea and New Caledonia, and prevent American supplies reaching Australia, she would be content. An attack on Hawaii means a large-scale naval battle, Maybe Japan doesn't want this yet. But Hawaii is a rich prize. With that in her hands and India neutralised—if not occupied—Japan can put her fingers to her nose at the United Nations. She would be astride the American Australian supply line and with her essential conquests completed, she could sit back and develop her newly won Empire." He pursed his fat lips and drummed with his glasses on the table.

"Yes. I think an attack on Hawaii or the islands round Australia, perhaps occupying part of the north of Australia, is next on the programme." ......of course, if the Germans broke through the Caucasus, and the British and American forces in India had to be switched across to Iran and Iraq, Japan would stop shaking the tree in India, and get the apple by cutting the tree down. She'd have to occupy the Eastern industrial side before Germany got across there."

He swung his heavy body round so that he faced us instead of the interpreter and spoke in English.

"You know, it's a question whether India becomes a......" he pulled at his bottom lip searching for the expression, "......ah......focal point of United Nations strategy, from where we can strike out east and west against Japan and Germany; or whether it becomes the connecting link in Axis strategy. If that happens—the war is lost and humanity's lost for generations."

The Cantonese woman in a stiff white blouse and black silk trousers came in with a big kettle, tossed the remains of our tea on the floor, and filled up our cups with hot tea. We drank tea, and PS took time off to show George and I how to crack the outer shell of water-melon seed with our teeth and extract the crisp inner white seeds. The seed is held vertically between the teeth and gently bitten until the black shell splits at the top, opening like two black lips, with the tiny white tongue of the seed peeping out, ready to be gripped ever so delicately in one's teeth, extracted and chewed. Around the legs of General Wang's chair and the chairs of the other was a steadily increasing pile of seeds mostly bitten through the middle, while George and I had accumulated a modest pile of seeds bitten off in the middle.

"Washington and London were warned that Japan would attack in December," Wang startled us by saying. "But they thought the warning was just 'so much Chinese propaganda'."

I'd heard hints of this story from Foreign Office sources, and pressed Wang for details.

Early in July, 1941, the Japanese Imperial Council met and decided to attack Russia towards the end of the year. Hitler had submitted the schedule for his Russian conquest, stage by stage—and it was agreed at which stage Japan would come in. Preparations were made for the attack. Reinforçements were sent along the Siberian and Inner Mongolian frontiers. Big tank manoeuvres were held. Things didn't go so well with Hitler's schedule, but more important still, Britain and America didn't take the situation in the Far East seriously. Britain and America only reinforced the Philippines and Malaya sufficiently to back up their diplomacy and not to face military thrust. They were bluffing when they put out reports of large reinforcements arriving here and there; big air strength being built up; and naval forces transferred. They didn't bluff the Japs. They knew exactly how strong we were at any given time. In October, the Imperial Cabinet met again, and decided because of the non-fulfilment of Germany's schedule against Russia, and because Britain and America had failed to strengthen their Pacific defences, to attack in the south instead of north. A plan of campaign was submitted at that meeting and accepted. Copies of minutes of the meeting were forwarded by us to Washington and London, but both governments thought it was a fake story. Britain and America were warned insistently through their embassies in Chungking that Japan was preparing for the attack, that when it came it would be sudden and treacherous, but still they were caught "as the Americans say 'with their pants down'."

He paused for a while, then looked at his watch, jumped up and said: "Well, if you're starting off tomorrow, you'll want to get to bed." And he went for the Cantonese woman to put lamps and bowls of water in our bedrooms.

Next morning, I wrote a message on General Wang's interview, and after going through it word by word with his interpreter, and making a few minor alterations, he agreed to let it go. I hoped to send it from India.

The SSO at Lashio opened his eyes very wide when we walked in and asked for sixty gallons of petrol, but after examining our chits, issued by GHQ, requesting all civilian and military officials to "render us every assistance and supply petrol and rations as required," he reached for his pen. I had a forty-gallon drum strapped in the back of my Jeep, and George had a twenty gallon. Tseng handed us a letter requesting YBR officials to give us what we needed in the way of tools, and we started out after lunch on April 6th. We took things easy for a start, and had to halt every few miles, till our loads settled down and petrol drums stopped shifting at every bend. High up in the mountains before we turned off the Burma Road to Bhamo, we met Bill Mundy, "Sunday Morning Herald", and Dan de Luce, coming back from Loiwing. They had a good laugh when we told them we were driving through to India—but they were the first correspondents to believe we were going to try it. We got to the barrier on the Loiwing-Bhamo road about 10 p.m. and found a long queue of trucks waiting for the barrier to lift at midnight. It was still one way and night traffic. With our small Jeeps we were able to manoeuvre through to the front of the column. Trucks were still rumbling through from Bhamo.

Many of the trucks in the queue were YBR and had big posters across their sides "China-Burma-India Highway", "We Build for Uni-nations' Victory", "Down with Japanese Aggression." Tseng's propagandist experts had been on the job, and it looked good publicity for the Shans to see these trucks pouring through, filled with road workers and equipment.

There were drivers of all sorts and colours, squatting round a big fire, waiting for the whistle to blow and the barrier to lift. Some had girls with them, and they huddled up close together, just out of range of the fire light. Kettles were boiling and tea was passed round. Chinese turning up their noses at thick brown stuff with milk and sugar, Indians scornfully passing on the Chinese unsubstantial-looking, discoloured water with green leaves floating on top. We dug out our coffee pot and primus stove. A crowd gathered round as we pumped the primus, and followed the coffee-making process with great interest. Some bolder than others stuck their noses close to the pot to smell our strange brand of tea. We squatted with the group round the fire, and wished we could follow the babble of talk. Some local Shans stood a little distance off, motionless, looking like Bedouins, with their brown blankets wrapped closely round their bodies, and pulled up in a hood over their heads. Each driver after he'd pulled his truck into line, had to register at a Police box, giving his name, truck number and showing his registration card. From 11-30 onwards, drivers started wandering back to their trucks, and engines were warmed up. Exactly at midnight, the whistle blew, one end of a bamboo rail was released from its hasp, and a weight the other end pulled it high up into the air. The race was on. We were well away in our Jeeps and thought we'd lose the rest of the trucks easily once we got to the bends. Apart from its narrowness and twistiness the road had very bad surface, with deep gutters across it. It had been surfaced in small sections, so that one drove over good road for half a mile, then twenty or thirty yards of bare rocks followed by another stretch of good road. The dust was terrible and in a Jeep the dust just pours in. We didn't want any trucks to pass us, otherwise we'd have had to wait till the whole convoy passed, and give them an hour for the dust to settle. We hurtled round hairpin bends—some of which described almost a complete circle—at dangerous speeds, skidding and banking, but those forward trucks kept right behind us. Spears of lights were probing and gliding over the whole countryside as scores of trucks twisted and hurled themselves along that terrible road. They had to make Bhamo in seven hours or else wait on the road till midnight the following night. My forty-gallon drum worked loose and each time I skidded round a bend it threw its weight on the wrong side and tried to push the Jeep over the edge. If I stopped to fix it, I'd either have trucks pass me, or I'd have to hold up the whole convoy. I managed to jump out once and keeping the engine running shoved a big rock in between the bottom of the drum and the side of the Jeep. This held it fairly steady and we could put on pace again. We travelled over thirty nightmarish miles before we "lost" the trucks, and our arms were aching with swinging the heavily laden Jeeps every thirty or forty yards, around hairpin bends. We arrived at Bhamo about 5 a.m., and had a couple of hours' sleep on the ground.

George's Jeep was not functioning well so we took it across to Standard Oil Co., where they decided it needed a new head gasket. This delayed us for two days, while they sent back to Loiwing for gasket material. At Myitkyina, we found the house of Steel Bros. Manager's had been requisitioned for Governor Dorman-Smith, who was due to arrive shortly. Latest rumour was that Government was shifting to Myitkyina, but GHQ was transferring to Shwebo, further south. I decided to take my baggage right through to India, rather than leave it behind at Myitkyina.

David Maurice hadn't arrived yet, but was on his way. I heard from an official, that at Mandalay there were several government launches; which the military wanted shifting to Myitkyina, immediately after the Mandalay bombing. They couldn't get crews for them. The Indians had cleared out and were legging it across country for India. Several times they collected men and put police guards to watch them, but at night they slipped overboard and swam away. Maurice volunteered to get crews and take the boats up the river, and soon collected enough for five launches. The Transport Officer wanted to put police guards aboard, but Maurice refused. He slept on one of the boats himself till they were ready to leave, and all the crews stayed with him.

"He's a queer codger, that chap Maurice," the officer explained. "Bit of a Buddhist or something, they say. He seems to get along with the natives alright though. I been told they'll do anything for him."

"He treats them as if they were humans, that's all," I said, and the TO looked at me as if I were a bit queer, commenting:

"Ah. You wait till you've been out East for a while."

Later on, when the British army was retreating through Myitkyina, it was David Maurice and his five launches that ferried them across the Irrawaddy. His boats had been dive-machine-gunned several times coming up the river, but his crews stayed with him. When he got to Myitkyina, the Japs were already at Bhamo sixty miles away. Most officials had cleared out, and Maurice was made River Transport Officer at Myitkyina. British troops were piled up on one side of the river, two thousand Chinese engineers, doctors and technicians from the Burma-India road project on the other bank. Ferries and launches had been sunk or turned loose to drift down the river. Maurice stayed and worked his launches till the last British soldier and the last Chinese were ferried across—the British to continue out through the Hukawng Valley to India, the Chinese along the caravan trail to Tengyueh and Kunming. From May 3rd to May 7th they worked non-stop, night and day, through countless machine-gunning and bombing attacks. Maurice had allowed the Indians to bring their wives and they cooked food which Maurice shared with the men, shovelling it into their mouths as they worked. When the last man was across, the Japanese were a few miles away. Maurice had grown a wild-looking beard by this time, and the Indians begged him to go with them to India.

"We shall put a fez round your head, teach you some lines of the Koran, and if we meet Japanese we'll say you're a Persian. With your beard and sun-tan they'll never know the difference."

He decided the risks were too great, and left with a party of Chinese on the long trek to Kunming, weaving in and out of the path of the Japs, who had crossed by this time into Lower Yunnan. The Chinese did their best to repay him for his services in ferrying them across the river by installing him at Kunming's best hotel, and not allowing him to spend a cent as long as he stayed in China. The USAAF flew him back to India, where he immediately volunteered to raise a levy of Burmans and carry on political work along the frontiers. He was turned down again.

But we've left the sequence of the story and must return to recount things as they happened.

George wanted to take one or two photogenic evacuee girls on the trip to make a better story. "Girls fleeing Jap Terror Across Head Hunting Naga Hills" was his idea of a good story for "Life" Magazine. He'd had two girls lined up in Maymyo, but mother decided to fly them out instead.. We almost persuaded a handsome brunette in Myitkyina to come with us, but she backed out at the last moment and asked if we'd mind taking her bedroll instead. She was only allowed one handbag in the evacuee plane. We took the bedroll and nicknamed it "Bertha" after the young lady, and later on whenever George was composing a specially good "shot" for "Life", he used to get mad when I suggested including "Bertha" in the picture.

We railed the Jeeps and ourselves down to Mogaung. There was a big YBR dump now established here, with lots of trucks lined up—waiting for petrol. We called in an old 'Doc' Wright—an American malariologist who'd fought mosquitos from the time of the building of the Panama Canal all over the world—and some other American doctors, who were superintending the establishment of coolie camps. They said we might run into two of their men who'd also left to see how close to India they could get. They fixed us up with axes, shovels, hoes and rope, and warned us we'd probably run into bother, because there'd been plenty of rain along the track.

CHAPTER XIX

We started off from Mogaung late in the afternoon and got some eggs and rice to eat at a Chinese shop, which had sprung up at Kamaing since I was last there. We passed several YBR trucks along the road, hauling rice. From Kamaing we had to put chains on, trucks had cut deep ruts in the dirt road, and these were now filled with mud. During my previous trip along the Hukawng Valley, I'd only seen one wheeled vehicle—a passenger bus which ran between Mogaung and Kamaing. This time, apart from trucks, there were scores of hooded ox-carts in convoys all pressing forward up the Valley. It was dark when we arrived at Shaduzup Village, and we were held up by a camp of nearly a hundred ox-carts, astride the road where it crossed the bridge. The drivers were just settling down for the night, and we regretted having to disturb them to shift their carts sufficiently for us to get our Jeeps through.

We shared a hut that night with half a dozen Chinese including one woman. There were two engineers, a radio operator and two doctors, going up the Valley on horse-back to establish camps and hospital service for the coolies. The woman was a nursing sister—wife of one of the doctors. We offered to give two of them a lift to Shingbwiyang, but they didn't want to break up the party. They were all young and seemed intelligent and enthusiastic. Next morning we got some pictures of elephants hauling logs for the bridge at Shaduzup, with ox-carts fording the stream and the jungle background. While we were taking the pictures a group of villagers came along, and I handed out some of the photographs I'd taken on the previous trip. They were wildly excited, when they recognised their friends and went scampering about until the whole village was present to gloat over the pictures. That made taking photographs easy in Shaduzup.

There were trucks on the road right up to Maingkwan, hauling and distributing rice. The local Kachins were making great money, building rice godowns. Everywhere along the track there were signs of activity. Several small tea stalls for the truck drivers had already been set up in the middle of the jungle. Villagers who'd formerly looked on our Jeeps with awe and suspicion hardly turned a hair now when great trucks went rumbling by. The track had been widened, bridges rebuilt or strengthened. Kachins staggered along with great bundles of palm leaves hanging down their backs and dragging on the ground—thatch for rice godown roofs. They looked like Maoris in their ceremonial feather cloaks, ready for a dance festival. We called in at the last missionary outpost of Burma—tended by the Darlington Brothers, who visited their flock on the backs of elephants. They had one young riding elephant "garaged" in a shed at the back when we arrived. We met the two American officers at Darlington's—but their Jeeps were headed back to Mogaung.

Their mud-bespattered vehicles didn't look too good to us. What one of them said didn't sound too good either.

"Boys, I'm telling you, you won't get another ten miles. You've no conception what things are like. It's only a mule trail. You'll get bogged in the mud or drowned in the rivers or break your necks crossing those crazy bridges. The guy who said he'd driven through to Shinbwiyang is just nuts."

"I'm sorry if it embarrasses you, but I was in the party that drove through last time."

"You mean to say you got right through to Shingbwiyang?"

"Sure, we did," I said.

"And we're going right through to India, this time," added George with much more confidence than I was beginning to feel.

"Well, I tell you, I met a crazy 'limey' up there, and he told me he drove through to Shingbwiyang. I was polite and pretended to believe him but I thought he was crackers. I wish you boys good luck anyway, but..." and he shook our hands and his head at the same time, as if we were going to a certain and terrible death.

Last time I'd passed through Maingkwan Mrs. Darlington had been away, having a baby, and she seemed to have made a good job of it. It was round and fat, and lay kicking its feet and gaping at us, as we devoured tea and cakes. Later mother and babe went out to India by elephant.

The natives in the Hukawng Valley had the most spectacular achievements of civilisation thrust upon them —all within a few weeks. Hard on the heels of our Jeeps had come more Jeeps and trucks and ox-carts, while overhead immense roaring birds flew daily steadily back and forth, as American and British planes ferried evacuees to Dinjan and carried drums of petrol to Myitkyina. The Kachins had accepted the planes as just one more consequence of this strange activity that was stirring up their lives. They'd give them a name which meant "winged boats" and many of them scarcely looked up as they soared past. We noticed that some, however, still shrunk into the protecting jungle, until the roar of the planes had passed away.

It wasn't till months later that our planes had to start bombing these peaceful, friendly villages. There weren't many people left then anyway. Those who survived starvation after the first onrush of starving looting troops, and cholera after forty thousand refugees had passed through, and camped, and left their dead there—had probably fled before the occupying Japs arrived. I should think, if I ever went back along that Valley again, and some survivors of the Hukawng Valley Tragedy recognised me as one of the first to show them the fruits of civilisation in the shape of a Jeep, they would take me and tear me into little pieces. I hope they would have sense enough to do it. With that first Jeep all their troubles started, and accumulated until the peaceful Valley was a horror of disease and the quiet jungle villages filled with the stench of death. And after that—the bombing planes. Ours first, and when our armies are again in the Hukawng Valley, there'll be Japanese bombing planes. The Kachins couldn't know all this was going to befall them when George Rodger and I passed through, so they were their simple, natural, friendly selves, helping us where they could.

From Maingkwan onwards we saw no more trucks, but hundreds of bullock-carts were moving in both directions. Trucks were dumping rice at Maingkwan, bullock-carts shifting it further ahead—as far as Shingwyiyang. The track was the one we'd covered before, but our improvised bridges were either replaced or strengthened, cuttings widened, holes filled in. We caught up with lines of pack mules and along one stretch swayed an elephant along with two people in the howdah on its back. It crashed off into the jungle as the Jeep approached, and two dahs, with which the passengers had been beating it, flashed into the air as they flung them away. Bullock-carts and rain had cut up the track terribly, and the going was very difficult. Many times we had to get out and dig the cars out of the bogs. Some places we tied our long, thick rope on to the front of the first Jeep, passed it round a tree ahead and tied it to the second Jeep, driving the latter backwards and hauling the front car forward inch by inch. Once we had the first Jeep over an awkward patch, we could haul the second one over with a straight pull. Rivers that we had forded on the first trip were beginning to rise, and at times water flowed right through over the footboards, but the Jeeps chugged away, blowing bubbles from the exhausts under water, rarely stopping as long as the wheels had traction.

For most of that second day it poured with rain, and we were glad of our heavy waterproof coats. We had tarpauling lashed over our baggage and provisions. At the Tanai river-crossing, there were fifty or sixty bullock waggons waiting to be ferried over. It was still raining steadily and most of the drivers were huddled together in a newly built rice-godown near the river's edge. I was delighted to see ferocious-looking, old "Grandpa" bringing the raft over so that we could carry our Jeeps on to the raft. As he led me down to the water's edge he grinned all over his terrible face when he recognised me, and nearly wept with delight when I gave him some pictures of himself working on the cutting we'd built on the opposite bank. He only left off gazing at his pictures to rush across and dance with rage at the inert drivers, and—with probably frightful Kachin oaths—ordered them to get their carts out of the way. We chatted away together and patted each others' backs, and I felt we understood each other perfectly without a word of common language. He had built a fine landing stage, with boxed-in approaches, filled in with rocks. Old "Grandpa" was a true artist, who took a legitimate pride in his handicraft. We had the Jeeps across in no time, and drove up a grand rock-paved cutting, and a new detour to "Grandpa's" village. I was genuinely sorry to say good-bye to the toothless old man, knowing I wouldn't see him again. He was a personality, and he had an artist's temperament and outlook. He had that difference between an artist and a workman, in that his work only satisfied him if it measured up to his own standards. We'd been quite satisfied with the first cutting we'd made. Old "Grandpa" had improved it because his own finicky standards weren't satisfied. He had the divine urge to improve and strive for perfection, and I've no doubt he kept on tinkering about with rafts and approaches and cuttings, until he was carried off by cholera or starvation.

We met two more Jeeps between the Tanai and Tarung Rivers, a Burma Government food controller and his assistant. We'd stopped at the top of a perilous descent, and were ploughing down through the mud on foot to see how deep it was at bottom, when we saw two more mackintosh figures doing the same thing from the other side. Coming through the jungle like that almost to our knees with mud, it was inevitable that someone should cry out:

"Dr. Livingstone, I presume."

I thought it was as well to mention immediately that I'd been with the first party to come through, in case they wasted more time telling us how impossible everything was. They'd got through nearly to Shingbwiyang by Jeep, but walked the last few miles and said the track got worse as we went on. North had shifted down from Shingbwiyang to Yawbang on the far bank of the Tarung River they told us. We were all anxious to get on quickly, so their Jeeps soon plunged down into the hollow and up the other side advancing sideways, valiantly climbing and slipping, but climbing more than they slipped, till with a sudden flirt of the back wheels they reached the top level and spun along, the two officials waving good-bye as they ploughed into the muck again. We got through alright and covered from head to foot with great mud splotches, arrived at the Tarung River about sunset. The rain stopped as we loaded both Jeeps on to the raft, and crossed the river. With the sun feebly shining through storm clouds, intensifying the dark of the jungle; the Naga Hills ahead looked sombre and menacing, stretching away to the horizon, dense and angrily purple. As we neared the pebbly shore a man and a woman walked across to meet us.

"Hello, North! I bet you weren't expecting me to drop in on you tonight." I yelled when we got near enough. He shaded his eyes with his hand......

"Is that Burchett? Well, well, well! This *is* a surprise," and turning to his wife: "What can we give them for dinner, dear?"

We made introductions as soon as George and I jumped ashore.

"But what are you doing here?"

"We're on our way through to India."

"Now look here, chaps. That's impossible. It's impossible to get to Shingbwiyang. Well, let's get up to our place first, while there's still a bit of daylight. You're going to stay the night with us, whatever else you do."

They piled into a Jeep each and we bumped across a neatly paved track right up to the North "menage". George and I had a dip in the river, and changed into clean and dry clothes. Mrs. North, brown of hair, freckled of face and cheerful, got things organised, worked out how a few square feet of space could be cleaned here and there, sufficient for us to lay out our bedrolls. The cook was set to work to find chicken for curry, and we turned out some tinned fruit and cream. After the first outbursts of "impossibles" North, as usual, became very energetic thinking out ways and means of helping us. He was certain, and by what he told us, I was certain too, that we'd not get far past Shingbwiyang. The "track" that was said to have been cut from Shingbwiyang to the Pangsao Pass, was a myth. Kachins and Nagas were supposed to have gone along and knocked the undergrowth down, along an old footpath which had been used many years ago, when troops were sent up to suppress the head-hunters and slave-owners. George and I both agreed we would go as far as possible by Jeep—and walk the rest. North thought he could arrange bearers, and rice supplies for us. For the time being we concentrated on our chicken curry and rice—with mango chutney.

"I'm sorry we can't do you better," apologised Mrs. North. "You see, we can't get any more rations here and I think we're going to get awfully sick of rice before long."

"You know, Burchett, you fellows brought all this trouble on our head," North grinned as he spoke. "If I hadn't happened to come up here with you chaps, they'd never have thought of dumping me in this hole."

"How long are you here for?"

"We're here till the blinking monsoon's over, anyway. We can't get any supplies here till then, unless a miracle happens and some come through from India. We've got to superintend the storing of all this rice you see coming along the tracks. Build godowns. I have to get labour. Good Lord, there's a lot of things to be done, and we're properly marooned here till it's all over. Tell us how things are going down below. Do you think I should try to get the wife back to Myitkyina and away by air?"

"You just try, that's all," murmured an indignant Mrs. North.

"I shouldn't say there's the slightest necessity. We might lose the lower part of Burma, but we'll certainly hold the North—at least till the monsoon starts, and I don't suppose even the Japs can keep on fighting through the Monsoon."

"Well, it's good to hear your chaps say that. You've been down on the front and you should know."

"By the way, we met a couple of American officers down at Maingkwan, who reckoned you were nuts for saying you'd driven through to Shingbwiyang."

"Did you meet those two crazy devils? D'ye know what they said when they got here? I invited them to stay the night and they said they couldn't. They had to push on to this place, Shingbwiyang, they said. They 'figgered' they'd have to buy up food supplies, and some warmer clothes and things there. Good Lord, they must be crazy. You should have seen their faces when I told them Shingbwiyang was a Naga head-hunters' village with about three thatch huts."

We talked far into the night, while North weaved plans for our welfare. He would have liked to accompany us to Shingbwiyang the following day but had to superintend the ferrying across the Tanai of all the bullock-carts. The "grand strategy" of the rice distribution was to push the bullock-carts as far forward as possible, and have convoys of them operating independently between the big rivers. From Shingbwiyang onward mule and pony trains would distribute through the Naga Hill tracts. The ox-cart drivers were beginning to rebel. They hadn't been told they were coming so far, and they knew once they got across the rivers, they would never get back until the monsoon was finished. They wanted to get back to their wives and children, back to the rice-planting. Poor fellows! They were just beginning to realise that they, too, were caught in the toils of war, toils from which they had little chance of wriggling free.

North was sending a messenger with us, and instructions to his clerk at Shingbwiyang to provide us with what bearers we needed and rice supplies. Our old friend, Shingbwiyang Du Hkawng, was to select the youngest, strongest and most intelligent Nagas he had—with some who knew the route to Ledo. We promised to try and send some rations back to North, when we got through to India.

It took us nearly a whole day to drive the twenty odd miles to Shingbwiyang. We got stuck in a river, two miles away from the village and were held up for a couple of hours while we dug away the sandy bank. We would never have got out, except for some Kachins and Nagas who came along and heaved on our rope. What a difference at Shingbwiyang! The framework of half a dozen huge rice godowns was already completed, and Kachins and Nagas of all ages were working away, hacking, splitting, thatching and binding bamboo, rushing the work to completion before the monsoon started. The old chief, Du Hkwang came over looking very grave and dignified. He'd been made chief of works, and was scrupulously superintending the construction. In contrast to the handful of people, when I was first there, there were hundreds of natives about. Du Hkwang had sent his runners out into the hills, and brought in every able-bodied Naga villager within fifty miles of Shingbwiyang. They were tough-looking boys, with thick mats of blackest hair, stocky figures and powerful legs with the bunched muscles of hillmen. The older men were slightly bent, as if they had spent most of their lives in a crouching position, and were now too tired to straighten up.

We left our Jeeps at the village and walked along a few miles of the track towards the Naga Hills. We weren't very impressed with what we saw, but determined to have a crack at it. We decided to take ten men with us in any case, and that night rice was weighed out—twenty pounds per man. They had to allow for another forty pounds each for our baggage and provisions. The chief had them lined up next morning, and they were a good-looking group—young and strong. When we'd signified approval, they squatted down and started making cone-shaped bamboo baskets. Each man had a yoke arrangement that fitted round the back of his neck and rested on his shoulders. They divided up our baggage—we had to have an extra man for "Bertha"—with great good humour, examining our leather zip-fastener suitcase with interest. Equality of distribution was judged by the old chief, and they started off, laughing and joking, yokes over shoulder, sixty pounds of rice and baggage bending their backs, and tightening the wide carrying bank which passed round the load and over their foreheads. They had one hundred and thirty miles to walk, according to the latest calculations of North, who'd worked out the distance from an old survey map. We reckoned we'd pick them up and carry them along in the Jeeps, till we got stuck, then they could keep on walking until nightfall, while we worked at freeing the Jeep. They had instructions not to move off next morning till we arrived. Our Jeeps were stripped of everything but one forty-gallon drum of petrol, and the road-making tools. We started off about an hour after the Nagas—and soon ran into trouble. I went too close to the edge of a solid-looking bank, which crumbled away and left my Jeep balancing on the edge, with the back wheel hanging over a twenty foot drop. We had to build a platform, and wasted nearly two hours' time getting it out. Difficulties piled up on us after that, and finally about midday we reached a sharp incline leading to a stream, filled with huge sandstone boulders. We knew we were beaten this time. Nothing less than dynamite and rock-drills could have burst up those boulders. Regretful we parked our Jeeps side by side, wrote a note to North as we'd agreed, and sent it back together with the keys of the Jeeps by a Kachin policeman, who'd accompanied us. The policeman promised to round up some workmen in Shingbwiyang and get them to build a shack over the Jeeps, till North could come along to recover them. We reckoned the YBR would be pleased to have them there, when their vanguard reached Shingbwiyang.

With our haversacks containing camera equipment and revolvers over our shoulders we started off on foot, gazing back sadly at our Jeeps, looking small and desolate, huddled together under the towering masses of jungle. They'd served us faithfully, and we felt to desert them in such an unfriendly environment—so far away from their accustomed world of tarred roads, petrol bowsers and mechanics, was a despicable act. We soon forgot about them, when our troubles started.

We were hungry, having breakfasted only on coffee. We'd had five hours' strenuous physical exercise, axe, pick and shovel work, and we realised we'd packed all our foodstuffs on the backs of our Naga bearers. Neither of us had done much walking for a long while. When I asked George what sort of a walker he was, he answered mournfully :

"I don't know. I always take taxis."

We knew we wouldn't catch our Nagas till evening—and we both had fears unvoiced at first, but discussed as the day wore on. The Nagas had everything we possessed, including, as we realised later, two hundred rupees—nice silver coins, which would string together beautifully for a necklace round Mrs. Naga's dusky neck. They knew all the paths, and were nearing their own country and villages. What if they chose to clear out and leave us? We didn't have a scrap of food, and we knew there was no chance of picking anything up along the track. There was one, at the most two Naga villages along the whole track, according to North, and they would have no spare food, even if the inhabitants were friendly. Most of them in these unadministered hill tracts had never seen a white man before. North warned us that since 1939 the government had been unable to send out its usual annual expeditions and he'd had reports that headhunting had started again.* Probably our hunger, and the unaccustomed strain of toiling up mountain paths, through tall jungle which blotted out the sky, caused us to exaggerate our fears. In any case we felt very despondent during those first hours of walking. George's watch had broken days previously, and the hour hand was missing off mine. Our first stage was about sixteen miles, and I reckoned averaging two and a half miles per hour; with a ten minutes' rest each hour, we should make the day's march by about sundown. According to the map we had a three thousand foot mountain to climb, and nightfall should find

*We regarded this warning as something of a joke. Luckily for our peace of mind, neither North nor ourselves knew that a few months previously, in October 1941 the Tsawlaw and Tsaplaw Naga tribes had carried out one of their most ferocious raids, bagging 150 heads.

us at a river, where the Nagas had been told to wait.

It was steamy hot, and that first hour's walking was very hard. I found a bottle of fruit pastilles in the bottom of my haversack, and we rationed them out—four at each hourly rest period. We heard, but couldn't see planes passing and repassing us, and reckoned the stretch from Myitkyina to Dinjan which took over an hour by plane, would take us a fortnight by Jeep and on foot. We had worked out the trip in eight stages, but allowed enough rations for two extra days—just in case of accidents.

We soon found that Naga headhunters weren't the only blood-thirsty creatures on our trail. Our legs were soon spotted with sores from leeches, which grew fat and bloated on our precious blood, before they dropped off. The difficulty was to stop the bleeding once we'd got rid of them. They bit a small triangular hole which couldn't close, and injected some of the secretion in their body which prevents blood congealing, and we were fearsome sights with blood streaming down our arms and legs. I was wearing shorts; so rolled my socks down over my ankles so that I could get off those above my shoes fairly quickly. George with his long trousers had a much worse time, and only knew he had a leech when it stung and by that time it was ready to drop off, curly, dark red and fat. They squeezed down into our shoes, and sometimes our toes squelched in blood. Arms and neck too seemed to be fair game for them.

Our haversacks became unbearably heavy and the straps cut into our shoulders. The path twisted up, unendingly. Sometimes the gloom of the jungle lightened a little and we thought we must be nearing the mountain top, only to find out that we were skirting a cliff face, and the light was filtering through from brushwood and trees covering a drop of hundreds of feet into a valley. Baboons shrieked at us all the time, mocking our poor efforts. Through bamboo thickets, along knife ridges a few feet wide with steep walls falling away on both sides down to rumbling gullies, clambering up sandstone ledges, green and slimy with sleeping moisture. The hours dragged out, each one seemed twice the length as its predecessor. The fruit pastilles made us thirsty, and toiling up the mountain face, we found no drinking water. We guessed it to be 5 o' clock when we reached the mountain peak. The descent was as difficult as the ascent, except for a wonderful few hundred yards where the track ran almost level, along thickly carpeted dry brown leaves, through magnificent arbour of tall teak trees. We had our ten-minute rest here, squatting on a log and pulling off our boots and socks to rid ourselves of the leeches clinging between our toes.

Down the steepest stretches, despite my stiffening muscles, I found it easier to relax and run. It was hard on one's breathing, but kinder on the legs. Several times we thought we saw signs of smoke that would mean our Nagas' camp, but it turned out to be mist in the valleys. It was getting dusk and we seemed to have gone down further than we'd climbed—which was disheartening for the morrow, when we knew we had to go at least as high again—when we thought we heard voices. Sure enough we dropped down from one especially steep section, and there was a rushing torrent hundreds of feet below, and on the other side of the torrent were figures moving about and blue smoke hanging low in the valley. We groaned with relief. Water to drink; water to bathe our feet; the Nagas were still with us; food; security; sleep.

The Nagas—we discovered there were now eleven

instead of ten—exceeded their duties as porters. They'd built a rough shelter for us, and had packed all our belongings under cover. They had a good fire going, and rice cooking. We grinned at them and slapped each other's backs and without a word of their language soon had excellent relations established. We had a wash in the river and sat around on the rocks with our feet and legs in the icy cold water. Leech bites which were still bleeding, stopped when we washed in the cold water, and blood and water cleared out the last of the poisonous secretion. The Nagas stood around with wide eyes as we opened tins, and especially when we lighted the primus under the coffee pot. They ran after the tins when we threw them away, and carefully wrapped them in leaves and tucked them away with their cooking tins. After that we distributed our empty tins among them in strict rotation.

To describe the day to day happenings on our tred across the Naga Hills would be as wearisome to the reader as the walk itself was to us. We settled down after the first two days to a regular routine. The Nagas with their heavy loads liked plenty of rest, while, I, with nothing to carry and used to long hikes, felt pretty fit once my muscles got used to their job again. George stayed along with the main party, while I went on ahead with one of the porters who carried only a small pack, including the "makings" for our coffee. We usually had a fire alight and coffee made, and had started building the night's shelter before George and the rest arrived. Once I went on ahead of the porter and ran into a band of really wild-looking Nagas. I could hear them crashing through a short cut, and I stopped short, thinking it was a leopard or tiger.

They stopped dead in their tracks on seeing me. There were three men and one oldish woman with drooping, bared, shrivelled breasts. One old man had a steel-hafted spear, the rest had dahs. We stared at each other and I managed a weak smile, wishing I hadn't given my revolver to the porter to carry. The old man with the spear tensed as I put my hand in my pocket, and they all looked at me with alarmed suspicion. I tried to muster a laugh and pulled out a handful of silver rupees. I handed them one each. They took them, but continued looking at me, rather than at the rupees. The youngest one—who I noticed was wearing a European style singlet—to my amazement then produced a packet of cigarettes and stiffly handed them to me. I took one and—breaking my non-smoking habit for the moment—lit it. Tension immediately slackened. Mama decorously flung a one-piece garment over her body, covering up her breasts. The youth opened up a bundle of cigarettes—five in a packet—and offered me half a dozen packets. He seemed hurt when I refused, so I took them. We all laughed then, and it struck me for the first time that laughter is the only true international language. I gave them some more rupees, and pointed my camera at my own head and clicked the shutter. I handed the camera to the old man to look at, while I examined his spear, and after that we were on the best of terms. They let me take a few pictures of them. Mother even unbent sufficiently to throw off her cloak again and display her well-used breasts. We shook hands all round and they padded away, chattering in great excitement. George, who'd been out of cigarettes from Myitkyina onwards, was a bit staggered when I produced the cigarettes later that evening.

On several occasions we saw tiger and leopard tracks in muddy streambeds. The monkeys never ceased shrieking during the whole of our trek. Occasionally we saw them swinging along, shouting and screaming at each other. Once I saw a big near-white, long-haired fellow sitting on the side of the trail. He obscenely turned his back on me and walked sedately and stiffly away. We came across two Naga villages. Several families live together in very long, single roomed thatch huts with low split-cane pleated walls. Each hut has a small unshaded platform in front where the family takes its meals and enjoys its leisure hours. There were many villages in this area according to old maps, but after the first punitive expeditions along this trail, most of the Nagas shifted further back, where they could go about their honourable head-collecting without interference. When I saw a village I always waited for the bearer, and allowed him to make introductions. I'd-taken his photos several times, and he was able to explain to the tribes people that no serious aftermath followed the operation. At the first village he collected a whole family on to the platform and I got several good "shots."

Our worst experience was a terrible hailstorm, which caught us—fortunately—just after we'd got under shelter for the night. We'd read of hail as big as pigeons' eggs, but this was the first time either of us had seen it. Huge round lumps of ice, composed of scores of hail stones frozen together, hammered down on our rough shelter, and shattered to pieces on the rocks in a nearby stream. They were followed by smaller jagged lumps of ice, that would have laid open a man's head, and after that normal hail and torrents of rain. The stream turned into a raging torrent during the night and crept uncomfortably close to our shelters, but as we were getting ready to turn out and shift to higher ground, it started to subside again. Every morning we started from a few hundred feet above sea level and climbed three or four thousand feet, then dropped down again by evening to a river. The only exception to our river camps was the day we reached the Pangsao Pass—4,122 feet—the highest mountain on our trip and accepted boundary point between Burma and India. As far as I know, we were the first white men to cross into India via the Pangsao Pass. From the summit of the mountain Pass we could see the dark, folded ranges of mountains. We only had the courage to look forward at the boundless view of mountains and valleys, still to be negotiated, after we'd looked backwards at those we'd already crossed.

Only occasionally did we see the sky, and although we heard planes passing and repassing every day, I only saw them once—three fat transports no doubt laden with refugees. Amongst them was Bertha, wondering if she'd ever see her bedroll again.

As the Nagas ate their way through their rice and the weight of our tinned food diminished, we made better time. They preferred taking the short cuts, that went straight up and down the mountain sides, instead of following the better graded trail. Their legs and sloped bodies never seemed at home on level stretches, and the steeper the pinch, the better they liked it. On the sixth day out from Shingbwiyang, we met some tea-planters, in charge of a big gang of coolies cutting a road in to the Pangsao from Ledo. Needless to say, they were amazed to see us, but said, we should never have come through those hills without an armed escort. They wanted a full report on the condition of the track up to and beyond the Pass. The tea-planters were the advance guard, preparing camps and sites for many thousands of Indian coolies, who were on their way to build a "Jeep" road to meet the road the Chinese were supposed to build from Burma.

They told us Ledo was only thirty miles away, but

if we were lucky we'd get to Timpang, 22 miles away and connected to Ledo by a light railway.

"There's a colliery manager there. See him and maybe you can get a hand-car and pull yourselves down to Ledo. There's a supply officer too, who might be able to help you. You'll have to get there about four in the afternoon, if you want to get a hand-car. If the manager's not there, just grab the first one you see and take no notice of anybody. Save you a good eight miles of slogging."

We got away about 5 a.m. next morning, and walked flat out. It wasn't so hilly, and most of the way there was a wide, well-graded track, which the coolie gangs had already cut. We passed hundreds of the latter trudging along, bundles on heads, making for the coolie camps further ahead and also Naga porters "supply convoys" carrying on their backs bags of rice for the camps. The jungle had thinned out and for the first time we had the sun blazing down on us as we walked. This was the first day, we cut down the bearers' rest periods but we were determined to finish the trek that day. Rocks were being busted out of the yellow earth, cuttings deepened, trees felled, bridges prepared —thousands of coolies, men, women and children were on the job, looking curiously at us, as we strode past. By midday we were passing through big coolie camps and hospital where malaria and dysentery cases were stretched out. Anti-malarial works were in process of being set up, but meanwhile a big percentage of workers were laid out. It was just 5 p.m.—knock-off time——when we came in sight of Timpani, and we were caught up in a stream of workers pouring down the newly made road towards the little colliery town. We found the manager's house, and hoped we might achieve the luxury of a cup of tea. We'd been frightened to drink any water along the road, because of all the dysentery, and walking twenty-three miles up and down mountains in the blazing early-summer Indian sun is no joke. The manager was away. As we walked out of his gate, with long faces, we met a tea-planter, who told us the Supply Officer would certainly want to see us and get a report about the track.

"Sorry," I said, "we want to push on to Ledo tonight. We'd hoped to get a hand-car from the manager, but now I guess we'll have to walk."

"Yes. You're too late for hand-cars now. But still, I think, you should see the SO. A few minutes rest won't hurt you."

"What do you think, George?"

"Might as well. We'll probably get some drinking water there, anyway."

We walked along the line to the SO.'s depot. The tea-planter hailed him.

"Hey! There is a couple hoboes here just dropped in from Burma. Want to have a word with them?"

A big fellow in shirt-sleeves with a note-book in hand and pencil behind his ear, came out and looked us over.

"Well, well, now you couldn't have dropped in at a better time. Come over and sit down. What's it to be—tea or cold beer?"

We didn't believe about the beer, till he yelled for a boy, who appeared a minute later, with a bottle of beer for each of us. It had just arrived with other stores from "down the line."

That was the most satisfactory ending to an expedition that I can imagine. We were worried as to how long it would take to find the right people at Ledo to supply our boys with rice for their return journey. The SO fixed them up on the spot. We paid them off, at double the agreed rate, and the SO gave every man five packets of cigarettes and two boxes of matches. They looked very tired, but very happy.

We asked about getting in to Ledo, but there was no chance that night. All the hand-cars had gone.

"You'd better have a rest here tonight, anyway. This case of beer's just come in, and a good blow out on beer will do you the world of good. You look like a couple of scarecrows."

And we did look ragged. We'd lost plenty of weight, I think mainly through the leeches causing such a loss of blood. Our feet and legs were covered with purple triangular blotches where they'd "bled" us. The bearers were just unlashing our baggage when we heard a whistle.

"By Jove, I believe that's another supply train," the SO yelled, jumping up and going over to the line. "If it is, I'll send him right back to Ledo with you, and I'll come along myself."

It was a supply train, and the Nagas—at first terrified at the noise of the puffing, grunting engine, approached it with eyes nearly bursting from their heads. Jeeps, trucks, aeroplanes—now a railway engine. We had a chain of interpreters who gradually broke Naga down through Assam dialects and Hindustani to English. We asked the bearers if they'd like to jump in the train and ride with us to Ledo. They were very fearful until we got in but then they followed us, clinging tightly to the sides as the train moved off. We left them at Ledo station, from where they wandered off, hand in hand, looking at the modest wonders displayed in the shop windows. We had to see the Station Staff Officer, who told us the local military commandant had received a telegram from GHQ Burma about us, and we'd had to go and see him. We went along and found the Colonel had been asked to get a complete report from us about our trip. We there and then dictated report as best we could, describing the route, state of ricers, walking time between stages, types of soil, where surfacing metal available, attitude of natives, etc.

"There's no question of you being allowed back into Burma," the Colonel said in answer to my query about planes from Dinjan, "as far as I can see, they're trying to get everybody out of the country. The Japs have broken through the Southern Shan States, and we'll probably have to use the route you travelled as an evacuation road.

"But hell, I've got to get back and be in at the death!"

"Sorry. Not as far as I'm concerned. Best thing you can do is to get to Calcutta. Maybe they'll fly you into Shwebo from that end. That's where GHQ is now".

He gave us a rail warrant for Calcutta, and a station waggon to pick up our baggage, and take us to Tinsukia, a junction some miles south of Ledo, from where we could get a train early the following morning. Back at Ledo station we found our Nagas, looking dazed but happier than ever, and faithfully guarding our baggage. A couple of hours of Ledo seemed sufficient for them and I think they were looking forward to returning homeward next day. After Jeeps and locomotives and cars in Ledo, they were fairly blasé about the station waggon. They helped us to the last, carrying our baggage out and stacking it in the waggon. They stood around, looking very forlorn as we drove away. Probably thinking as they'd looked after us so well in the jungle, it was up to us to look after them in this strange new world. The SO assured us he'd see they got a ride back to Timpani and got started on the road back to their hills.

CHAPTER XX

The manager of the Great Eastern Hotel didn't look very pleased to see us, as we tramped in, still wearing the same clothes we'd worn on our trek. We'd wired for rooms, otherwise I don't think he'd have let us in. Later, when evacuation by road was in full swing, they became used to ragged, dirty individuals in uniform, arriving and demanding rooms. The day after we checked in at the Great Eastern, I went down with malaria, and had a miserable five days before the fever left me. There was no question of getting back into Burma. Public Relations Office told me all correspondents had been ordered to get out as best they could. The only thing to do was to hang around and get stories from evacuees as they came through.

Towards the end of May—about three weeks after we arrived in Calcutta—I was sipping an iced squash in the Great Eastern lounge, when someone tapped my shoulder—and it was Mrs. North.

"I thought it was you, but wasn't quite certain, you with your new uniform and all," she chuckled.

"How on earth did you get here? Sit down and have a squash. But, my God, I'm glad to see you. I've had a very guilty feeling since I arrived here, and Burma cracked up like that, especially after all the "cheer-up" stories we told you."

"Wasn't it awful? We had no idea. Were just settled in at Shingbwiyang, waiting for the coolies to arrive. We had most of the rice stacked away and expected to have no more shifts till the rainy season was finished......"

"Say. Did you get those Jeeps out?"

"Certainly we did. I learned to drive one, and they were very useful running to and fro from Yawbang to to Shingbwiyang......Well, there we were with nothing to do but wait, when on May 8th a runner arrived from Ledo, saying a plane would come over next day and drop food by parachute. That there were five hundred Europeans and ten thousand Indian refugees on their way up the Valley. That was the first idea we had that things weren't going alright. I wanted to stay on, but Clive was so insistent I thought I'd better go after all. He said he'd stay on and distribute food to the refugees. You should have seen those Nagas when the 'pyen li,' winged boat, as they called it, circled round and shoved sacks of food out onto the clearing between their huts. They dropped rice—and we were made about this at first, seeing the hundreds of bags we already had, but when we opened up the sacks, these were full of tins of bully, biscuits, milk, tea, sugar and cigarettes. The rice stopped the tins from bursting open, and the bags were only half full so's the rice didn't burst out either." She paused to sip her squash.

"You remember old Du Hkawng, the Chief of Shingbwiyang?"

"Of course. He was a fine old boy, and provided the beaters for our trip."

"Well, he said he'd take me to India, and provide ten good men for an escort. All those that went with you, wanted to go, and he took some of them. By the time we set out, we'd picked up twelve more. It was like a royal tour. Word had passed round that Du Hkawng was taking out the wife of the "White Chief," and wherever we stopped, Naga chiefs came down and brought us eggs and chickens. They were really wonderful. It slowed down our trip a bit, because we had to play up to them and exchange speeches."

"I didn't know you spoke Naga dialect as well?"

"I don't, but Du Hkawng speaks Kachin and Naga, so he interpreted, always looking very grave and dignified. After three days some Tommies caught up with us. They'd been convalescing at Myitkyina and were told to 'skip it' while they were lucky, so the Nagas insisted on carrying their kit as well.

"The rivers were all up and it rained pretty heavily. It was very embarrassing for me. Several times I had to swim rivers with all the men. When we got to the frontier, there was a detachment of the Assam rifles, and the officers wanted to give me an escort and send Du Hkwang Shingbwiyang back. The old chap looked as if he'd take the lot of them on single-handed. Stood very straight and told them he'd promised the 'White Chief' to take his woman to Ledo, and take her to Ledo he would. Anybody else would take her over his dead body. I told them they'd better let him go, if they wanted to avoid a row. So, of course, he came on with me. It is eight days altogether."

"And what are you going to do now?"

"Back home to England and Macclesfield. As soon as I can get a boat."

When anybody tells me—and sometimes I've believed it myself—that the spirit of adventure and initiative in England is dead, I think of Mrs. North. A slip a freckle-faces, wispy brown-haired girl from Macclesfield. Never been away from England, and hardly out of her home town, until she came to Burma in 1940, to marry a Burma Frontier Service Official. Learned to speak one of the most difficult of the Burma dialects, was on excellent terms with the primitive Kachin people, joined in their tribal songs, games and dances, and faced a hundred-and-thirty-mile walk alone with the reputedly savagest natives in the whole of the Far East. That takes 'guts' with a capital 'G.'

On May 24th, a group of weary, filthy-bearded men dumped their bags down in the hotel lobby, and demanded rooms. They represented the greater part of "Uncle Joe's Mob," as Stilwell's staff were dubbed. They were a thin, haggard-looking bunch compared to when I last had seen them in Maymyo. The story of their twenty-four-day trek has been well told in Jack Belden's book, "Retreat with Stilwell." Belden accompanied them throughout their trip and is best qualified to tell their tale. My first enquiries were about "Doc" Seagrave and his nurses; they were alright, the Burmese nurses stood the hardships better than anyone. The indefatigable "Doc" was already at work again, establishing a hospital near the frontier to look after the Chinese army, as it came through in bits and pieces.

The most spectacular of the party was Col. St. John, whom I had known from the time he first arrived in Chungking with the Magruder Mission. I remembered him as a full, red-faced, hearty fellow, weighing about fifteen stone, looking like an advertisement for Bovril drinkers. Now he had a tremendous greying beard, his clothes hung as if all their supports had been withdrawn, his face was pallid and hollow. He'd had to be carried part of the way and the others told me they "sure thought he was a'gonna." I went up to see him after he'd had his first decent sleep for a month. He was recovering his normal boisterous spirits.

"Boy, was that a step. I'm telling you that was something. If anybody brings rice near me again, I'm gonna disembowel 'em with a chopstick. We're pleased to see that British Officer who fished us out of the Naga country."

Capt. Fred Eldridge, Stilwell's Public Relations Officer, also a fifteen stoner reduced to twelve, took up the story, and being a journalist himself, remembered the important details.

"Yes, they did a good job and no mistake. Sent in parties along every trail we could possibly have taken. One of 'em was sure to get us, and by God they did. Did we have a celebration that night? Remember those pigs, Colonel?"

"Best meal I've ever eaten," and Col. St. John smacked his pallied lips at the memory of the thanksgiving feast they'd had with two pigs bought from local villagers.

"That 'Limey' political officer Sharp, was a grand guy. What he knew about that country, and the way he got on with the locals was something to see," continued Eldridge.

"They'd organised things fine. The day after we met Sharp, his follow-up party arrived with twenty-four horses for wounded—just in case—and five hundred bearers to carry our gear. Just too bad those fellows had nothing to carry. We'd dumped everything, typewriters, cameras, tommy guns, even most of our food. All we had was just what one man could lump, and after a few weeks on rice and tea, I'll tell you, you can't lump much."

"How did 'Uncle Joe' bear up?"

"Hell, that was one picnic excursion for him. He's just made of steel wire, rubber and concrete for guts. It was the big boys like the Colonel and me, couldn't take it so well. Eh, Colonel?"

A few weeks of Calcutta was enough for me. After months of intense activity where one had some feeling of participation in misery, tragedy and suffering, it was difficult to settle down and join the ostrich with head in the sand, and nether parts well exposed......Dinner jackets and evening dresses, clubs and shining cars, hotel orchestras and cocktail parties, conversations centring around shortage of whisky and gin, more rigid distinction between various grades of European society than the Hindus had with their caste system. Clubs open to "burrah" sahibs, closed to "Chotah" sahibs. All the infinite gradations from the pukkah pukkahs down the scale, to semi-despised Europeans "of the country" and Anglo-Indians. The "Saturday Club" where only "pukkahs" could be members. Where one had to submit to examination by the Club Committee, and only if one's antecedents and reputation were "quite-quite" irreproachable, could one become a member. If one married, one must resign and present one's wife to an examination board, which judged whether wifie's antecedents were sufficiently respectable to permit hubbie's re-acceptance as member. There is a good story about a well-known military man, a member of "Saturday Club", who married, resigned, and duly presented his wife before the Board. After some days he received notice that his wife having appeared before the Board and been found satisfactory they could both become members of the Club. The Officer replied saying that his wife, after inspecting the Club Board, had decided *she* didn't want to become a member.

Such was Calcutta, at the end of the Burma campaign, with the Japs likely to launch an attack on India at any moment. Calcutta, 1942 front-line city. Such had been Singapore, Rangoon and Hong Kong.

The last straw as far I was concerned came one Saturday night at the Grand Hotel. I'd met an Anglo-Burmese girl, of good family and education, whom I'd known in Rangoon. I took her to dinner and dance at the Grand Hotel, and saw a blonde English girl I'd dined with the previous evening, sitting with an RAF Officer. In between dances I went across to their table intending to ask when a mutual friend of ours was returning to Calcutta. She looked as if she'd never seen me before, and without replying to me, stood up with assumed dignity and asked her escort, to take her away. He winked at me as he helped her into her coat, and shrugged his shoulders as much as to say:

"Sorry, old boy. Bloody silly, I know, but what can I do ?"

I'd been swimming and dining with this girl and another friend the previous day, and wondered if I'd contacted leprosy in the meantime. I walked slowly, and wonderingly across to my table. The Anglo-Burmese who was at least as well educated and certainly more intelligent than the blonde girl, had seen what happened and said without bitterness:

"That will teach you to take an 'Anglo' dining and dancing with 'Pukkah' people again. I should have warned you, but thought you knew."

"Don't be crazy. That's got nothing to do with it. That girl must be ill or suffering from a memory lapse."

"Try to get any of your other 'mem sahib' friends here to recognise you, and see what happens. But don't try too hard; or else we'll both be embarrassed."

I was on nodding acquaintance with plenty of people round the tables, mainly officers and their girl friends. There weren't so many 'eligible' girls in Calcutta and one soon knew most of them. As we danced round the floor, I made a point of nodding and smiling at several I'd recognised. The officers grinned back uncomfortably, and the girls looked through me, frozen and unsmiling. Only one, unusually intelligent and gracious and slightly unconventional, gave a sign of recognition in a half smile, half frown, which said: "Naughty, Naughty, We're scandalised."

Quite innocently, I'd committed the only really unforgivable sin in an Indo-European city. Cheating, forging, raping, whoring, perjury, deserting from the Army, any of these sins could be readily forgiven a man by the Mem Sahibs, but "flaunting" a "half-breed" in their faces, sets a man beyond the pale. As one explained it to me.

"We don't mind you sleeping with them, but don't for God's sake drag them around in our hotels and restaurants, where we've got to sit and eat and dance with them. If you do, then don't blame us if we cut you."

The mem-sahibs of India have co-operated in self-defence on a scale never achieved elsewhere. They whisper and pool information and act with a unity worthy of a better cause. Woe betide the man who breaks the moral code established by the mem-sahibs' unofficial mutual defence association. A word to home, club or office will wreck his career, outlaw him from his clubs and make him a social outcast. The virtue of a white skin, is the only "superior" asset many of them possess and once the legend of its all-superior attributes is destroyed, the mem-sahibs might as well pack up and go home. The Indian climate—alas—wreaks ruin with their skin and complexion. The only thing that could save them—a little sun-bathing—has to be avoided like a plague, in case their skin becomes suspiciously brown. Suntam so eagerly sought after at home is shunned like leprosy in India. When they go to Poona, or Darjeeling or Simla or Srinagar, mem-sahib might find herself avoided, might overhear a group at bridge......

"My dear, that Mrs. M. S.......Don't you think she looks a little *dark*?"

"That's what I thought. She doesn't *look* quite like an Anglo, but one can't always be certain, the way some of them get themselves up."

"Yes. I remember that nice young Captain Swoofs Puffington......Hmmm. It was a pity. Ended his career, you know. An Anglo, of course. And I always did say, it was just a mistake he made. The little minx......It's terribly hard to tell sometimes."

"Well, I don't know. I can always pick them. I have a *feeling* about them."

This uncharitable, superior attitude to the Anglos was sickening. Many of Anglo-Indians and Anglo-Burmans had done excellent jobs in Burma, staying at their posts when "pukkah" Europeans who should have had a higher sense of duty and responsibility, skipped off to save their white skins. They formed the vast body of executives and white-collared workers, who—never able to occupy the highest positions—carried the main burden of administration and commerce. They kept the trains running, manned the fire-brigades and ambulances. Anglo-Burman and Anglo-Indian nurses and telegraph operators performed heroic jobs up till the last, and when the collapse came many of them were left to find their own way out of Burma. In India, they found themselves still society's outcasts, no claims on an Indian or Burman community, shunned by Europeans.

CHAPTER XXI

I asked to be transferred back to China, where fighting had broken out in Kiangsi and Chekiang provinces. Early in June I flew over the "hump"—the sixteen thousand feet Himalayan "foothills" to Kunming and Chungking, and a fortnight later left by plane and train for Hunan province. From there I started a three months trip, by bus, sedan chair, horse-back and foot through China's frontline areas, "covering" the Kiangsi-Chekiang campaign. With a Chinese woman of letters, a well-known poetess as interpreter—of Chinese life and customs as well as language—I travelled right across China from Chungking to Foochow on the Pacific Coast, returning to Chungking in time to accompany Mr. Wendell Willkie northwards to the Yellow River Front. If the Japanese provide me with another opportunity of writing a book, I'll write about my experiences in China during that time. I stayed in China nearly five months, mostly travelling about. During the time spent in Chungking, I saw and talked with most of China's present—and future—leaders, including Generalissimo and Madame Chiang, Madame Sun Yat Sen, General Chou En Lai, and a host of lesser known but important individuals. To attempt to cram even an outline of those months into this book would be an insult to the subject matter, so I'll skip a few months and jump back to the Kunming aerodrome on October 24th.

I had arranged to do a bombing trip with the American Air Force. Two other correspondents were also going, Teddy White of "Life and Time" Magazine and "Newsreel", Wong, celebrated Wide World newsreel camera-man. I'd left Chungking three days previously in an RAF plane, bound for Kunming, but we'd been diverted to Chengtu—the old Tibetan capital near the Tibetan border—and then twice turned back because of bad weather, ice forming in the wings, and October 26th we had taken off early in the morning, followed along the snow-crowned lofty Himalayas, and landed in at Kunming, just as the air raid warning was posted up. The big field was jammed with planes, and they did a fine job clearing them off. Rows of fighters left the ground together, without using the runways. B 25 bombers and big Douglas transports roared down the runways at split second intervals. Over sixty planes left the field in about fifteen minutes. One B 25, just cleared the runway, dropped back like a fowl with a broken wing, and dragged along flat on its belly in a cloud of red dust. The pilot had got excited and pulled up his landing gear too soon, and the big bomber flopped back—fortunately not exploding its bombs—and skipped on its undercarriage ripping off both propellers. The RAF plane which had brought me, zoomed off with its nose pointed towards the hump—bound for India. With a bag in each hand, I walked across to the fields behind the aerodrome, hoping to get well away from the petrol dumps before the bombs began to fall. The bombs did not fall that day. Eighteen Jap bombers were turned back long before they got to Kunming, but they effectively upset my plans. The other correspondents—on account of the alarm—had taken off with the bombers ahead of schedule bound for the field from which the raid was to be made. I was annoyed because this bombing raid was to round off my trip to China. Then I was going back to India. They raided Hong Kong, and I wasn't so annoyed about missing the trip, when they told me afterwards the plane I was to have gone in was shot down—the first bomber lost in China up to that time. I left for India next morning in a transport loaded with tungsten for America's war industries.

It was a cloudy morning and we had to fly high to avoid missing some awkward peaks which poke up unexpectedly considerably over sixteen thousand feet. The pilot, Lieut. Benjamin told me that if I felt my breath getting short, I'd better go up front and he'd give me a whiff of oxygen. He and the co-pilot both wore oxygen masks, but there were no tubes for the radio-operator or myself—the only other occupants. There wasn't much to see among the clouds, and I reckoned if we did scrape the plane's belly out on a peak, we would't know much about it. Once I happened to look across at the radio-operator, and he was slumped across his desk, fast asleep. I told Benjamin, and he took off his mask and yelled: "I guess he's passed out. We're pretty high here. I'll chance it and dive down a couple of thousand feet. Hang tight."

I went over and shook the operator, and found even that bit of extra effort made me gasp. He looked dopey and listless, but brightened up as we dived out of the clouds into clear air—at about fifteen thousand. The mountains and valleys looked fine below us, gleaming peaks, white folded hills, black crevasses and—deep down—purple and green woods and what looked like cultivation patches. There was a high ridge ahead, which looked just about the right level to scrape our belly. We started to lift to clear it, when the co-pilot jabbed Benjamin's arm and shouted:

"There's three planes away over there."

Benjamin looked in the direction his "co" was pointing and grunted......"Hmmm. Radial engined fighters. Probably Japs. This is where we do a bunk." And the plane curved steeply upwards feeling for the clouds again. The other planes either didn't see us, or else weren't interested. We plunged into the soft cotton-wool comfort of clouds again with visibility extending to about the tips of our wings. We saw no sign of them again, and Benjamin thought they might have been p. 47's, an American radial engined high altitude fighter. We didn't land at Dinjan as I'd expected, but Dum-Duma about 50 miles to the east. We got in about midday, and went across to the officers' mess for lunch and a sleep. The three hours' high altitude flying left me feeling as if I'd finished a three-day-and-night non-stop rail journey. I'd just got to sleep when I heard the rattle of machine-gun. I thought I must be having had dreams at first, but poked my head out of the window, and there, sure enough, was a fighter plane a few hundred yards away, diving with its machine-guns blazing.

"Hey. There's a Jap fighter out here." I yelled, and Benjamin and other officers came out in their pyjamas.

"Thought I heard something......"

"There's three of them over there. Look at 'em, diving and playing merry hell. Wonder what they're after."

We couldn't hear the guns then, could only see the diving.

"They don't look like our ships. Guess it must be the RAF practising."

"The one I saw was a Jap plane," I persisted. "I could tell by the way the wings were away up forward. I think I even saw the red disk, but I'm not certain."

"Don't be funny. How would a Jap plane get over here without us knowing?"

We talked on the verandah for a while, and they

persuaded me I was wrong; so we went back to bed. Half an hour later an ambulance crunched up the gravel-drive and a white-faced doctor whom I'd noticed previously at the 'drome when we got in called out:

"Hi. C'mon you guys. There's a raid on. There's a helluva bunch of bombers over Dinjan."

They piled out then, pulling trousers as they went—literally caught with their pants down this time. Several of us jumped in the ambulance, others grabbed Jeeps, and we went back to the aerodrome. The boys were at action stations as we drove in. A Negro with a Bren gun, squatting in a slit trench, called out in a high-pitched voice:

"Yes, Jus'let those ole sons o'bitches come this way. Ahm ready frem Ah am. Ahll sure punch a string o'lead through their guts, they come this way. If Ah get 'em on the sights a' this lil baby, they'll wish they stopped home."

"There's about fifty planes over Dinjan now and eighteen more supposed to be on their way here," a lanky sergeant told us as we walked up to the control tower.

"Couldn't you give us a warning?" someone asked the radio-operator, when we went inside.

"Hell, I just got the signal, and looked up and there were eighteen of the sunzubitches, sailing across just south of here. One of them got knocked out by ack ack a bit further over."

"What were those fighters diving on, over towards the hills?"

"That was Joey Walker. He was just loading up here, when the planes were sighted. He'd 15 drums of petrol on not tied down or anything. Thought he'd scoot for it. Just as he got up, three fighters peeled off the bomber escort and took after him."

"Did he go down?"

"Dunno. Seemed to be going alright last I saw of him. Keeping right down low skimming the tree-tops. They should a got him, though. Funny we didn't see his petrol going up all the same." (Joey Walker turned up at Kunming five hours later, grinning all over his face. He thought it was a great joke the way the Japs missed him. The fuselage and body of his plane were pattern stitched with machine-gun bullets, but no serious damage done. He later got a D F C).

This was the first Japanese raid on the Assam area. Though they did no damage at Dum Duma, they played havoc with grounded transport and Tomahawk fighters at Dinjan and satellite fields. A couple of fighters managed to get up in the air but several were shot upon the field. All in all it was a pretty bad day for the USAAF. I felt sick inside. The first day-back in India after five months absence and seeing exactly the same thing happen as had been happening all through the Burma campaign. The Japs, of course, picked their day and time—Sunday after lunch—and it looked as if every war theatre had to have its own Pearl Harbor. One had hoped that the British and American air forces had suffered sufficient Pearl Harbors in Burma, to have learnt a lesson. There'd been plenty of warning signs at Dinjan. Jap observation planes had been over daily for several days previously. I had a hot story to get back, but due to an unfortunate series of incidents I never filed a message, despite the fact that I was the only correspondent on the spot.

I'd hoped to get a plane from Dinjan the following day for Calcutta, but at 2 a.m. Benjamin woke me up and said as fighter protection was now "non es" in the Dinjan area, those transports still able to fly were to leave for Allahabad before dawn. They expected—rightly—

that Japs would be over again next day. We took off at 6 a.m., still with our load of tungsten. That was the finest flight I've yet made. We hugged the snow-capped Himalayas for almost the whole journey. The rising sun turned the gleaming peaks pink, later rosy red. The sun was already high up in the heavens when we got our first glimpse of Everest, lofty, austere and remote. Its immense gleaming pile held the stage for a long time, changing shape and contour as we passed round it scores of miles to the south. In front and behind were other transports keeping their respective distances unfalteringly, through nearly a thousand miles flight, as though strung on a knotted string, India's face stretched out beneath us—flat and green, intersected by twisting brown lines of rivers, and tiny hairs of a railroad.

We landed about 11 o'clock. A Jeep buzzed across and an officer asked me where I wanted to go. I said either Calcutta or Delhi was good enough for me.

"We've nothing Calcutta way, but there's a crate going to Delhi in half an hour. Hop in the Jeep and I'll see you aboard."

We left about midday, two officers and lots of luggage and mail bags, and more bags of tungsten. The precious powder indispensable for steel hardening, and hardly won from the Chinese soil near Kanchow in Kwangsi province, has a long and romantic voyage from those Chinese mines to munition factories in the United States.

We'd been travelling over three hours and I thought it was time to come down at Delhi, so I strolled up to the pilot's cabin and asked him what time we were due at Delhi.

"Delhi? We're not going to Delhi. This ship's bound for Karachi. If you want to get off before you can, of course, but shut the door after you."

Karachi was about the last place in India I wanted to go to. We came down at 5 p.m., having flown nearly two thousand miles, right across the widest part of India in ten hours. Things became very formal at Karachi.

"Did I have a movement order?"

No. I had no movement order. The CO at Kunming whom I'd known since he arrived in China, just called a pilot over and told him to take me through to India.

"I was supposed to be let down at Delhi," I complained.

"Yeah, I know. That was a mistake. The pilot got the wrong orders. He was supposed to have stopped off there. That's too bad for you, of course. We can't do anything for you here. You'd better go and see the adjutant at headquarters."

They gave me a car and sent me in to headquarters, where sympathetic adjutant heard my tale. He wanted movement orders and warrants and things, but was satisfied with my card showing accreditation to Stilwell's headquarters. The adjutant wanted to be very helpful, but he just couldn't get me on a plane. My priority rating wasn't high enough. I had no Indian money, having expected to land at Calcutta or Delhi where I had bank accounts—but the adjutant fixed me up with money, a hotel, a car whenever I needed one—everything in fact except a plane to Delhi. After two days' delay hoping each day to get away, the adjutant admitted the best he could do for me was to put me aboard a train in *two* days' time. I was bound to submit any stories concerning American activities to US censorship in Delhi, before putting them over even the local wires, so could do nothing with my Dinjan story. If

I'd anticipated the delay, I'd have posted a story from Karachi, the first night. I tried to phone through to the Delhi "Express" correspondent, but couldn't get him. Five days after landing in Karachi, I reached Delhi, with a uselessly stale story in my pocket.

I'd had dysentery and malaria several times in China, and tearing around on horse-back and on foot in the hottest time of the year in China, most of the time living on soldier's diet of rice, twice daily, had made me thin and peaky. Doctors told me I was suffering from debility, undernourishment, fatigue, vitamin deficiency and other oddments. The only thing that was holding me together at all, in fact was a telegram from Australia, informing me that my wife and three-year-old son and heir, had received permission to join me in India. They were already on their way out. That one, together with vitamin injections, and food rich foods stuffed into me every hour of the day, while I lay in bed, or basked in Delhi's magnificent winter sunshine, soon pulled me round. In a few weeks I'd added pounds to my waist-line and was fighting fit again. A lazy life, lying around on the lawns of Delhi's lovely garden surrounded Hotel Cecil, swimming, not too strenuous games of tennis, for a while beautiful month. My family arrived early in December and I extended my convalescent holiday long enough to run across to Bombay and collect them. My son not having seen me for sixteen months, inquired somewhat doubtfully of his mother if I was his daddy, but politely accepted our assurances.

Most of the Burma correspondents had drifted away. Dan de Luce and George Rodger had been clamorously acclaimed when they returned to the States. With lecture tours, special articles and radio talks, they were the first to tell the American public of the "Battle for Burma." Belden, whose hollow cheeks had filled out and rounded, and whose melancholia and taciturnity had disappeared under the spell of action in Burma, was finishing off a book and left for the States soon after I arrived. Bill Mundy of "Sydney Morning Herald" had gone to the Middle East. Alec Tozer of "Movietone News" was in Chungking. Only Darrell Berrigan, the inimitable rotund Alfred Wagg of "Allied Newspapers", Vic Thompson of London "Daily Herald" and myself were left of the Burma "gang."

One day I ran into David Maurice. He'd had a bad bout of amoebic dysentery during his Odyssey through Northern Burma and China. After recovering from that he was on the point of leaving for Australia when Burma government acquired him to help direct their propaganda service. He was enjoying his job, putting across some of the ideas he'd been trying to drum into people's heads while he was in Burma. He thought Burma government had learned a lot through its past errors, but didn't feel too sure about things in India.

"The thing that makes me mad," he said, "is that while Burma government in chastened mood have admitted their mistakes and try to correct them, we seem to be making the same sort of blunders here in India."

"Well, you must admit, India's a more difficult problem than Burma ever was. I used to think the issues were clear cut here. Get out and give the Indians their independence. It used to look easy enough from Melbourne or London, but it's not so easy when you get here. Christ, you should talk with Jinnah, and Rajagopalachari, Sapru and Ambedkar and Congress people. Every one of them wants something different, and each one's completely uncompromising in his criticism of the other. Maybe in the past we have created problems and consolidated and exploited natural difficulties, but recognising that doesn't make it any easier to solve the problem in ten minutes now."

"I'm not talking about political problems at all. One of the greatest stumbling-blocks here is the personal relationship between the British and the Indians—between whites and coloreds. At the best we're patronising. At worst—and that's pretty often—we're arrogant and domineering. At the best the Indians feel resentful, at the worst bluddy hostile. Any British Tommy thinks he's a perfect right to go into a shop and call the proprietor a thieving black bastard. Maybe he is too, but would he stump into a British shop and call the proprietor a "thieving white bastard?" Even white children draw away from Indian kids as if they'd the plague—which maybe they *have* got. But don't forget the Indians didn't *ask* white children to come to their country. The Indians feel aliens in their own country, just by the way we treat them. If you took the Indian man-in-the-street and talked to him about Pakistan, Mahasabha, Congress or Hindustan, he'd probably not understand what you were talking about. If he did he'd probably be bored. But ask him if he'd like to kick an Englishman in the pants, or heave a brick at him, and he'd say: 'Brother, lead me.' "

"We're so bloody superior all the time. The burrah sahibs will talk in loud voices about the dishonesty, untrustworthiness, inefficiency 'never trust 'em old boy' sort of stuff in their offices with half their Indian staffs drinking in every word. D'you think that doesn't breed resentment? If you correspondents paid more attention to this sort of thing, instead of trying to find some magic formula for joining all India's political loose ends together, you'd do a damn sight more good."

I took a quick trip up to Simla, where the Burma reconstruction government was "exiled." It was brutally cold, and the first snow of the season was beginning to drift down as I left the rail motor at Simla Station for the Governor's offices. Shivering, blanketed rickshaw coolies were stamping their feet and blowing on their hands outside the station, and I hired one of them to pull me to the Government of Burma's offices. I was surprised when four of them wheeled the rickshaw across, and after tucking me in, two pulled in front, the other two pushing behind. When we got on to the main street I saw that all the rickshaws were of the four men class. Simla is built all over a mountain, its streets are narrow, twisting and steep and pulling a rickshaw load around those streets is hard work, even for four coolies.

Governor Sir Reginald Dorman-Smith wasn't in his office when I arrived about 9-15 a.m., but came in soon after, shaking the snow off his furlined coat. He wasted no time in formality, but took me straight into his room where a "sweeper" was belatedly trying to inject life into a coal fire. He immediately called in a Secretary to make arrangements for me to see without delay everyone from Burma Government I wanted to interview. It was freezing cold, the snow was whirling down thick and fast, and I'd only the light uniform I'd brought up from Delhi. The Governor apologised for the fire......

"We're very short of fuel in Simla, and I don't have my fire lighted till I arrive. Normally we'd be down at Delhi through the winter, but there's a shortage of office space and housing there, so we decided to stick it out here."

We got down to tin tacks almost immediately. I didn't want to be away from Delhi for long and Simla's cold reception made me determined to leave that evening, if possible.

"What's going to be Burma's status after we've retaken the place?" was the first question I asked him.

"That's nothing to do with us, of course. That's a question to be settled by His Majesty's Government."

"I take it we don't expect the Burmans are going to welcome us with open arms. Maybe they want the Jap out, but wanting them out and wanting us back are two different things. Wouldn't it help your case and the army's too, if we had something to offer the Burmans?"

"I agree with you indeed. We'd be in a vastly stronger position if one definite promise was made—some goal regarding Burma's status. Something which will be attained by the Burmans within a stipulated time limit. I very much hope some such statement will be made by HMG in the near future."

"What is your approach to this problem of reconstruction?"

"We realise we've made a hash of things in Burma. Not just within these past months, but over a period of years. We've done a bad job, and we want to correct that. Burma's suffered through being a member of the British Commonwealth of Nations in that she's been through a particularly horrible war and been allowed to fall into Japanese hands. We have to make that up to her, and so arrange things in Burma, that the Burmans themselves will want to remain members of the British Commonwealth of Nations. We say: 'If we're going to hand Burma over to the Burmans, let's do it gracefully, but let's first put the country in order, so that economically as well as socially and administratively, it will be a credit to its guardians. That's our approach to the problem. To recognise that we should make reparation to the Burmans for what they've suffered, with the 'arriere pensee' that we hope they'll want to stay within the British Commonwealth."

"What are you going to do with Burmans who've co-operated with the Japs; those who've fought in the

Burma Independence Army, for instance?"

"We're against reprisals. We feel that if we recognise—and we do—the country's right to strive for independence, we can't be too hard on this Burma Independence Army. Many of its members have been influenced by genuine patriotic motives. Others joined up because of the bad economic situation. The army gave them a living. We draw a distinction between such people and those who are traitors and acted purely in Japanese interests."

"What about administration? How are you going to implement your ideas for putting the country into good shape?"

"We're not going to be cluttered up with an unwieldy instrument as was the last Burma government. Government will be more direct. I shall be assisted by equally represented Burman and British advisers, and all the way down through the district and village administrations our District Commissioners, Assistant Superintendents etc., will be assisted by Burman advisers, stepping up from the smallest unit to government itself. Something like the Soviet system of village, regional, district councils leading up to the Supreme Soviet itself."

"Will these Burman advisers be nominated from above or elected?"

"The people themselves will choose them. Of course, we're only in the blue print stage yet. Details of organisation have still to be worked out. The important thing is that the people who are now working out the future administration and development of Burma, are those who'll be responsible for putting it into operation. They're for the most part young men—our reconstruction secretary is thirty-six and there are many younger. Only those older men have been retained, whose experience is useful, and who've remained young at heart. They're enthusiastic, as you'll see when you've spoken with them. They like and believe in the Burmans. Each will be responsible for setting into operation that section of the general plan which he himself has designed."

I saw most of those connected with the Burma Reconstruction Government, and, lunching with Mr. MacDougall (Counsellor to Governor) I asked if he'd heard anything of Clive North.

"North? Why, yes. North did a magnificent job in the Hukawng Valley. He only came out recently—at the end of October. He's been a pretty sick man since."

I said I'd like to see him and hear of his experiences.

"I don't know if he's out of hospital yet, but I'll send a peon round and find out. If ever a man earned a decoration North did. Saved the lives of thousands of refugees. He was in bad shape when he arrived here though, I can tell you."

North came over an hour later. After our first warm verbal embraces, I explained, I wanted a long but quick talk with him, because I had to leave for Delhi by the evening train.

"But that's impossible," and his high brow furrowed in consternation. "You can't possibly hear all I've got to say in an hour or two."

I laughed. "Ever since I've met you, your first reaction to any proposal is that it's impossible. If it wasn't that you yourself immediately proceed to prove that the thing's possible, I'd hold it against you. By the way, I met your wife after she came through in May, and later read in the "Daily Express" the story I'd sent about her. They published it together with a rotten photo of her too. But let's hear your story."

"By Jove. What a time I had after she left. The

very next day after the refugees started pouring in. The first were the Indian labourers already at Shingbwiyang, and who wanted to bolt when they heard other refugees were on the way. I sent 80 of them with two of our officers to build rest camps at the Namyung River and the Pangsao Pass. Then troops started arriving and by the middle of May, troops and civilians poured in at the rate of 800 daily. Convalescent tommies and garrison troops from Myitkyina, Europeans, Anglo-Indians and Indians. Some were sick, others half starved. It was raining only slightly by then and the going up the Hukwang wasn't too bad; but lots of them when they got to Shingbwiyang took one look at the Naga Hills ahead, and lay down and died. With nothing really the matter with them.

"Fortunately we had plenty of rice at that time, and I rationed it out. Volunteers dragged dead bodies away into the jungle. Sometimes they just piled wood on them where they lay and burnt them. Those that were fit didn't stay long at that time. Two or three days rest and most of them pushed on to get across the Naga Hills before the real rains started. After the first rush was over I left an officer in charge at Shingbwiyang and went down the track to Yawbang on the Tarung River. Lord, was that a terrible trip. Dead and dying people everywhere. Cholera had started. I was terribly scared I'd get it too. Everytime I saw a dead body, I'd hold a handkerchief over my mouth and run past it. Some were sick, others only exhausted. I could do nothing for them, only help those who could still stagger along. At the Tarung, the Kachins were doing a grand job, with rafts and boats shifting about a thousand people across daily. I went on down to Taihpa at the Tanai River, and the same thing there. Do you remember the old chap you called 'grandpa'?"

"Sure, I do. I have a great affection for that old chap."

"Well, he did a grand job with his raft, setting people across. Refugees were piled up at the river crossings, and were living in most of the Kachin houses and barns. One official told evacuees to stay at Maingkwan till the rains stopped, while the RAF had dropped leaflets printed in Hindi along the route urging everyone to make for India, but they didn't know what the hell to do. Most of them were making for India as fast as they could.

"Further down the track towards Maingkwan I met a Captain who said he was escorting Bishop Strachans Home for Girls; he said he'd gone ahead for supplies and help, so I helped him buy stuff from the Kachins and collected what rations were available and sent him back. I got two elephants with mahouts to take the girls and their kit up to the Tania River. The girls didn't arrive, and I heard afterwards they'd gone on foot. The Captain escorting the party had pushed on ahead and left them. Things were going from bad to worse. Food at Shingbwiyang and Yawbang was running out, and then I got a note sent by a Kachin chief, that ravenous Chinese troops had arrived at Shingbwiyang. They'd been seven days eating nothing but grass, and were raising hell at the food depots.

"It was middle of June when I got back there. The refugees had occupied all the Kachin and Naga huts. There were about two thousand, I suppose, by that time. Most of the Chinese had grabbed some rice and gone away. All our military and government officials had gone straight on except a couple of RAMC privates, who stayed and helped me. One chap especially, Katz, should get the VC. Risked his life time and time again. The RAF started dropping food again, but we had a job collecting it. The Chinese started shooting at us so's they could get the food themselves. There were people dying everywhere. We had an average daily death rate of about twenty. We bullied friends and relatives of the dead to do the burying, and those unclaimed were burned on the spot. We had to inspect the huts daily, because morale was so low, people were eating and sleeping in the same rooms with putrefying corpses. What a mess it all was. Katz and I tried to ration out jobs and withhold food from those who shirked their work. We had to organise a guard to protect those who picked up the rations dropped from the air. Katz established a "hospital" with little except clean water. When he was out of action for a few days with a nail in his foot, I appointed the other RAMC private to run it. After several days, I had a look and there were nearly as many dead as living patients. The building was burnt down later, and we had to clear out another shack for a hospital. It wasn't till July that the RAF dropped medicines by parachutes. Later they dropped a doctor and two nursing orderlies also, so we had some sort of hospital organisation after that.

"More of the Chinese army arrived, the men practically crazy with hunger. There was a mad scramble when bags of rice were dropped. Once I was standing with a Chinese officer and we saw a group of men tearing open a bag of rice on the dropping ground, only six yards away from us. The officer shot the men with his revolver, but this had no effect on another group a few yards further away. They were just ravenous. In August the RAF dropped some tarpaulins, so we built new shelters with tarpaulin roofs. I'd heard that the remnants of Bishop Strachans Girls' Home had arrived at Yawbang, but I'd too much on my hands to do anything for them until I got Kachin reinforcements from the surrounding hills. I sent them down the river in boats, but by the time they got there, there were only seven of the original party left.*"

"After the main rains were finished, two Gurkhas arrived from Ledo. They reminded me of the doves that were sent out from the Ark to find dry land. They'd

---

*I learned of the full details of Bishop Strachans orphans much later. The story of their sufferings is the most tragic of the war. Several of them were killed early in the Burma campaign when the Japs bombed the train in which they were travelling, at Pyinmana station. This was on the first day of their evacuation. They were subsequently pushed from pillar to post over the country as the official appreciation of the military situation changed. Eventually about sixty of them reached Upper Burma, northwards of Myitkyina. One group of 25 of the younger orphans were taken into the wild "triangle" area, behind Sumprabum, where they were discovered by the Japs. The latter behaved decently to the children and left them much-needed food when they left. Afterwards food became scarce, and seven of the little girls died. The rest suffered terrible hardships before they were ultimately rescued by British officers with elephants, and they were taken to a point from which they were evacuated to India by air, in October 1942.

36 of the older girls treked through from the Sumprabum area into the Hukawng Valley, and it was this group which North vainly tried to save. They travelled for a fortnight through blinding tropical rain, clad in pitifully thin frocks, subsisting on a cup of tea before they set out in the mornings and a plate of rice at the end of the day's march. By the end of a month they had reached Yawbang, where the officer-in-charge and a non-commissioned officer left them to seek aid in Shinbwiyang. The officer tried three times to return to them, but unsuccessfully. Eventually he died in Shinbwiyang. At Yawbang, a non-commissioned officer and the two civilian officials in charge of the orphans died, and one by one the girls exhausted by their frightful hardships, suffering from disease and hunger, lay down and died. Seven eventually reached Shinbwiyang when the rains ceased, but of these only one succeeded in reaching India. The rest died either at Shinbwiyang, or during the final trek over the Naga Hills.

come to look for their families. The fact that they'd been able to get through from India in nine days made everyone anxious to get going again. I sent another party of Kachins and Gurkhas to help at the Namyung river-crossing and made preparations for the grand exodus. Everyone got ten days as rations as well as aspros, quinine and cotton wool, etc. They started to move off on August 28th, nearly four months after the Japs had occupied Myitkyina. As they shifted out, more that had been held up further down the Hukwang through the worst of the rains started to come in. They had terrible tales to tell, of people being drowned in mud, too exhausted to pull themselves out, of looting and robbing. Indian women arrived with torn noses and ears. Looters had snatched out their rings and jewels. Several Kachins ferrying refugees at the crossings had been killed by troops firing at them trying to force them to give them preference. One boat had been sunk by rifle fire. An old Shan hobbled up to me one day and showed me where he'd been shot by a soldier. Mounted troops had cut Kachin crops and fed them to their horses, thrown the ripe grain on the ground so's the horses could more easily feed. In almost every case officers had hurried off and left the troops to get out the best way they could, so there was little discipline. Near Maingkwan whole villages were looted and burned down.

"Most of the refugees now arriving continued on to India, almost immediately after drawing rations. I stayed on until all but those who couldn't travel had evacuated and then I left. Darlington, you remember the missionary from Maingkwan?, came in to relieve me. I was just about finished with malaria and dysentery by that time. I must say I never expected to come out of that lot alive."

"How many refugees do you reckon passed through Shingbwiyang?" I asked.

"At least forty thousand, I'd say, and that's not including the Chinese armies."

"My God, what a time you've had. Well, that'll teach you to go looking for new routes to India. Say, what do the Kachins get out of this? And the Nagas?"

"God knows. We can't even start to estimate what they've lost. Hundreds of them—especially women and kids—have died. Their villages have been destroyed. They'll certainly never rebuild them anywhere near the Hukawng Valley Road again. They'll get as far away from us as possible. That so many refugees were saved was due entirely to them. They sold and gave freely their goods and services. And what did they get? Disease, starvation and even bullets. These people can never be recompensed for what they did and what they've suffered. They were under no compulsion to do anything. They knew that government had ceased. They'd seen the officials and the army legging it out through the Valley. They gave their help because people needed it; just as they helped us when we went through."

"What happened to old Chief Shingbwiyang Du Hkwang?"

"He was wonderful right through. Never complained and worked like a trojan. He kept his people together and used his influence to bring other tribes in to help us. I've recommended he be given an inscribed grass-bound percussion gun. I reckon there's no higher reward in this world that he can imagine than a new gun.

"Another chap who should be rewarded is a Gurkha sweeper, who organised a sanitation squad. His main job was dragging out corpses and burning them. The

Gurkhas as a body were the best of the refugees who camped with us. They got on well with the Kachins, and their own settlement with houses they built themselves. They hunted and shot game in the hills. It was darned good to see the way they looked after each other. Several times, where heads of families had been killed, you'd see one Gurkha escorting several families of women and children in addition to his own. But I must admit they were pretty cunning at pinching rations. The Chinese were the worst for that. One day I was out of my hut for an hour or two, and when I came back everything seemed alright. Afterwards I discovered 24 bags of rations had been swapped for 24 bags of useless tea. Another time, while I was away from Shingbwiyang about four thousand newly-arrived Chinese armed with rifles and hand grenades tried to loot the rice godowns, but this RAMC private held them up and outshouted them till their officers came and took charge of the situation."

I jumped up looking at my watch. "I'm terribly sorry, North, but I'll have to rush and catch that train. We little thought all this was going to follow that innocent trip of ours up the Hukawng, last February, did we? What are you going to do, by the way, when we go back into Burma?"

"At present I'm submitting proposals for the future administration of the tribal areas. I hope to do something for my poor bluddy Kachins again."

From some information I'd picked up among the Burma government people I was more than anxious to hurry back to Delhi—and on to Calcutta and further. It was still snowing hard as I left Simla, and it looked more like some Tyrolean village than an Indian hill station with its pointed fir trees, heavy with snow and its steep white hills fading away into lowering yellow snow clouds. It was the 17th of December, and it looked as if the "exiles" in Simla would at least have a homely, traditional English X'mas.

CHAPTER XXII

I stayed in Delhi only long enough to pack bags, pick up my family and entrain for Calcutta, where we arrived the Sunday before Xmas. That night we went to the pictures to see the voiced version of Charlie Chaplin in "The Gold Rush." We'd just reached the pathetic scene where Charlie was serving up his boots for dinner, twirling the laces round his fork as though they were choicest spaghetti, when the "banshee wail" of the sirens sounded. It was my first visit to Calcutta since June, and I thought at first, it was a practice alert. There was a good-looking moon up, however, so we took no chances and hurried back to the hotel where the boy was sleeping. Bearers were banging brass gongs, rattling and hammering on hotel doors, people yelling and rushing down the corridors, but the infant didn't even turn over.

Outside, from the Great Eastern verandah, I could hear the heavy, alternating doom-ba-doom-ba-doom of Jap bombers, on their first and long-awaited visit to Calcutta.

I walked along the footpaths where ARP wardens were kicking the pavement sleepers to life. Most of them sat up rubbing their eyes, then turned over and slept again. Others rolled over behind the anti-blast walls. Fifteen minutes after the sirens sounded, bombs began to fall. They didn't seem very big ones. Taxis were still cruising about, so I grabbed one and drove in the direction of the bombing. The planes were away by the time we got there. One small house was on fire in Wat Gunge (in the docking district) but ARP workers were on the spot and the fire was soon out. There wasn't much excitement.

Next day, I happened to be in the Port Commissioner's office when a deputation of wharf-labourers arrived to petition for an increase in wages. The leader said to me......

"We don't mind staying and working, even if they do bomb us, but we want food in our bellies and decent shelters. At present we've got neither."

I never stayed to find out how far their complaints were justified but left that evening for Chittagong, en-route for Burma once again. Fighting had started in Arakan, and although I'd counted on spending at least this Xmas with my family, I could hardly afford to miss "covering" the first round of the campaign to drive the Japs out of Burma.

Within three weeks of their arrival from Australia, my wife and son were plunged into the middle of war. Fortunately they had a very mild baptism. The Japs bombed Calcutta for several successive nights. They dropped a couple just outside the Great Eastern, but the boy never woke up to know a raid was in progress.

Xmas day, I spent back in Burma, at an advanced operational headquarters on the Arakan front, after running into a fairly heavy bombing at Chittagong on the way through. I'd nursed a huge Xmas pudding all the way from Calcutta, and by the light of Kerosene lamps, supplemented by the winking behinds of thousands of fireflies, headquarters staff and myself demolished the plum pudding. Mellowed with extra Xmas rations of rum and beer together with a bottle of whisky someone had treasured for the occasion; with a pack of jackals yapping and howling round the outer perimeter of the tents, stiffness and formality softened and tales passed round of where this or that one had spent his last Xmas. For several, it was their first Xmas spent under canvas and everybody became sentimental as their thoughts drifted back to home, and former, peacetime Xmas celebrations. For my part, I cursed myself for a fool. The General told me there was no activity of any sort. I might as well have stayed in Calcutta and spent Xmas with my family. Our troops had occupied two villages, Maungdaw and Buthidaung without resistance from the Japs, and a period of inactivity was expected.

On Boxing Day, Gordon Waterfield of Reuters arrived, and we decided to go and see what was to be seen at Maungdaw and Buthidaung. With a Public Relations Conducting Officer we left on the morning of the 27th for Buthidaung driving over a road specially built by our engineers for the Arakan campaign, arriving at Buthidaung in the evening. The Brigadier there told us how the Japs had prepared to hold the place. Two days before the occupation, the Japs were sighted digging trenches and preparing. They left in a hurry was seen by half-fried rice dishes lying about, particularly the brothel showed signs of hasty flight. The Japs had taken the Japanese and Maug girls with them, but left the walls covered with pictures and photos of geisha girls. The troops eagerly souvenired these—and other more practical moments.

The next important village—the only one left before Akyab—was Rathedaung, thirty odd miles down the Mayu river from Buthidaung. A young lieutenant had taken a patrol into Rathedaung on Xmas night, and prowling about in the moonlight had found no signs of Japs. A local told him that about fifty Japs and several thousand Maugs had left the day previously. The

Maugs are Buddhist tribespeople living in the Arakan Hills, between Akyab and the Indo-Burma frontier. For generations, they've perpetuated a bitter feud with the Bengali-type Moslems inhabiting the frontier districts. The Moslems were helping us, partly because they lived more on the India side and we'd had more contact with them, partly because so many of the troops we were using in that area were Moslems. The Japs naturally exploiting the ancient feud, had armed the Maugs, and set them against the Moslems and us.

The Lieutenant had reported back to headquarters that the Japs had left so the Brigadier had decided to occupy the place. We asked if we could go down and he agreed. The advance troops were to shift into Rathedaung that night, the main body the following day. The Mayu is a tidal river and as we'd just missed the evening tide, we had to wait till the early morning—at 4 a.m. We were loaned a fine big sampan, and after a dinner of bully and rice at the Officers' Mess, we went over to our boat, accompanied by the PRCO and a young staff major, who also wanted to investigate the situation at Rathedaung. As we neared the river, we could hear dull explosions in the distance. Hwoom! Hwoom! Hwoom!

"Sounds like the Japs are evacuating Akyab," said the Major. "If that's not ammunition dumps going up, I'll eat my hat."

Waterfield and I opined, it might be a battle going on at Rathedaung.

"Not a chance," said the Major, "That's not guns. I'll swear the Japs are carrying out demolition works. Those are ground explosions we can hear."

Hwoom! Hwoom! Hwoom Hwoom Hwoom!

"Maybe we're bombing Rathedaung, or they're bombing us. Isn't it a bit far to hear anything from

Akyab? It's about sixty miles away isn't it?

"About that. But the air currents in these hills are very peculiar. If you get them the wrong way you can't hear anything a few miles away. Other times you can hear things scores of miles away, quite plainly. That's what makes it so difficult working wireless hear—especially at night."

Hwoom! Hwoom! Hwoom Hwoom Hwoom!

"Must be a mighty lot of ammunition dumps they're blowing." Waterfield said. "Sounds to me more like heavy mortar fire."

"That's what I was thinking," the PRCO agreed.

"I'm sure it's gelignite explosions from demolition works. I'd better send a chit back to the Brigadier," and the Major scribbled a note and sent it back by sepoy to headquarters.

We laid down to sleep in the bottom of the boat, with the sound of the explosions still in our ears. It was bitterly cold on the river, and I was glad to zip fasten myself into my newly acquired sleeping bag. We, and that includes the two sampanwallahs (boatmen) and the sepoy escort, overslept, and it was 6 a.m. before we shoved off from Buthidaung. Waterfield and I cursed because we'd wanted to hitch up with a supply column seventeen miles down the river. It was due to move off with the afternoon tide. We'd lost two hours of tide, just sufficient to prevent us catching the supply convoy.

There was a fairly heavy mist on the river, which is about one hundred yards wide at Buthidaung. Until the sun came up, we could hardly see either bank from midstream. The sampanwallahs, each wielding two oars, stand on a small platform at either end of the boat, and keep up steady effortless rhythm, shoving the heavy sluggish craft slowly but surely through the water.

We lay comfortably enough in the bottom of the boat, sleeping for the most part till the sun beat down and made it impossible. We rigged up a shelter with bamboo poles and towels, so that we could squat in the shade. One couldn't help but admire the boatmen, as, naked to the waist, brown backs glistening with sweat and sunlight, they never faltered in their slow, even strokes, for all the heat of the sun. The boat, made of teak, was about sixteen feet long and very sturdy. Even rowing with the tide, progress was only about three miles per hour, against the tide, almost nil.

We halted about midday, soon after the tide changed and had some bully and biscuits washed down with tea made on Waterfield's spirit stove. We had a short sleep on the bank, and towards 4 p.m. started off again. We'd missed the supply column, of course, but hoped to make Rathedaung not too long after it arrived. Almost as soon as we got into midstream again, we heard planes, and could see six bombers, circling about where we reckoned Rathedaung lay. It was too far away to distinguish the planes but we saw them circling for some time, then diving deep down, and we heard the thud of exploding bombs. We reckoned they were probably Jap bombers having a crack at the supply column with which we should have been travelling. We congratulated ourselves that we hadn't contacted them after all. Then we saw six fighters coming across our way.

"I think they're Japs," I said. "They look like Zeros to me."

"No, no. They're our new Mohawks. They've got radial engines just like Zeros," said the Major.

Waterfield and the PRCO, were silent, but gazed anxiously at the planes.

"I'll swear, they're Zeros. They've got their wings well forward and have a squarish look about them. I've seen plenty of them." I persisted, "This reminds me of an argument I had with the Americans at Dum Duma....."

"It reminds me of a story my father tells," interrupted the Major, "he was having an argument with the postmaster at Bedford, about some planes flying overhead. He said, 'They're Jerries, I tell you.' The postmaster got angry and said, 'Don't be foolish man. Think I don't know our own boys when I see 'em?'......"

I didn't hear the end of the story, because Waterfield interrupted "Well, I'm sorry boys, but they're Japs alright. There's the red disk."

And as he spoke, the planes manoeuvred into single file and passed a few hundred yards in front of us, the dull red disks plainly visible on their tails. They turned in a wide sweep to come round the back of our boat.

"I guess they won't worry about a single sampan, anyway," the PRCO commented optimistically.

I was trying to pull Waterfield's big bulk into the space under the rear platform, where I was already crouched. Waterfield is six feet and a few inches tall and broad to match. He didn't fit very well under the platform. The PRCO and the Major, were poked half in and half out of the recess at the other end. Waterfield had lighted the spirit stove ten minutes previously, and the water was boiling. He bent over it.

"Well, I think I'll make some tea anyway," he said. "I always think it better to do something at a time like this."

He put some tea in and stirred it round, replacing the lid on the kettle. The planes sounded to be much lower down and coming towards us from behind.

"Better put out that spirit stove in case it's knocked over," I suggested.

There was an intensified roar of diving planes.

"By God, they're coming at us," yelled the Major. His and the Lieutenant's eyes were fixedly and fearfully staring at the rushing planes. Waterfield squatted, impassive as a Buddha, lifted down the kettle and blew out the spirit stove.

I was amazed to notice that the one oarsman I could see, was still rowing with the same steady rhythm, his back contemptuously turned to the planes.

It sounded as if the plane was going to dive right into our boat. I hoped to the last split second, that they were diving down only to see what we were. There was an awful hammering sound and instantaneously I felt as if someone had swiped me good and hard across the back, with a cricket bat.

I have to admit, I yelled, "Aaaah, I'm hit."

Confused thoughts tumbled head over heels through my mind. "This must be the end. Bullets in the back. Can still think and feel. What a pity! Just when family at last arrived. If first plane does this what'll be left after sixth? Hope I get clean knock out. Not gradually shot to pieces."

All these thoughts flashed past in a split-second. I looked up and realised the sampanwallah was still rowing as if nothing had happened. The plane was just zooming up a few score yards ahead. The others seemed alright, but the two officers were still following with fascinated eyes the course of a second plane. Another terrible hammering. This time I saw blood pouring down Waterfield's arms, and a plane tore through the air twenty feet above our heads. A face under a crash helmet peered round at us as the dark shape hurtled by.

The sampanwallah's oars were crossed, and he was leaning steadily forward on them, still rowing.

"Are you badly hit, Gordon?"

"I don't think I'm hit at all, am I?"

Another maddening roar, cut short by the clatter of a thousand hammers belting over one's head. A grey, brown shape flashed, screaming past. I thought, "Thank God, I don't have to watch them swooping down like the Major and PRCO do." There was a big gash in my leg, this time, right alongside my knee, and warm sticky blood was trickling down my right arm. I didn't remember feeling anything hit me but just huddled my head in my hands as the plane roared by.

The sampan wallah had disappeared. The oars splintered near the top hung listlessly at the sides, jerking a little with the action of the tide.

Another and another plane. The Major jerked his body, straightened out and turned over on his back, but I could see no blood. Waterfield was bleeding from his side, arm and leg. Another roar and rattle. The Major quivered slightly and turned on his back again, a red patch spreading under his right shoulder. His eyes were calmer now as he watched the next plane coming, but his face was greenish white. Light showed through holes all round the boat. Warm drops dripped on to the top of my head and I thought of the sampan-wallah and sepoy on the platform above me.

The first plane followed the sixth one round again so closely that I thought I must have miscounted the number of them. Alongside my knee was a gaping bloody hole. The trouser leg was well torn and I was sitting in sickening, slimy blood up to my hip. As the bullets rattled and hammered through and across the boat, I was reminded of a day in Australia, when I hung suspended over a river, arms clasped round a railway sleeper on a bridge, while a goods train rattled and hammered past, a few inches over my head, the terrible noise of the wheels clattering over the rail joints, beating into my brain.

I gave up counting the attacks. It seemed endless.

I didn't know how bad my back wound was, but cautiously feeling with my uninjured arm, discovered a biggish patch torn out of my shirt, and bits and pieces of lacerated flesh all over my back. There wasn't much blood.

For a while there was a pause, and we thought the planes had gone. I fumbled for a scrap of paper and pencil to write a note to my wife—just in case. I'd just started to write when the PRCO yelled that the planes were coming back.

I felt very bitter about having gone away when I could have spent a comfortable Xmas with my family in Calcutta. I didn't see how any of us could survive another round. It was tempting the fates too much. The boat was pretty well riddled with holes. I noticed particularly one big one right through the stern, probably caused by the first burst that got me in the back. Good, stout, water-logged teak had, fortunately, taken the main force of it.

When it was all over, the PRCO jumped up and grabbed the oars and pulled up into the bank. We were all amazed that we could stand up. The PRCO was covered in blood, but didn't think he was hit at all. There were no signs of sampanwallahs or the sepoy. We managed to hobble over the side and clamber through the mud, upon to the bank. The PRCO carried out a quick inspection. The Major had three big holes in the back of his right shoulder, and another small one right through the shin-bone. I had about a dozen holes in my back and right arm and one big and two smaller gashes in my right leg. Then he looked at Waterfield.

"Sorry, old boy, but it looks as if there's a piece of your lung sticking out there on your shirt."

"Well, I don't feel too badly, you know," said Waterfield, "but then, I've heard that really bad wounds don't hurt so much at first."

"You'd better lie down and keep perfectly still, till I can get help."

The Major and I were already lying down in long grass, hoping we'd be invisible if any more planes came over. We could hear them machine-gunning further down the river and prayed they wouldn't return. The sepoy and one of the sampanwallahs dragged themselves near us, blood caked down their faces and body. The other sampanwallah was hit, and fell into the river, they told us. They didn't see him again. The sepoy was hit in the arm and legs, the sampanwallah had one bullet right through his cheeks, and also in his legs. The PRCO felt himself carefully and could only find a few skin-deep scratches. The Japs had dived down very low but flattened out before they fired. Most of the bullets must have travelled straight across, just above our body line. Waterfield cursed loudest when he found they'd sent a bullet through a metal jug of rum he had been carrying.

The attack started at 4-33 and by 4-50 we were out on the bank. The first thing was to get help. The PRCO went off on foot, down towards the front. The Major knew of a dressing station at the next village. He came back after an hour, very distressed to say that he'd been blocked at a creek. Some villagers had gathered round us by the time he came back and two of them offered to row him down in the sampan, so he set off again.

We weren't feeling so well by this time. Muscles were beginning to stiffen and it started to get cold. We had no tunics, only light shirts and trousers and in the hurry had forgotten to get our blankets and bedrolls out of the sampan. One old native, with a cotton wool beard came over and clucked sympathetically when he saw our wounds. I was shivering as if I had fever, and the old chap took the blanket from his shoulders and laid it over me. Some small boys came running across with brass pots of water, and what must have been a precious family heirloom—a glass to drink from.

The sun went down. It grew darker and colder, and our discomfort increased proportionately. Minutes passed like hours, hours like ages. Soon we were all shivering and groaning. The natives gathered wood and bamboo and built a fire for us. Although I'd skipped out of the boat nimbly enough, I found I couldn't drag myself over to the fire, so the fatherly old fellow who'd given me his blanket, and who must have been devilishly cold himself without it, brought two blazing bamboo sticks and held them near me.

Just as the pain and cold and stiffness were getting unbearable, we heard the creak of oars, and a few minutes later a cheerful voice.

"Now, which of you chaps is most badly hurt."

We told him he'd better first have a look at Gordon Waterfield because some of his guts were hanging out.

The PRCO came along with armfuls of blankets, apologising for the delay in getting the Medical officer. The first casualties—we were within a few hours of being the first wounded in the second Burma Campaign—from Rathedaung had just arrived at the dressing station, and they were in the middle of attending to them when the PRCO arrived. Our chaps had run into trouble at Rathedaung and the explosions we'd heard the previous evening were part of a fierce and bloody battle. The Japs had set a trap for us by pretending to have withdrawn. They'd actually left the village, but occupied the overlooking heights and pumped shells and machine-gun fire into our chaps as they tried to land. The PRCO was recounting scraps of news he'd picked up when Waterfield called out......

"Boys, I'm a cheat. That bit of 'lung' you saw, was only a bit of skin and shirt mixed up together. I've only got surface wounds. Hardly a thing the matter with me."

We all laughed with great relief at that. It was the only laughable incident out of the whole thing so we made the most of it.

The MO was quick and efficient. Working by torchlight, supplemented by bamboo flares held by willing natives, he quickly hacked away shirts and trousers, pulled out bits of surface metal and applied field dressings. He had brought stretchers and Indian orderlies with him, and as soon as we were bandaged they lifted us back on stretchers, into the sampan. Few bullets had penetrated below the waterline, and the few holes there were, had been plugged. Our volunteer oarsmen rowed us down to the dressing station where we each got a jab of anti-tetanus and morphia. While we were waiting for the PRCO to get a report on the fighting, another sampan pulled up with a couple of wounded North country lads. They said the going was "fookin' hard at the front."

"Ay. Japs chooked every fookin' thing they had at us. They wooz oop on 'eights an' twas like cross on football ground with enemy in grandstand. When we chooked oop hand grenades they toombled back an' went off 'moongst our own lads. Japs joost dropped grenades over top an' rolled mortar bombs down on oos. Eeeh, t'wasn't 'arf a mook oop tha't wasn't."

We left the dressing station on the 11 p.m. tide, headed back for Buthidaung. We'd travelled a couple of hours maybe when we heard a sampan creaking along. Somebody called out to us. We replied, and immediately a bullet "whanged" across the boat. We thought it must be Japs, despite the British challenge. It's a favourite trick of their's to challenge in English and fire in the direction of the reply. We had a Mill's bomb and two revolvers on board and the PRCO grabbed the Mill's bomb, ready to toss it into the bottom of the boat if it came within range. Then an unmistakably English voice rang out......

"Sorry, chaps. That shot was an accident."

The Major recognised the officer, who explained the boat was part of a mountain battery convoy, moving down to the front. They warned us that a few boatloads of Japs were supposed to have pushed up through the dark and landed on the river bank ahead of us. We should keep a sharp look-out, they said.

We creaked slowly on up the river. The moon came up and I cursed it heartily, wishing the morphia would make me sleep. I wasn't in much pain but the thought that we might at any moment run into a bunch of Japs, kept me awake. The Major and Waterfield were fast asleep, but the PRCO and I didn't shut our eyes all night. By daybreak the tide had changed, and we were still a couple of hours away from Buthidaung. We were just starting to pull into the bank when we heard planes coming again. There was not much undergrowth, but we reckoned the mists on the river would hide us from the air unless a plane came dangerously low down. The PRCO went off on foot to headquarters to take back a report about the Rathedaung situation.

When the sun got higher and the mists cleared away we didn't feel too safe in the boat and when we heard planes next time, Waterfield and the two sampan-wallahs, with great difficulty, got our stretchers out and up onto the bank. Somebody fired a couple of shots as they were struggling with the stretchers, but whether at us or not, we didn't know. After laying us under some trees and covering us with green branches, the sampanwallahs towed the boat downstream, and we felt reasonably safe from planes.

About midday, a wizened old native came along with a bucket of shrimps. He brought the disturbing news that there were three launch-loads of Japs a few miles down the river, and they seemed to be headed this way. That was bad news indeed. At first we thought we might get the boatmen to carry us inland and pull the sampan further down stream so as the Japs would think it abandoned. But we feared they might occupy Buthidaung and we'd be completely cut off. After further questioning the old man with the shrimps said the Japs had steamers, so we decided to start off in our sampan and keep a sharp look-out for steamer smoke. There were so many bends in the river that we thought we'd see the smoke long before the steamers hove in sight, and we'd have time to get ashore and hidden inland. At least we'd be a mile or two nearer Buthidaung. The boatmen fetched the sampans and they and Waterfield juggled us in again. The tide was with us so we made steady progress, and though we heard planes several times, none came near us. I was extremely plane-conscious by this time, and the merest sound of one, sent shivers up my spine.

After we'd been going half an hour, Waterfield saw a puff of white smoke, and not far behind it, another one. The sepoy, rather uselessly loaded his rifle, and we told the boatmen to pull into the shore. The Major was the only one who spoke Hindustani and he was in a good deal of pain at that time, so we had difficulty in making the boatmen understand what was happening. After a few moments we got matters straightened out and the boatmen said the smoke couldn't be coming from steamers, it was too white. We rounded another bend and Waterfield saw the smoke came from burning haystacks.

That was the longest and most anxious journey of my life—although it only lasted a couple of hours. We expected planes to swoop down, or Jap launches to round a bend behind us, at any minute. Eventually Waterfield said he could see in the distance the red roof of the District Court House at Buthidaung. Fifteen minutes later another sampan drew alongside and the PRCO and a Medical officer, jumped aboard. The MO jabbed us with morphia again while the PRCO explained a sampan had been sent down for us as soon as he arrived, but by mistake they picked up the two BORs we'd met the previous night.

We soon pulled in to Buthidaung jetty and were loaded into an ambulance for the emergency dressing station. I was lying on the table in a rough operating theatre when, through the window I caught a glimpse of two radial engined fighters hurtling down at us. I called out......

"Hi! Look out! There's a couple of Jap fighters."

The MO said, "That's alright. They're our new Mohawks."

The planes dived down near the roof and flattened out, while I waited for the clatter of machine-gun bullets.

"I've been caught too many times like that," I said. "They reckoned the planes that shot us up were Mohawks at first, but they were Army Zeros, and I bet those are too."

But the MO was right. This time they *were* our planes. He went out to look at the red, white and blue discs as they passed next time. I took my anaesthetic without protest after that.

From the pieces of copper picked out of my arm and back, and by the size of the Major's back and my leg wounds, it seemed we'd stopped some of the Jap's 20 cannon shells. The stuff that lodged in Waterfield's and my back and arms must have been from their explosive bullets. (Xray has since confirmed that half a dozen pieces of explosive bullet passed through my back and into the chest linings, just missing my heart. Another ten or twelve pieces are scattered round my leg and arm).

The same night, we were packed into an ambulance and sent seventeen miles to Maungdaw on the coast, where the Major and I spent several days before transferring to a hospital ship and started our seventeen-day Odyssey by steamer, train, ambulance, river-boat and train again, to the base hospital. Waterfield, heroically only stayed at Maungdaw long enough to have his wounds dressed, then went straight back to the front again. Five days after he was wounded, he was back at the Rathedaung front, limping around on sticks, with a partially stiff arm, but still well enough to dictate Reuter's despatches.

On the hospital ship, I shared a berth with a young officer who'd been accidentaly wounded. We lay in Maungdaw Harbor for two days, and my nerves were still a bit jumpy when I heard planes buzzing about. The young Lieutenant was not long out from England and had peculiar ideas about Jap chivalry.

"But, dash it all, old boy. The Japs wouldn't attack a hospital-ship. At least they're gentlemen in things like that. I simply refuse to believe all these atrocity stories they tell about them."

We weren't attacked, because no Jap planes came over while we were in Maungdaw, and we steamed across to Chittagong without incident. The hospital-ship returned for another load and this time the Japs *did* come over and *did* attack the hospital-ship—dropping several bombs alongside and spraying the decks with machine-gun bullets. Fortunately they did no harm except slightly to injure one orderly. The ship was painted white and clearly marked with huge Red Cross signs.

By a strange streak of irony, at Chittagong Hospital, I was placed in bed alongside a wounded Japanese airman. He'd been shot down over Chittagong the same day his colleagues attacked our sampan on the Mayu. I had a talk with him through a Canadian interpreter, but he had little to say, except that he thought the war would last a long time. The interpreter said this was the first time he'd shown any interest in life. On previous days he'd always requested a knife or revolver so's he might kill himself, but this day he was eating oranges and smoking cigarettes brought by the interpreter. Food as near Japanese as possible was specially cooked for him, and quite rightly, of course, he had the same medical attention as our own people. I hoped that our wounded prisoners of war, in Japan, received comparable treatment.

When I finally reached base hospital, I was sentenced to about three months in hospital. I am the only one of our party that can feel somewhat grateful to the Japanese. If those six fighter pilots hadn't provided the opportunity, this book would surely not have been written—and probably those readers who've struggled through this far, will be muttering......" and that would have been no great loss.

CHAPTER XXIII

EPILOGUE

The Japs beat us in Burma because man for man they were better fighters than we were. I don't mean braver fighters, but better. Man for man the Japanese is naturally better adapted for jungle fighting—cynics may say because it's not so long since he emerged from it. On top of natural adaptability, he has better training, better equipment and better organisation backing him. His communications are so far ahead of ours that there's no comparison. A platoon that goes out on patrol has at least two men expert in map-reading, and has wireless communication with headquarters. Patrols operate far ahead of the main body; if it sights enemy in force, it can whistle up planes and reinforcements within minutes. If it finds a break in our lines, within a few minutes the main body of their troops are pouring through the gap. Patrols don't have to return to headquarters to report.

During a campaign the Jap soldier carries five days' rations of food with him; supply brings up a further fifteen days'. At that, he eats better and more sustaining food than our troops with their interminable unimaginative bully beef and biscuit—the only rations I've ever seen our chaps eating. We laughed at the Japs' beef and soup powders, but they've more substance in their meals of meat powders and rice than our biscuit and bully.

If we're going to fight another jungle campaign in Burma without better food arrangements, and anti-malarial protection, we're heading for trouble again.

The most successful weapon the Japs use is the trench mortar. These can be carried easily—I've seen Chinese with mortars in two sections slung each end of a bamboo carrying stick and the Japs use them with extreme accuracy. They seem to be able to lob mortar bombs on batteries, trucks, launches and buildings with deadly precision. I've no idea of the respective mortar strength per unit in the Japanese and British armies in Burma, but I know the Japs always seemed to have plenty, when and where they needed them. Their all-round fire power per unit was much heavier than ours because of their superiority in automatic weapons. I hope in this respect we'll be at least as well equipped as the Japs when we go back into Burma, but the equipment during our first counter-attack in Arakan was something of a disappointment to all of us who had observed the first campaign.

The Japs at least had no monopoly of courage last time. Our British and Indian troops had every reason to suffer from lowered morale. With no air support, ill-trained, ill-fed, no proper medical care, always retreating, usually outnumbered, outfought, fighting without hope of relief, there was never a question of them shirking an engagement. Quite the contrary. I met a group of disgruntled Gloucesters—I think—returning from Pegu one day. They'd been convalescing at Maymyo and hearing their mates were in trouble at Pegu, tore down to the front to give a hand, sick and wounded as they were. They were most indignant when they were ordered back to hospital. Another group were cut off near Tavoy, and walked over a hundred miles arriving at Nyaunglebin, the day before we counter-attacked and retook Shwegyin. Gaunt with hunger and fatigue, they heard the action against Shewgyin was coming off and begged to be allowed to take part. They did. Such instances of highest courage could be multiplied by the thousand. No, there was nothing wrong with the fighting spirit of our troops.

Their courage deserved better equipment, better support, above all better organisation. Better organisation than that which blew the bridge over the Sittaung River too soon, leaving the best part of three brigades—the main part of our army in Burma—caught on the wrong side of the river; that left 300,000 gallons of petrol, bombs and repairable planes at Moulmein aerodrome, later to be used against our men. Better organisation than that which allowed Burma to start the war with only twelve days' supply of coal in hand for the railway. The normal reserve was three to four months' supply, but "someone had forgotten to order." Although there were large private stocks, big dumps were abandoned when we evacuated Rangoon, they were not requisitioned and the railways did not run to capacity during the campaign because of fuel shortage, and thus contributed to the difficulties of our troops.

We'll certainly have more aeroplanes next time—and I hope better co-operation between army and air-force. I remember meeting a wounded KOYLI who was being evacuated on a train on which I was travelling. I asked him how he got hit.

" 'Twas this way, sir. We knew Japs wuz waiting in a patch uv joongle. We wuz told: 'at 5 o'clock we're goin' ter shell that strip. Quarter past RAF's goin' ter bomb tem. 'alf past you boys are goin' in ter clean 'oop the rest with bayernets.' Ay that was alright. Cooms 5 o'clock we sent over few shells alright. Quarterpast 5 no fooking planes, but cooms' 'alf after 5 an' poor bluddy oos goes in with bayernets, joost the same. Eeeh, an 'japs don't arf give oos soom 'oorry oop. Wuz joost sitting there with mortar bombs und machine goons waitin' for oos."

Time and again one heard the same story. All laid on for planes to come—and they never came. The troops blamed the RAF. They couldn't know that we had about half a dozen planes operating at that time, planes that should never have been flown; that the RAF in Burma were flying more hours per week in worse planes than in any other theatre. Planes that collapsed when they tried to land because tyres were shot to pieces. That even poor old "Lizzies" (Lysander-Army-Co-operation Planes) hovering about at 100 miles an hour, were being used for bombing flights. Usually it was the Japs flying machines of ours they'd captured.

On the eve of the Eighth Army's great advance from Egypt to Tunisia, General Montgomery received War Correspondents in a tent on the outskirts of El Alamein. Amongst other things, he said:

"Other things being equal, the side with the highest morale will win, and I am confident in the morale of my men. The soldiers will never let you down—never."

And that's the way it was in Burma. The soldiers never once let us down. Unfortunately other things were not equal, and so the side with the highest morale didn't win. But our troops never let us down—they themselves were let down—mainly by circumstances, but not always unavoidable ones. Next time, I hope we're going to make circumstances match the valour of our fighting men.

Perhaps our greatest defeat in the Burma campaign was our failure to mobilise Burmese public opinion against the Japanese. We were most careful not to allow a breath of anti-Japanese propaganda before the Pacific War started. Burmans were almost encouraged to look on the Japanese as our friends—and because Chinese propaganda was prohibited the inference was that the Chinese were not our friends. Burmans and Indians saw Japanese ships in Rangoon harbour till within a few days of the outbreak of war being loaded with zinc, tin, wolfram and lead. Even after hostilities started no intelligent propaganda was handed out to the Burmans.

For years past, British civilian authority in Burma was too prone to divide people into a pro or anti-British category. The 'pros', of course, were purest white, the 'antis' blackest black. We'd have done better to classify them as pro or anti-Fascist, or pro- or anti-Japanese. If we'd done that we would have found, surprisingly that the anti-British were mainly also anti-Japanese. The pro-British were often pro-Japanese also. The "pros" were mainly those who didn't care who ruled the country as long as their jobs or businesses flourished. I could quote long lists of those holding government positions under us, now holding similar positions under the Japs. The chiefs of the Nippon Police—distinguished from the "Free Burma" Police—in Rangoon, Mandalay Kyaukse and Shwebo, for instance, are all former assistant or deputy superintendents of the Burma Police Force. Those who were anti British before, are now mostly actively anti-Japanese. They were anti-British because they wanted independence. They're anti-Japanese for the same reason. I know there is a surprisingly large proportion of the population in Burma who hate the Japanese, and are willing to co-operate with Britain and the Uni-nations to get the Japanese out.

Here is a statement from a leading Thakin, who escaped to India, hoping to contact democratic forces here, and help to oust the Japs from Burma.

"I have been anti-Imperialist, not anti-British, for a long time. I am by conviction anti-Fascist. By Fascism, I mean the worst possible form of Imperialism. Of the two Imperialisms, British democratic Imperialism is preferable to the Japanese Fascist type—if we must have one of the other. I, therefore, come to help the British in their fight against Fascism but I cannot say I want to invite the British once more to rule Burma. I am all for Burmese freedom. I, as an anti-Fascist, am prepared to help Britain and her allies against Japan and the Axis even if it means helping an Imperialist. My countrymen......are not politically conscious enough to distinguish between Democratic Imperialism and Japanese Fascism......In my personal opinion they (my countrymen) will only turn against the Japs if Britain promises them their Independence. There are now signs that...... anti-Japanese feeling is rising, but this doesn't mean that there is pro-British feeling in Burma."

I think that is an honest statement which puts the situation in a nutshell. This particular Thakin came with some others to India, some time after the Japs took over. He represents a big body of educated opinion, and an influential section of the Burma Independence Army, which he claims is largely anti-Japanese.

"We came," he says, "to find out how we can co-ordinate our activities with what the United Nations forces proposed to do......how we could help the Uni-nations if the Uni-nations help us. It's our idea that Uni-nations' anti-Fascist propaganda in Burma can best be handled and made more effective if it came from patriots and public men like us, rather than government servants. I could talk over the radio in my own name and could send over leaflets signed by me......we ourselves are not bargaining with the Uni-nations for Burma's Independence but we cannot guarantee success with the masses or the BIA (Burma Independence Army) without a promise of independence and/or the application of Cripps' proposals to Burma. We are prepared to work on the Uni-nations' Anti-Fascist Front unconditionally for the sake of our political opinions, but the BIA and the masses are not all of our views. We and the masses are prepared to let the "status quo" exist during the war, but we and the masses want independence after the war. Even if independence is not promised, we on our part are willing to work for the cause of the Uni-nations."

The Burmans are dissatisfied and disillusioned with the Japanese for obvious reasons. As David Maurice had forecast, as soon as the Japs had the British out, they wanted to dissolve the BIA. This latter army was raised by the 32 Thakins who went to Japan in 1940. They were trained and commissioned by the Japs and raised about one thousand troops on the Siam border. It was they who led the primary attack on Burma at Victoria Point. We had reports at the time, of Siamese troops using elephants, but actually it was the BIA. They occupied Victoria Point and Tavoy and the whole of the Irrawaddy Division, setting up their own administrations as they went. The first clashes occurred with the Japs at Moulmein, quite early in the Burma campaign, when the Japs at first objected but later agreed to the BIA establishing their administration at Moulmein. They recruited followers as they advanced arming them with weapons abandoned by our troops and later the Chinese. By the time the Burma campaign finished, the BIA numbered about 30,000 men, armed with rifles, Tommys, Brens and mortars. They wear varied uniforms but all carry a red, green and yellow tricolour armlet with a peacock inset. The army is divided into regiments, each regiment officered by Burmans, but with a Japanese "adviser." I have heard several well-authenticated stories of clashes between the Japs and BIA. At Pyinmana, for instance, there was a small battle when the Japs tried to disarm a section of them. Several Japs were killed and Burmans were wounded, but the BIA were allowed to keep their arms.

The Japs soon made it clear that the Burmans were not going to have things their own way. Independence was not possible during wartime. Burma had to help the Japs win the war first. A four-stage political programme was announced at a meeting in Maymyo on June 3rd presided over by the Japanese CIC—General Ida. A committee was appointed by Ida with the following announced objectives......

(*a*) To prepare for a Central Government of Burma, with a view to mobilising the full resources of the country for the victory of the Japanese.

(*b*) To prepare a constitution ensuring that friendship between Japanese and Burmans will be perpetuated.

The four stages towards independence included

(1) the formation of a Preparation Committee, (2) the establishment of a Co-operative Committee, really a Puppet Government. This was as far as Burma advanced towards independence during the war. After the war a provisional government was to be formed for an indefinite period, leading to the fourth stage of independence. There is no stipulation when this fourth stage was to be reached. To make quite clear their intentions, the Japs, however, are taking over complete control of Customs, Railways and Currency for a preliminary period of fifteen years.

Later in response to considerable Burmese agitation, Tokio announced that Independence would be granted by the end of 1943. But the Burmans would have to pay for the whole cost of the campaign, as well as an indemnity of three thousand rupees for every Japanese killed to date in Burma, and those who would be killed in future fighting. Only the Japanese can estimate the cost and losses of the campaign, and Burma will be saddled with such an enormous debt that she'll be completely economically dependent on Japan, even if she is given a bogus political independence. Of course, Railways, Customs and Currency will still be controlled by the Japs.

Small wonder that the Burmans are bitter and disillusioned about all this. The educated classes see clearly that Burma is further from real independence than ever before. Those that were loudest in supporting the Japanese before are now loudest in their abuse of them.

The small man on the land, who was completely apathetic during the fighting, now had a grudge against the Japs. For the first time, he feels directly imperialist exploitation. His way of life is changed to fit in with Japan's economic needs. Japan wants cotton. The peasants, in the drier regions of Burma now have to switch from food-crops to cotton. Formerly, no matter how bad things were, he at least grew his food. Now he'll have to depend on what the Japs give him for his cotton, to buy rice for his family. The first blow has been dealt to his own economic independence. Peasants are notoriously conservative and this forced change from generations of rice cultivation is bound to breed resentment.

It is the Burmese women, however, who are most deeply affected by the Japanese occupation. A casual visitor to Burma might think that women there occupy the same lowly status of most women in the East. He will notice a Burmese wife walking several paces behind her husband in the street. If he visits a Burmese home, he will see how the male members of the household eat first, with the women-folk waiting on them hand and foot. Probing deeper, he'll discover women pray that in their next existence they may be men, so as to have a chance of attaining Nirvana. Despite this apparent lowliness, there are very few countries in either the New or the Old World, where women have such a high status as in Burma.

Economic, social and political laws in Burma are based on complete equality between the sexes. Boys and girls have equal rights in inherited property, the oldest *boy or girl* receiving one quarter of the inheritance, the rest of the children equally dividing the remainder. If husband or wife dies, the joint property automatically reverts to the survivor. When Burmans marry, husband and wife each acquire half the others' possessions. Divorce can be obtained by mutual consent without recourse to costly courts of law. The joint property is equally divided and after the separation neither are worse off economically than before. Only where one partner is proved guilty of misconduct, and this is made ground for divorce, is his or her share of the property forfeited. Burman men can have any number of wives—if they can afford them. The taking of a second wife is considered justification for the first wife suing for divorce unless she has first consented. Once she has accepted the second wife thus tacitly endorsing polygamy in principle, she can't make the taking of third or fourth wife ground for divorce. Nor can the second wife claim divorce because a third or fourth wife is taken. Marriage is also by mutual consent. No registers need be signed nor ceremony observed. Marriage is recognised when two people live together and are accepted by the community. Women have free entry into all professions and politics. Neither marriage nor motherhood is considered a bar to holding any postion in the State service—as it is in so many countries.

Burmese women have attained a higher stage of emancipation than women in any other country except Soviet Russia. Perhaps on account of this the White Salary Commission attached to the International Labour Office at Geneva, reports that no Burmese women have been found in the world's great brothel centres, where women of almost every other race and nationality abound.

Daw Mya Sein, the portly, cheerful intelligent "Queen Wilhelmina of the Burmans," who is now in exile working to clear the path for the eviction of the Japs insists that this absence of Burmese prostitutes abroad is the crowning proof of the correctness of Burmese economic and social equality of the sexes.

Japan and Burma are at the opposite ends of the pole as regards women's rights. In no other country do women occupy such a lowly and abject position as in Japan. They are reduced to slaves and prostitutes, and have no social, economic or political rights. In marriage, they are liable to be dismissed at any time, and sent away with no obligation on the husband's part to support them further. They are tolerated only so long as they give pleasure and service to their lords and masters. Once they fail or cease to do that, they are thrown into the gutter.

The effect of the impact of Japanese customs on Burmese women can well be imagined. At Toungoo, for instance, the Japs demanded of the Administrative Committee established by BIA that they should hand over their daughters together with other girls, for the Japanese officers. The Committee promptly resigned and disappeared. There have been countless cases of rape and forced abductions of girls. In an attempt to demonstrate Jap methods, parents have been forced at bayonet point to watch rapings of their children. No matter how hard the Japanese High Command tries to restrain its minions, Japanese contempt for women, cultivated for hundreds of years, can't be abolished overnight. They have simply never learned decent respect for women's rights. Burmese men and women alike are outraged by the Japanese attitude of racial arrogance plus their assumption of male superiority.

We have a more fertile field for fifth column activity in Burma than ever the Japs had—and it is up to us to use. Last time the Japs had on their side a tiny proportion of people who believed they helped themselves to independence by helping the Japs. The overwhelming mass of people didn't care two hoots either way, who won. They helped us when we passed through their districts. Doubtless they helped the Japs when they came along. Burmans are naturally kindly and their religion encourages them to do goodly works. I've never been refused food or water in any part of Burma and have often given offence by offering payment. No doubt the Japs found the same thing. But because they were well supplied with Burmese-speaking guides, they got far more out of the apathetic Burmans than we did.

If a promise, backed by the United Nations, were given the Burman people, that within twelve months of the cessation of hostilities they would be free to choose their future relationship with Great Britain—dominion status or independence—I'm convinced we'd have the Burmese people and the thirty thousand strong Burma Independence Army wholeheartedly with us. There is no excuse, as there is in India, for postponing such a promise. There are no irreconcilable communal issues. There are representatives of the Burma Independence Army and the Burmese people in India now, waiting to take such a promise back into their country. They are certain of what the results would be.

If we don't do it, we're going to have the same trouble all over again. At best, apathy. At worst, open hostility. The difference in degree between Japanese or British domination will probably seem insufficient for any mass struggle by the Burmese to throw off the one for the other. Maybe, although personally I doubt it, the Burmans would sooner suffer greater economic and social hardships and prefer to be exploited by fellow-Asiatics, than live under higher standards and endure the superiority assumed implicit by the possessors of white skins.